GOD
AND THE
EVOLVING
UNIVERSE

GOD AND THE EVOLVING UNIVERSE

The Next Step in Personal Evolution

JAMES REDFIELD

MICHAEL MURPHY

and SYLVIA TIMBERS

BANTAM BOOKS

LONDON · NEW YORK · TORONTO · SYDNEY · AUCKLAND

GOD AND THE EVOLVING UNIVERSE
A BANTAM BOOK : 0 553 81481 8

Originally published in Great Britain by Bantam Press,
a division of Transworld Publishers

PRINTING HISTORY
Bantam Press edition published 2002
Bantam edition published 2003

1 3 5 7 9 10 8 6 4 2

Grateful acknowledgement is made to the following
publishers and individuals:
Coleman Barks, for permission to quote from 'The Dream That Must be
Interpreted', translated by Coleman Barks, with John Moyne, from
The Essential Rumi, published by HarperCollins, 1995.
Copyright © Coleman Barks.
Yale University Press for an excerpt from *Long's Day Journey into Night*, by
Eugene O'Neill, published by Yale University Press, 1955. Copyright as an
unpublished work, 1955, by Carolotta Monterey O'Neill.
Jonathan Star, for permission to reprint 'Seek That', by Jelaluddin Rumi, and
translated by Jonathan Star and Shahram Shiva, from *Two Suns Rising*,
published by Bantam, 1991.

Set in 11/12.5pt Palatino by
Phoenix Typesetting, Burley-in-Wharfedale, West Yorkshire.

Bantam Books are published by Transworld Publishers
61–63 Uxbridge Road, London W5 5SA,
a division of The Random House Group Ltd,
in Australia by Random House Australia (Pty) Ltd,
20 Alfred Street, Milsons Point, Sydney, NSW 2061, Australia,
in New Zealand by Random House New Zealand Ltd,
18 Poland Road, Glenfield, Auckland 10, New Zealand
and in South Africa by Random House (Pty) Ltd,
Endulini, 5a Jubilee Road, Parktown 2193, South Africa.

Printed and bound in Great Britain by
Clays Ltd, St Ives plc.

We dedicate this book to the many pioneers and heroes who have set the stage for a deeper understanding of human nature.

CONTENTS

ACKNOWLEDGMENTS

We would like to thank the following people for their contributions to this work: John Austin, for his handling of schedules; Phil Novak, for his research and aid in compiling information on the world's great religions; John Diamond, for his constant vigilance in finding a home for this project; Mitch Horowitz, senior editor at Tarcher/Putnam, for his deft stewardship; Jeremy Tarcher and Joel Fotinos, for their vision of this book; and especially Phil Cousineau, for his many hours of research and organization.

AUTHORS' NOTE

Today we stand poised at a threshold in human history. The shock and horror of terrorism continue to haunt us, reminding us of the alienation and hatred that have too often characterized human history. Yet, at the same time, we see reflections of the best in human nature, as people around the world continue to hold a vision of peace and justice as they demonstrate the love and heroism that reflects a greater humanity.

We believe we are on the brink of a new understanding of who we are as human beings, an understanding that includes the depths to which we can plunge when we fail to pursue our greater potentials. In a sense, a new urgency has been declared in our search for self-awareness. During the last four hundred years, science has opened the world to us with discoveries our ancestors could not have imagined. It has revealed the nature of distant galaxies, the structure of subatomic particles, and the evolutionary process that brought our universe from a tiny seed to this immense and still-expanding cosmos.

But the threshold we've now reached involves more than our physical existence. Irresistibly, we are called upon to join our exploration of the evolving universe with an equally daring and disciplined exploration of the inner life. In spite of the negative actions of a few, there has rarely existed a wider interest in mysteries of the soul nor so many experiments in personal transformation.

Such experiments are happening around the world, informed by discoveries in psychology, anthropology, and medical science as well as once-esoteric knowledge from every sacred tradition. They are increasing in number and sophistication today because there now exists more publicly available knowledge about our transformative capacities than at any time in human history. The nature of spirituality and the inner life is coming more clearly into focus, bringing us a vision of human transformation that is unprecedented in its scope and beauty.

Our aim in writing *God and the Evolving Universe* is twofold. First, we want to add depth to the popular understanding of our human potential by discussing a wide range of capabilities and experiences that are now available to us, all of which can be more readily sustained through disciplined intention and practice. And second, we want to suggest that a widespread actualization of these capacities would herald the dawning of a new evolutionary step – a step as significant as the emergence of life from inorganic matter and the rise of humanity from the first tiny cells, a step that would bless us with spectacular new abilities and levels of experience.

We believe that humankind's exploration of the inner life, in its infancy now, can reveal new frontiers of creativity, antidotes for hatred and alienation, and possibilities for cultural transformation beyond those we presently imagine. As we present this picture of further evolutionary advance, we contend that history is not merely cyclical, but that it is going somewhere and, indeed, that it has been struggling all along toward higher ends.

In Part One we survey the high points of this remarkable journey. We begin with a look at the mystery of how

12

we came to be on this planet in the first place, and at the world's astonishing evolution from the Big Bang to the appearance of life on Earth to the emergence of humankind. We then briefly chart some of the great turning points of human history that have prepared us for the evolutionary step we can now foresee.

In Part Two we discuss the emergence of extraordinary human capacities, looking not just at how they feel and impact us, but also at ways in which they seem to seek integration with other emergent attributes in a manner that can ultimately lift us to a greater life.

In Part Three we offer a vision of how the cultivation and disciplined maintenance of these aspects of human nature could contribute to the renewal of institutions and culture, to an expanded communion with other levels of existence, and toward the eventual transformation of the body itself.

And in Part Four we suggest specific exercises, which we believe can facilitate personal and social transformation. We include A Guide to the Literature of Transformation, which includes important classic and popular books that have helped set the stage for a new vision of human possibility. We hope that this information will help you explore the extraordinary life that is your birthright.

Come join us as we explore an evolution that has not only brought us to where we are today, but is ongoing – and calling us to participate.

J.R., M.M., S.T.
Fall 2001

Part One

Awakening

1

THE MYSTERY
OF OUR BEING

For many years, a new worldview has been forming intuitively in the hearts and minds of people around the world. Though this emerging picture of our place in the universe has not been fully articulated, it is based on a central perception that we have capacities for a greater life than most of us have realized – a life that seems essentially joined with the evolution of the universe itself. We sense this connection, many believe, because we and the world are unfolding from the same transcendent source and are secretly moved to manifest more and more of our latent divinity.

THE EVIDENCE OF EXPERIENCE

The awakenings that inspire this view of the world, which come to us in many ways, can be enriched by reading various philosophers, scientists, saints, and sages who have opened new perspectives on human nature and the universe. As we shall see, the visions and practices of these pathfinders are available now in great abundance. However, the intuitions and insights that most typically lead us to a sense of our unfulfilled capacities and their relation to the Transcendent come not from books but from direct experience. For many, such openings come during prayer or meditation. For some, they arrive through counseling or other activities designed to help us through difficulty. But just as often they appear when we least expect them – at play, at work, or in moments of reverie. But no matter what the moment's trigger was, or its hidden roots, our ordinary way of being in the world suddenly blossoms into the extraordinary.

We might be walking in the woods on a summer day with sunlight streaming through the trees when everything is seen in a new way. Colors seem richer. Trees and bushes stand out with a more vivid presence. Sounds are magnified and we smell fragrances we hadn't noticed before. The woods are suddenly magic and alive. In that instant, we enter a world that is usually unseen. Was it hallucination? Or is this how the world would always look if our senses were more developed?

There are other kinds of experience that call us beyond the familiar. Have you ever sensed a friend's thought before she said it or known who would soon call on the phone? Even if such events seem trivial, they point to powers we tend to neglect. Have you ever pictured a significant turn in your life and been amazed when it actually happened? When such things occur, we are filled with a sense of something uncanny – a higher intelligence, a destiny that wants to be actualized in us.

And there are awakenings that are stranger still. Some involve contact with a distant or deceased loved one – through an urgent whispering in the night, a fleeting vision, a fragrance unique to the loved one, or an immediate and disturbing sense of his or her nearness. Several recent Gallup polls have shown that more people than we think have experiences such as these, as well as glimpses of luminous worlds beyond the range of our physical senses. And there are moments even more compelling when our very identity shifts and we are lifted to a larger, more encompassing sense of our self. We know more than ever before who we really are and what we are meant to do. We and the world share a common end, a secret source, and a mighty journey.

Sadly, though, these moments pass. A veil drops. We return to our normal awareness. But we cannot entirely forget such awakenings, however brief they may have been. Even as their memory fades, we are haunted by them. Again and again they whisper to us, reminding us that more awaits us. What larger life do they reveal? Is our present existence all we are meant for? What greater destiny do we and the world share?

In the chapters that follow, we will explore such awakenings and ways in which we can follow their lead. For it is the case, we believe, that they begin to reveal a greater life pressing to be born in us. Through practice, what they show us can be nurtured and eventually integrated as a permanent aspect of our being.

But to do this we must appreciate their fundamental significance and the social forces that work against them. We need a philosophy that gives a context for them and guidance for their development. Superstition will not do. Dogma will not help us. We need a vision that will stand the test of time. To understand what these haunting moments point to, we must draw upon our best resources, including science, religion, philosophy, literature, and the arts. We will turn to all of these resources in the chapters that follow.

And there is no better place to start than with science and the mystery of evolution. Experiences such as those we've described shake our world, and suggest a depth to our existence often lost in the everyday business of life. We are led to revisit the perennial questions. Who are we? How did we get here? Where might we be going? The story of our evolving universe, which grows in magnificence every day, gives us an indispensable foundation for addressing such questions. The universe *is* going somewhere, and its momentum was triggered in the first instant of the Big Bang.

THE STORY OF EVOLUTION

We began
as a mineral. We emerged into plant life,
and into the animal state, and then into being human,
and always we have forgotten our former states,
except in early spring when we slightly recall
being green again.
That's how a young person turns
toward a teacher. That's how a baby leans
toward the breast, without knowing the secret
of its desire, yet turning instinctively.
Humankind is being led along an evolving course,
through this migration of intelligences,
and though we seem to be sleeping,
there is an inner wakefulness
that directs the dream,

and that will eventually startle us back
to the truth of who we are.

RUMI
thirteenth century

Science has enjoyed no greater triumph than the discovery of evolution. In showing that the universe unfolded from a tiny seed and gave rise to life and human-kind, it has found a truth that unites the discoveries of many fields, including astronomy, physics, geology, biology, paleontology, anthropology, and psychology. And in making this discovery, science has provided a

20

unifying context for the transcendent abilities described in this book. The human longing and capacity for a greater life is an emerging part of the evolution story.

That story goes something like this:

Some fifteen billion years ago, from a mysterious something no larger than a single atom, our universe exploded into existence and within a second was millions of miles across. Try to picture it: enough energy to form our entire cosmos racing outward at ever-accelerating speed, blossoming with light, and coalescing to form successive generations of stars that create ever more complex elements. It is an image that stretches our mind to its limits: The energy in that first seed gave rise to this entire universe, now trillions upon trillions of miles across with stars and galaxies too numerous to count. Step by step, for some ten billion years, it set the stage for evolution to take a great leap forward. A new kind of existence would emerge on Earth.

In the waters of our primordial seas, organisms appeared that were different from the complex molecules that had preceded them. They could move through their own volition, reproduce themselves, and contact their surroundings with new sensitivities. Evolution had entered a new stage. Life had begun. Single-celled creatures populated land and sea.

And from these improbable tiny life forms, over the course of four billion years, there came bacteria that filled the atmosphere with oxygen, which made multicelled plants and animals of many types possible. Among these complex organisms were fish, whose gills evolved into the lungs of amphibians that could breathe the Earth's abundant oxygen and begin to move on land. From these first terrestrial creatures came reptiles and dinosaurs, birds and mammals, and the primates that would evolve into *Homo sapiens*.

Though science has not yet revealed all the ways in

which this evolution took place, we now know that increasingly complex life-forms appeared on Earth, with capacities to sense their surroundings, process information of many kinds, manipulate objects in their environment, move with agility, and care for their young in ways that exceeded their ancestors' abilities. These capacities developed until evolution was ready to take another leap.

In Africa there appeared an animal that stood erect, used tools with care, and began to speak. A new kind of species had appeared, with a brain greater than any before it and a capacity for self-transformation that was new on Earth. It created intricate social groups, discovered fire, told stories of its origins, and painted pictures that haunt us still. It looked to the stars and the spirit world. From its very beginnings it began to sense a divinity beyond the reach of its senses.

We can look upon the appearance of our species as a third stage of evolution, analogous to the emergence of matter and life, because in it something new came into being. Self-reflection and inwardly directed change were added to the processes governing the development of earlier life forms. This increasingly self-aware creature often felt others' pain. It began to long for a greater life. And through the fire that grew in its heart, it eventually set foot on the moon, beamed timeless music toward the stars, released the power of the atom, and built the complex human world growing inexorable around us today.

The universe has traveled a mysterious journey from its birth. It went from darkness into light. It became a cosmos of a trillion galaxies in which matter gave rise to living things. And then, just a moment ago on its cosmic scale, one of its creatures started to wonder who it was, where it had come from, and where it might be going.

THE FACT OF EVOLUTION

The epic of our evolving universe, which is often retold by scientists, theologians, and philosophers, is a still-developing story. But no matter how it is described or what theories are proposed about it, we know that evolution is a fact. The universe was born with the Big Bang and over the course of many billion years gave rise to matter, life, and humankind. Though we do not know all the details of this stupendous unfoldment, we know that it happened. That the universe evolves has been proved according to the most rigorous standards.

Scientists, for example, have found exciting fossil remains from thousands of plant and animal species ranging in size from microscopic organisms to *Tyrannosaurus rex*. Paleontologists have greatly improved their estimation of fossil ages using carbon dating and other methods so that they can determine with increasing precision when life began and for how long particular species flourished; and in doing this, they have mapped the progression of species from the simplest to the most complex. Geneticists have refined their understanding of the genetic mutations and recombinations that cause variations within plant and animal populations and give rise to new species, while geologists have learned how climatic and geological changes affect the evolution of life.

And astrophysicists have discovered that the cosmos itself is evolving, leaving records in the sky of its marvelous past, while astronomers gradually map its contours and reveal to our increased astonishment how it gives birth to new galaxies, stars, and planets as well as distant objects that remain mysterious to us.

Meanwhile, paleontologists and anthropologists are learning more and more about humankind's emergence from our primate predecessors. They have found, for example, that by one hundred thousand years ago our species had diverged from its immediate relatives with a brain as large, a hand as dexterous, and a physique as agile as ours today. Like the evolution of the cosmos as a whole and animal species on this planet, the development of our human ancestors is becoming increasingly evident, and all the more mysterious for it.

Viewed as a whole, these discoveries form an increasingly awesome panorama and a wondrously detailed view of life's advance. According to Ernst Mayr, the eminent historian of biological thought, evolution 'has been confirmed so completely that modern biologists consider [it] simply as a fact.'

HOW THE UNIVERSE IS EVOLVING

But in spite of the ever-growing evidence that evolution is real, some people still deny its existence. One cause of such misunderstanding is a failure to distinguish evolution-as-fact from theories of how and why it is happening. We know that the cosmos, animal species, and humankind are evolving, but we are still learning about the ways in which evolution works.

It is important, for example, to remember that Charles Darwin's discovery that living creatures have evolved from a common ancestor must be distinguished from his theories of how that happened. Darwin (and his fellow naturalist Alfred Russel Wallace) proposed that among plants and animals, those individuals best adapted to their environments generally survive in greater numbers and have more offspring than organisms that are less well adapted. By increasing the relative number of their more successful genes among members of their species, organisms improve the survivability of their species. Darwin

24

believed that all species emerged through this process, which he called 'natural selection.'

However, the more scientists have learned about the history of living things, the more they have had to refine and broaden their theories to account for evolution's complexities. Contrasting evolutionary theory at each of the three Darwin centennials (1909, the hundredth anniversary of Darwin's birth; 1959, the hundredth year after publication of his landmark book *The Origin of Species*; and 1982, the hundredth anniversary of Darwin's death), Stephen Jay Gould wrote:

. . . 1909 marked the acme of confusion about how evolution happened in the midst of complete confidence that it had occurred.

[But] by 1959, confusion had ceded to the opposite undesired state of complacency. Strict Darwinism had triumphed . . . Nearly all evolutionary biologists had concluded that natural selection, after all, provided the creative mechanism of evolutionary change. At age 150, Darwin had triumphed. Yet, in the flush of victory, his latter-day disciples devised a version of his theory far narrower than anything Darwin himself would have allowed.

[Some] experts even declared that the immense complexity of evolution had yielded to final resolution . . . [But] now [in 1982], Darwinian theory is in a vibrantly healthy state. Confidence in the basic mechanism of natural selection provides a theoretical underpinning and point of basic agreement that carries us beyond the pessimistic anarchy of 1909. But the constraints of an overzealous strict version, so popular in 1959, are loosening. Exciting discoveries in molecular biology and in the study of embryological development have hinted at modes of change different

25

from the cumulative, gradual alteration emphasized by strict Darwinians.

Gould himself contributed to this break with strict Darwinism. With Niles Eldredge, he developed a scheme of evolutionary development called the model of punctuated equilibria, which modifies Darwin's emphasis on the gradual change of living species. Darwin believed that new species developed gradually over enormous periods of time, but his view was at odds with the fossil record, which has many gaps between species. To account for this discrepancy, Eldredge and Gould (as well as other biologists) have proposed that such gaps remain in the record because new species develop rapidly, usually at the edges of their ancestral populations, and for that reason leave relatively few traces of their transitional forms. If they do not develop in this manner, they will be reabsorbed into the species from which they arise. 'Lineages,' Gould wrote, 'change little during most of their history, but events of rapid speciation occasionally punctuate this tranquility.'

Another change in evolutionary theory is underway among scientists studying self-organization, the tendency observed among both inorganic and living forms to create orderly, self-perpetuating patterns. Until recently, most evolutionary theorists, following Darwin, believed that natural selection worked with *random* changes in living things to produce species best adapted to survive in a given environment. But reflecting the newer view, biological theorist Stuart Kaufman wrote:

We have all known that simple physical systems exhibit spontaneous order: An oil droplet in water forms a sphere; snowflakes exhibit their six-fold symmetry. What is new is that the range of spontaneous order is enormously greater than we have supposed. Profound order is being discovered in large, complex, and apparently random systems. I believe that this emergent order underlies not only the origin of life itself, but much of the order seen in organisms today. So, too, do many of my colleagues, who are starting to find overlapping evidence of such emergent order in different kinds of complex systems.

Most biologists, inheritors of the Darwinian tradition, suppose that the order of ontogeny (the development of organisms from fertilized egg to adult) is due to the grinding away of a molecular Rube Goldberg machine, slapped together piece by piece by evolution. I present a countering thesis: Most of the beautiful order seen in ontogeny is spontaneous, a natural expression of the stunning self-organization that abounds in very complex regulatory networks. We appear to have been profoundly wrong. Order, vast and generative, arises naturally.

[If] this idea is true, then we must rethink evolutionary theory, for the sources of order in the biosphere will now include both natural selection *and* self-organization.

To repeat, evolutionary scientists realize that evolution has features that remain mysterious to us. We emphasize this because our basic proposals about human transformation do not stand or fall with the changes of evolutionary theory that will come with new scientific discoveries. Our acceptance of evolution as a reality must not be limited by the fact that evolutionary theory is incomplete.

As you will see in the pages that follow, knowledge of how evolution has brought us to where we are and continues to operate in human affairs can help us create practical ways to realize our greater potentials. If we deny that it is a fact or dismiss it as irrelevant to our further development, we forfeit a wondrous inheritance.

THE MEANDERING COURSE OF EVOLUTION

In ancient Turkey there was a river called the Meander that had more twists and turns than a corkscrew. That legendary body of water gave us a verb we still use today to describe looping and languorous journeys such as those we see in the evolution of species and the long, tortuous paths of human change.

But though it meanders, evolution also progresses. And more than that, we believe, it is possibly en route to a stupendous transition. In this book, we present evidence that points toward such an event, evidence that another evolutionary step is tentatively beginning in the human race, both spontaneously and through deliberate practice.

The meandering course of evolution from the Big Bang to living species to the appearance of humankind has created the inorganic, biological, and human worlds, which can be seen to comprise three evolutionary stages or domains. In this progression, evolution itself has evolved, first when matter gave rise to life, and second, when life produced *Homo sapiens*.

The evolutionary theorists Theodosius Dobzhansky and Francisco Ayala have called these two watershed events instances of 'evolutionary transcendence' because in each of them there arose a new order of existence. 'Inorganic evolution went beyond the bounds of [its] previous physical and chemical patternings when it gave rise to life,' Ayala wrote. 'In the same sense, biological evolution transcended itself when it gave rise to man.'

The appearance of life and the emergence of humankind marked the beginnings of new evolutionary eras. They were made possible, though, by countless changes that preceded them. For example, the creation of new elements in exploding stars and the subsequent formation of complex molecules on Earth made living cells possible, and the evolution of land-roving vertebrates from fishlike ancestors led to the development of primates, which, in turn, evolved into *Homo sapiens*.

A principal architect of evolutionary theory, G. Ledyard Stebbins, described many small and large steps of organic evolution, distinguishing minor from major advances of living things. There have been about six hundred forty thousand of the former, he estimated, and from twenty to one hundred of the latter during the hundreds of millions of years of plant and animal development. Though such estimates only approximate the actual number of advances that have occurred among living species, they reflect the immense complexity of evolutionary progress.

We cite Stebbins here to draw an analogy at the heart of this book. We believe humankind is also evolving by minor and major steps toward another epochal change. To our way of thinking, the evidence suggests that a new evolutionary domain is tentatively forming in the human race. This emerging domain, like the emergence of life from inorganic matter and humankind from animal species, has been made possible by countless advances large and small, from the birth of spiritual awareness among our ancient ancestors to recent scientific discoveries about our still mostly untapped capacities for extraordinary life.

But given human ignorance, free will, and perversity, this advance is not guaranteed. As we have said, evolution meanders – and has sometimes nearly come to a stop. In the first microseconds of its birth, for example, after a first cosmic collision of matter with antimatter, the universe was left with a relatively small surplus of material particles – but without that surplus the universe would have been nothing more than pure energy. There would have been no elements, no stars, no planets, and no place for life as we know it to evolve. This was among the first of many events that can be seen in retrospect as hazardous close calls in our cosmic adventure.

The Earth's collision with a meteor sixty-five million years ago was another close call. It enabled our mammalian ancestors to flourish by causing the dinosaurs to vanish, but if it had been more severe, no mammals – nor any *Homo sapiens* – could have developed on our planet. And in the human sphere, entire cultures have disappeared, while others have endured for long ages without significant progress. At all its levels, the evolving universe has been filled with both narrow escapes and long periods of time that give no evidence of lasting advance.

The same principle holds for the evolutionary possibilities we are exploring here. Ecological disaster, cataclysmic war, unforeseeable diseases, extraordinary social upheavals, or other catastrophes could so diminish life on Earth that few people or institutions would have the will or resources to cultivate the extraordinary capacities at the heart of the evolutionary advance we foresee. Such events could destroy the conditions for any kind of widespread human progress, let alone a third evolutionary transcendence.

In short, *neither animal nor further human evolution is automatically progressive*. Progress occurs when there is change toward a *better* condition, however that improvement is defined, whereas biological and human evolution is sometimes regressive and often leads to the extinction of entire species and cultures. Biologists such as George Gaylord Simpson and Francisco Ayala have proposed criteria by which animals can be judged to have progressed, among them an increase of adaptive behaviors, development of more efficient sensory organs, increase of energy level as in the warm-bloodedness of birds and mammals, growth of information-processing skills, improved care for the young, expansion into new environments, and progress in individualization.

Similarly, there are many criteria by which to judge individual human development, whether physical, emotional, moral, cognitive, or spiritual, as well as standards by which to assess the progress of human cultures, such as care for the young and the weak, promotion of individual rights and liberties, social justice, prosperity, artistic expression, stewardship of animal life and the environment, and religious freedom. By these or any other criteria, many individuals and cultures will be judged *not* to have developed beyond their predecessors, and some have even clearly regressed.

And the same principle holds for the development of extraordinary human attributes. Long experience in the sacred traditions has shown that ecstasies, illuminations, and supernormal powers provide no guarantee of lasting goodness and growth, and many contemporary studies have shown that meditation, psychotherapy, and other ways of growth do not automatically transform those who undertake them. Whenever we propose that progress *might* or *could* occur, we do not mean that it necessarily *will*. Further human advance depends on us, even if there is reason to believe the scales are tipped in favor of it.

A HIDDEN TELEOLOGY

As we have noted, evolution has clearly demonstrated many kinds of progress. Observing this obvious fact of our universe, many scientists, philosophers, and theologians have asked if evolution has a telos, a fundamental aim or drive to manifest the increasing complexity evident in the development of elements and stars, the creatures of Earth, and the emergence of consciousness in our species. As we will see, many such thinkers have concluded that this is the case.

We share their view. In spite of the randomness evident in the world around us, which can be seen as a kind of dice rolling, we think the dice are loaded. With all its meanders and close calls, our evolving universe has given rise to ever-greater complexities in the material world and the growing capacities of humankind. To see this can give hope in times of doubt, optimism in the midst of negativity, and courage to tap our deepest potentials.

At the core of this book is our belief that the universe has a telos, a fundamental tendency to manifest its latent divinity. Though evolution suffers many close calls and wanders at every level, it has given rise for billions of years to greater and greater capacities among the Earth's living things. To say that evolution appears to meander is not to say that it has no direction. Indeed, many attributes of living things exhibit clear lines of progress *across* evolutionary domains.

For example, a single-celled organism's dim perception of the outside world, the improved human vision produced by sensory training, and the extraordinary visual acuity reported by certain athletes and mystics exhibit an apparent continuity. This development of perceptual ability has unfolded for some four billion years, though improved sensory capacities among our animal ancestors were produced by natural selection and their further development in us requires our uniquely human consciousness and intention, deliberate training, and the ego-transcending gifts, or graces, of transformative practice.

In other words, the ability to perceive environmental stimuli continues to develop even though it is shaped in different ways at different stages of evolution. And the same principle is evident among other capacities. Bodily awareness, movement, information processing, and other abilities that are shaped by natural selection during animal evolution can be amplified by human discipline and at times, it seems, by higher powers.

In Part Two, we develop the idea that all of our human attributes, each of which has evolved from those of our animal ancestors, are capable of further development. Taken as a whole, such advances suggest that evolution is influenced by purposes or agencies that to some extent transcend and subsume the mechanisms presently recognized by mainstream science. The multibillion-year development of such capacities suggests that nature indeed has a telos, a tendency to go beyond itself, a drive or attraction toward greater ends.

If this universal tendency does indeed exist, it must have been operating from the Big Bang through the development of the inorganic world to the advent of life and human consciousness. And it must be with us still. Humans have long sensed that something transcendent calls us on, often framing their intuition in myth, poetry or philosophic speculation. In the next chapter, we will see that this intuition has developed since the Stone Age.

2

A HISTORY OF HUMAN AWAKENING

Evolution entered a new domain with the appearance of humankind. Intelligence, communication skills, and other attributes of animal life advanced dramatically as our species formed newly creative social groups, harnessed fire, developed new tools, learned to speak, and tried to make greater sense of the world around them. As their capacities developed, our ancestors awoke to the Transcendent and began to advance toward the truth of their higher nature. This evolution began in the Stone Age and accelerated during the civilized era, often meandering, sometimes regressing, but preparing us nevertheless for still another evolutionary leap.

In this chapter, we will briefly review some of the great turning points that constitute this general advance. In this we will not try to be all-inclusive, for such an attempt would take us beyond our competence and the scope of this book. We are not trying to be definitive here in our judgments about the relative importance of history's great cultural flowerings. Our intent is simply to suggest the continuity of humankind's growth in consciousness, its irrepressible drive to exceed its apparent limitations, and its ever-astonishing capacity for further development. We have had extraordinary predecessors. Countless pathfinders have opened frontier after frontier for us to explore. By reviewing the advances they have made, we can better appreciate our possibilities for growth, our insistent urge toward a greater life, and the evolutionary adventures that await us.

SHAMANISM

There was a time in the history of our Stone-Age ancestors when the development of their abilities began to accelerate. Paleontologists date this flowering to a period some fifty or sixty thousand years ago. More swiftly than ever before, our forebears elaborated language, toolmaking, art, and their approach to the spirit world. Shamans were central in this awakening. They were at once medicine men or women, visionaries, masters of the ritual, artists, and guides to realms beyond the senses.

Early evidence of the shaman's existence can be found in painted caves such as those at Lascaux, Pech-Merle, and Les Trois Freres, where he is depicted as a figure masked to suggest a bird in flight, a wizard-beast, or other numinous forms that expressed his extraordinary powers and consciousness. Such images, some of which were painted more than twenty thousand years ago, combined with many studies of shamanism among still-existent peoples, show that shamans have long been the primary mediators in their communities for contact with the spirit world.

Shamans have long derived their central place in Stone-Age cultures from knowledge of healing medicines and rituals, from abilities to assist their tribe in the hunt, and from their use of spells for love and battle. But their chief importance for our purposes here is their capacity to enter ecstatic trance as well as altered states of waking consciousness, from which they gain powers to heal their fellows, interpret dreams, and bring their community into closer rapport with worlds beyond the reach of the ordinary senses.

Studies in Siberia, Central Asia, Australia, Africa, and the Americas have shown that there are remarkable similarities between shamanic practices in different parts of the world. The members of most Stone-Age cultures believed, for example, that while in trance shamans can journey to various heavens and underworlds, communicate with supernatural beings, liberate spirits of the dead, and retrieve lost souls. From such journeys, it is said, shamans learn how to heal both physical and spiritual ailments, locate animals clairvoyantly for the hunt, help relocate his tribe if that is necessary, and assist his tribe in other ways. With the supernormal powers they receive from beyond, they can better preside over rites of passage associated with birth, adolescence, marriage, and death. Such powers exhibit a pattern that becomes more distinct, as we shall see, in later sacred traditions, but with Stone-Age shamans, they appear in organized fashion for the first time on Earth. In shamanism, we see the first institutionalization of visions and practices that open humankind to other worlds, extraordinary powers, and contact with the Transcendent.

Shamans find their vocation in various ways. In some cultures, they inherit the role from a parent. Some are 'wounded healers,' having come through madness, seizures, deformity, or life-threatening illness with healing insights and powers. But in most cases they experience initiatory practices and ordeals that produce altered states of consciousness, a sense of transcendent identity, and other extraordinary attributes. Imbued with special authority, they help to heal the sick, preside over sacred rituals, and provide guidance to the spirit world.

In many Stone-Age cultures, shamans have become living, ever-present symbols of the Transcendent. In this they are the forerunners of the prophets, saints, and seers who gave rise to the world's great religions and the other visionaries who have led humankind's awakening to the extraordinary capacities described in this book.

THE ANCIENT MYSTERY SCHOOLS

Many thousands of years after the birth of shamanism, the human awakening to the Transcendent that began in the Stone Age was kept alive in centers of religious ritual that emerged in Greece, Syria, Anatolia, Egypt, and Persia. These 'mystery schools' involved adoration of various deities, rites of spiritual transformation, and elaborate religious dramas based on sacred marriages of the gods and their deaths and rebirths.

According to the eminent scholar Karl Kerenyi, 'participation in the mysteries offered a guarantee of life without fear of death.' During annual and seasonal mystery festivals, such rituals revealed a vision of eternity and the source of life. At Eleusis, a place famous for such events, the participants experienced a dramatized reenactment of the abduction of Persephone and her reunion with her mother, Demeter, the goddess of agriculture. Though the initiates were under injunction to never speak of what they saw, poets such as Pindar and Sophocles echoed these rapturous words of the Homeric hymns when they described what the Mysteries revealed: 'Blessed is he among men on earth who has beheld this.'

Another important Greek festival, which was held in honor of Dionysus, the god of the vine, reflected humankind's fascination with death and resurrection.

During passion plays in ancient Egypt, participants observed a sacred drama enacting the rebirth of the god Osiris in the underworld with the help of the goddess Isis and the birth of their son. In the mysteries of ancient Persia held in honor of Mithra, a sacred bull was slain to guarantee the fertility of the earth and initiates consumed bread and water that represented the body and blood of the divine and signified the mystery of eternal life. Rites such as these were also celebrated among Germanic tribes that worshiped Woden, and by the Celtic Druids. Their prevalence in early Christian times is reflected in Saint Paul's famous statement regarding the gospel of Christ, 'Lo, I bring you a mystery.'

Greek philosophy, too, was influenced by such rites. Such influence can be seen in Plato's famous parable of the cave and passages from several of his Dialogues. In his dialogue *Phaedrus*, for example, Socrates says:

> But then there was beauty to be seen, brightly shining, when with the blessed choir . . . the souls beheld the beatific spectacle and vision and were perfected in that mystery of mysteries which it is meet to call the most blessed. This did we celebrate in our true and perfect selves, when we were yet untouched by all the evils in time to come; when as initiates we were allowed to see perfect and simple, still and happy. Purer was the light that shone around us, and pure were we.

These festivals and rituals nurtured humankind's witness to the Transcendent in civilizations that came after the Stone Age and preserved initiatory practices such as those that the shaman had preserved for humankind. They kept alive our intuitive sense that the soul is secretly connected with the divine and, like the great awakenings that were to follow, they pointed countless people toward a greater life to come.

THE VEDIC HYMNS AND UPANISHADS

Human consciousness, we believe, made another significant advance with the emergence of Vedic culture in India during the second millennia B.C.E., It is difficult to date the origins of its founding scriptures exactly, though most scholars now agree that they were composed and passed along orally by the Aryan invaders of northern India. They are the oldest body of religious texts used today in something close to their original form.

The Vedas are divided into four bodies of text, the oldest called the Rig Veda. They include hymns and prayers to the gods, injunctions for sacrificial rites, formulas for healing and nutrition, mythologies of ancient India, spiritual philosophy, and instructions for yogic practice. Their teachings have long been considered the ultimate authority in Hindu India, the wellspring of religion, philosophy, and literature, but their teachings are uneven, having evolved from the superstitious beliefs of ancient India to understandings of human nature and transformative practice that have never been surpassed in depth and subtlety. The results of this evolution are most evident in the body of texts called the Upanishads.

These teachings, which make up the final part of the Vedas, are spiritual treatises composed by poets, mystics, and philosophers rather than priests between 800 and 200 B.C.E., though some were composed in Sanskrit as late as the fifteenth century C.E. The Sanskrit word 'upanishad' refers to direct spiritual instruction, literally 'sitting at the feet of a master.' Such instruction leads the aspirant to direct experience of the Ultimate, or Brahman, which in essence is one with atman, the deepest self. This core teaching is famously summarized in the Chhandogya Upanishad, where the aspirant, Shwetaketu, is told 'thou art that.'

It is often said in these sacred texts that this realization can best be sustained through yogic practice. But according to the Katha Upanishad, 'The way is as narrow and hard to traverse as the edge of a razor. Not through much learning is the atman reached, not through the intellect and sacred teaching.' Only through direct experience, which yogic concentration and meditation can produce, can we know atman, our essential self, which is one with Brahman, the transcendent and omnipresent reality. This is the core teaching of the great Indian texts. According to them, the deepest mysteries of existence cannot be penetrated by intellectual exertion alone, but only through spiritual vision, which involves direct experience of the ultimate in its eternal being (*sat*), knowledge (*chit*), and joy (*ananda*).

The earliest vedic hymns celebrated the mystical link between human life and the Transcendent, but the Upanishads carried that teaching to new heights, establishing an intimate relationship between master and student, and poetically teaching that every human being can experience transcendent knowing and identity. That we can, through transformative practice, realize our oneness with the divine, in both its immanent and transcendent aspects, was memorialized in scripture for the first time on Earth in these Indian texts.

TAOISM

From the seventh to the fourth century B.C.E. in Asia, Greece, and the Middle East, there was another extraordinary surge of intellectual and spiritual creativity. As we have seen, Vedic culture gave birth to the Upanishads. In China, Taoism arose. In India, the Buddha flourished. Among the Jews there appeared several of the world's greatest prophets. And in Athens and other Greek city-states, philosophic speculation made an evolutionary leap. Some philosophers have called this period the 'Axial Age' in reference to the dramatic ethical and spiritual turn that occurred among peoples across half of the world. Never before had so many cultures advanced at once in religion and philosophy. This unprecedented period of human history contributed countless insights and practices that are preparing us still for what could be another evolutionary leap.

It is said in the *Tao Te Ching*, the central scripture of Taoism, that the meaning of Tao cannot be captured in words. As its author, Lao-Tzu, wrote, it is 'the mystery beyond all mysteries.' However, the word 'tao' means way, in the sense of water finding its natural course or clouds moving with the wind. Taoism teaches that nothing in life is static, that all is in dynamic flux, and that inner peace and well being can only occur if a person comes into harmony with this fundamental feature of worldly existence.

The *Tao Te Ching*, which was composed in the sixth century B.C., gave voice to the coalescence of Chinese philosophy and shamanism that grew into the religious-philosophical culture of Taoism. Its teachings, though metaphysically elevated, gave rise to many practical arts, among them the geomantic practice of feng shui (literally 'wind and water'), which helps architecture and land-scaping find accord with the world's natural contours and forces; the art of calligraphy, in which the student is taught to trust the hand's intuitive flow in creating beautiful script; the martial art of tai chi, which is based on movements that harmonize the body with *chi*, the subtle energy that pervades the universe; and Taoist art, which highlights the harmony, power, and beauty of the surging currents that pervade the universe (sometimes represented by the yin-yang symbol and magical beasts such as the dragon).

Taoism emphasizes the cultivation of *chi*; the right use

of *i*, or will; the practice of *wu-wei*, 'non-doing,' or flowing surrender to deep nature; and *tzu jan*, disciplined spontaneity. In concert, these give rise to wisdom, joy, beauty, and goodness. But in cultivating them, you cannot 'push the river.' To seek spiritual liberation with brute will or excessive self-consciousness will only bring failure. As the third-century B.C.E. sage Chuang Tzu put it, 'Easy is right. The right way to go easy is to forget the right way and forget that the going is easy.'

Taoism brought new subtlety and depth to the arts of everyday life, and through its influence on Zen Buddhism and Asian culture in general it has given us many ways to cultivate the world's natural beauty and grace. Its influence, for example, can be detected today in the rediscovery of 'design with nature' in architecture and gardening, and the emphasis among environmentalists on 'biomimicry,' in the use of herbal medicines and acupuncture, and in modern psychology's interest in 'flow.' More than any sacred tradition before it or any since, Taoism has elaborated a philosophy, an aesthetic, and a set of practices that promote harmony with the natural structures and rhythms of the Earth and human nature. The values of Taoism are important for our vision of further human development. If we do not distort its philosophy of *wu-wei*, as some of its followers have done by remaining passive in the face of wrongdoing, we can benefit from its celebration of the divine immanence.

BUDDHISM

In the fifth century B.C.E., Buddhism emerged as a reform of Indian religious culture, and has been both a laboratory and disseminator of liberating disciplines ever since. Its founder was Gautama Buddha (the Enlightened One), who during the sixth century B.C. taught in many parts of

India. Born an Indian prince, he grew up surrounded by the pleasures of a royal court, but after he married and had a son, he encountered death, poverty, and injustice outside his palace walls and began to long for a life with greater consequence and meaning. According to legend, he left his family and privileged life, practiced intense asceticism for six years, then sat beneath a bodhi tree vowing to remain until he was free from the world's bondage. And there he remained until he found enlightenment and the principles of his subsequent teaching.

These principles comprise the Buddha's four 'noble truths.' The first is that all life is marked by suffering (*dukha*), the second that suffering is caused by desire (*kama*), and the third that release from suffering, or *nirvana* (literally, 'blowing out' the flames of desire) can be realized. The fourth noble truth is that the way to nirvana can be found in the 'eightfold noble path,' which includes right understanding or view, right thought, right speech, right action, right livelihood, right effort, right concentration, and right mindfulness. Each of these has been elaborated in various ways as Buddhist practice has evolved in different schools, but their essential unity of purpose endures in the Buddhist commitment to ideas and disciplines that produce freedom from suffering and spiritual ignorance through detachment and wisdom. The Buddha emphasized practical ways to realize nirvana rather than metaphysics and, though Buddhism has given rise to some of the world's most elaborate and sophisticated philosophies, this emphasis has endured through the centuries. As it developed, it spawned a powerful ethic of service to those in need. This spirit of compassion has been accentuated by the doctrine of the bodhisattva, the enlightened being who forgoes nirvana until all beings are freed from suffering.

Buddhism has produced many philosophers, saints, and sages, among them: Ananda, who according to legend was the Buddha's foremost and favorite disciple; Ashoka Maurya, who reigned as emperor of India from 269 to 232 B.C.E., giving support and prominence to the Buddhist community while helping to spread Buddhist teachings beyond his empire's borders; Nagarjuna (ca. 150–250 C.E.), a philosopher held in such high esteem by segments of the Buddhist community that he is sometimes called 'the second Buddha,' and who is recognized as the founder of the Madhyamika (Middle Path) school, the influence of which helped give rise to the Mahayana ('great vehicle') traditions of China and Japan; Bodhidharma (470–543 C.E.), an Indian monk who personifies the entry of Buddhism into China and is remembered as its 'First Patriarch'; Padmasambhava (eighth century C.E.), the founder of Vajrayana Buddhism, the main religion of Tibet, who is venerated in the Tibetan tradition as Guru Rimpoche (precious teacher) and who was said to have transformed the demons and gods of indigenous Bon shamanism into the protective deities of the Tibetan Buddhist pantheon; Milarepa (1052–1135 C.E.), Tibet's most celebrated poet-yogi, who after overcoming great adversity in his youth studied with the famous guru, Marpa the Translator, and spent twelve years alone in a cave until he reached enlightenment; Dōgen (1200–53 C.E.), a founder of the Soto branch of Zen and one of Buddhism's greatest and most influential philosophers, who believed that meditation practice, or *zazen*, not only leads to enlightenment but *is* enlightenment; Matsuo Basho (1643–94 C.E.), considered to be the founder of haiku, a short form of poetry used to express moments of spiritual illumination and reveal the deeper essence of everyday things; Hakuin (1686–1769 C.E.), who adopted Buddhism at the age of eight and was a principal teacher in Zen's Rinzai school; and the fourteenth Dalai Lama, who left Tibet in 1959 to work for the survival of his people, human rights, world peace, and nonviolence.

Buddhism's greatest gifts to us now come from its wealth of transformative methods, the ethical teachings these involve, and the intimate secrets of practice preserved in its various lineages. For more than two millennia, Buddhism has gathered an immense lore of human development related to the emergent capacities we will describe in Part Two. This immense body of experience has its roots in the yogas of ancient India, but incorporates innumerable discoveries from the shamanism of Tibet, Siberia, and Mongolia; from Taoist and other Chinese traditions; from the Zen Buddhist schools of Japan; and from other sources. This is the case in part because Buddhism has adapted well to different cultures. In Sri Lanka, Burma, and Thailand, it accommodated the otherworldly asceticism which had spread from India. In Tibet it incorporated the teachings of the ancient Bon cult, which had its roots in shamanism and spirit worship. In China, it blended its essential teachings with the earthy Taoist emphasis on 'non-doing,' beauty, and the practical arts. In Japan, it found accord with the warrior culture of the samurai with its emphasis on courage, high energy, and mindful concentration in every action.

In making these and other cultural adaptations, Buddhism has often gone beyond the insights of its founder and early practitioners, and in so doing it has become an immense repository of liberating practices and insights about our greater potentials. Among these are the meditative disciplines of South Asia's Theravada Buddhism, the visualization and energy mobilization techniques of Tibet, and the mindfulness training of Zen, all of which are widely used today not only in Asia but in Europe and the Americas. Through the centuries, Buddhism has had a genius for adapting transformative disciplines to various cultures so that they are more

45

widely accessible. As understanding of our emergent nature grows, it will incorporate more and more discoveries embodied in the various schools of Buddhist practice.

THE GREEK MIRACLE

As Taoism and Buddhism began to develop in Asia, Greek city-states and their colonies were flowering on the shores of the Mediterranean Sea. Wealth generated by Greek enterprise supported developments in politics, philosophy, mathematics, history, and the arts that laid many of the foundations for Western culture. Democracy made its appearance in Athens, the epicenter of this cultural awakening, and has remained a political ideal for nations around the world. New schools of philosophy arose in conjunction with mathematical discoveries and observations of the physical world that anticipated the methods and findings of modern science. Greek historians, dramatists, and masters of rhetoric gave rise to a sense of the individual's rights and potential greatness that would help inspire the European Renaissance. And through Pythagoras, Plato, and other thinkers, Greek culture produced a marriage of speculative metaphysics with mystical insight, psychological acuity, and the spirit of science. From these historic developments came the integral spirit we need to explore the complexities of our evolving world and human nature.

To name the great figures of ancient Greece would take us beyond the scope of this brief history, but a few are especially important for our vision of human possibility. Let us begin with Pythagoras, who lived from about 580 to about 500 B.C.E. For him, there was no difference between 'science' and 'religion.' To understand the nature of physical things and their relation to the human soul was, for Pythagoras, a spiritual activity. He founded an ascetic brotherhood at Croton in Italy that was dedicated to the study of mathematics, self-inquiry, disciplined habits, and the contemplation of the cosmos. This integral practice, he believed, exalted the soul and drew it closer to eternity. Several discoveries in geometry are attributed to him (his name graces a famous theorem). He devised the theory of intervals in musical scales and imagined intervals between the heavenly bodies that harmonized to make what came to be known as 'the music of the spheres.' And his teachings about the transmigration of souls influenced Plato, the Neoplatonists, and other philosophers.

Socrates (470–399 B.C.E.) was an electrifying figure in Athens during the time of its greatest flowering. He was a physically and spiritually vigorous man who once had fought bravely for his city-state, a prominent critic of conventional opinion, and a prime originator of dialectical inquiry in thought and conversation. His liberating skepticism was reflected in his supposed response to an utterance by the Delphic oracle that no man was wiser than Socrates. If true, Socrates responded, it was because he alone knew that he knew nothing. Most conventional assumptions about the world, he claimed, had to be questioned. The unexamined life was not worth living. His relentless efforts to stimulate self-inquiry and examination of social norms caused the Athenian authorities to banish him from Athens, but following his guardian spirit, or *daimon*, he chose death instead. Socrates has been a moral and spiritual exemplar for Western culture. He dramatized dialectical inquiry, which came to be called the 'Socratic method'; helped lead his most famous student, Plato, to philosophy; and has inspired acts of ethical integrity for two and a half millennia.

In the words of the English philosopher Alfred North Whitehead, all western philosophy is a series of footnotes

47

to Plato, and most historians agree that no Western philosopher has had more influence than Socrates' great pupil. In his Dialogues, where Socrates is often the main speaker, Plato explored the timeless questions about our identity and the means by which we acquire knowledge. He also proposed practical ways to live a good life, improve education, and govern social and political activity. In this he was highly imaginative and often playful, putting forth his questions and proposals in a richly suggestive variety of ways. Though his opinions about various subjects changed during the nearly forty years he wrote, several consistent themes mark his work. We learn, for example, largely by *anamnesis*, the remembrance of things we knew before we were born to this world. Our course in life is informed by a guardian spirit, or daimon, as Socrates taught, which can be a stern taskmaster but is accessible through self-understanding. By means of dialectical inquiry (*dianoia*), the practice of virtue, and contemplation, or direct perception (*noesis*) of the true, the good, and the beautiful, the soul can find wisdom and eternal life. Plato founded a school on his family's land, near the Grove of Academus. Called the 'Academy,' it flourished in Athens for nine hundred years and nurtured the Platonic philosophy that has influenced the world ever since.

Aristotle (384–22 B.C.E.) was Plato's greatest student, but eventually questioned certain aspects of his teacher's metaphysical scheme, including his Theory of Forms, which held that there existed eternal ideas with which worldly things imperfectly corresponded. Aristotle's genius was wide-ranging. He created a formal logic that was central in the development of Western thought. He classified plant and animal specimens with an exactitude that helped set standards for later biology (some two thousand years later, Charles Darwin called him 'the greatest biologist of all time'). His *Poetics* virtually invented literary criticism. His writings on ethics have been among the world's most influential. And his emphasis on the careful observation of living things, the inorganic world, and human nature helped give birth to scientific method as it is practiced today.

In spite of their differences, Aristotle and Plato shared many views. They both celebrated self-inquiry and virtue as the bases of wisdom and human fulfillment, and claimed we can learn to contemplate and thus 'see' (through *noesis*) the eternal activity of God. Both of them recognized the mutual entailment of the virtues, that courage without prudence, for example, is suicidal, or that justice without mercy is cruel and brutish. They were the two greatest philosophers of ancient Greece, bringing to the world unprecedented intellectual range and flexibility in their integral embrace of the physical, social, moral, and spiritual worlds. Their influence endured not only among Platonists and Aristotelians but also among thinkers of other persuasions.

Their simultaneous influence can be seen, for example, in the works of Plotinus, the founder of Neoplatonism who flourished in Rome during the third century C.E. and is considered by many to be the greatest Western philosopher between Aristotle and Thomas Aquinas, a stretch of one thousand five hundred years. The Plotinian doctrine, that the world and each human soul have their origins in 'the One' and press always for return to their source, profoundly influenced subsequent pagan, Jewish, Christian, and Islamic mystical philosophy and practice. The writings of Plotinus (collected by his disciple Porphyry in six nine-part books called the *Enneads*) remain important catalysts today for thinking about human nature and its relation to the Transcendent.

Ancient Greece contributed much to a vision and practice of many-sided, or integral, transformation. Without the democracy first modeled in Athens, we would not have the freedom for self-inquiry and experiment, nor the guarantees of rights and liberties we need for the exploration of our further reaches. Without the playfulness, fertility, and spirit of science we find in Greek philosophy, we would not have the combination of intellectual flexibility and exactitude we need for theories and studies of the human potential. Pythagoras, Plato, Aristotle, and other Greek thinkers were avatars of the integral spirit. They showed the world how to join social understanding, philosophic speculation, the practice of virtue, and mystical insight in comprehensive views of the cosmos and human nature.

THE JEWISH PROPHETS

The great Jewish prophets of the Axial Age, who lived between the ninth and fourth centuries B.C.E., broadened the conception of a tribal Yahweh to make Him the God of all peoples. For Isaiah, Yahweh was the One God, the Power beyond all powers who encompasses and yet utterly transcends the forces of nature. Not to be captured in images, He aches for his creation, cares for it in ways humans cannot grasp, and demands that his people bear allegiance to his love and eternal principles. This broadened conception of deity reinforced the idea that all men and women, including the poor, the sick, and the oppressed, are equal children of the Living God. For Isaiah, Micah, Amos, Jeremiah, and Elijah, we are called by Yahweh to resist injustice and care for those in need. Only through righteousness can people reflect the radiance of the God who is their Creator.

Not all Jews, of course, held this inclusive view of their maker. But the witness of Isaiah and the prophets who shared his universality of spirit brought a powerful vision to humankind of a single, personal God actively involved in the world. In spite of distortions by bigots and religious zealots, that vision has for two thousand five hundred years been disseminated by Judaism and its offspring, Christianity and Islam. 'Pressing for meaning in every direction,' wrote Huston Smith, an eminent philosopher of religion, Judaism stood witness to freedom and justice in human affairs and 'laid the foundation for social conscience that has been a hallmark of Western civilization.'

The great Jewish prophets saw that ethical standards must be met if people were to live together peacefully. At this threshold in history, when might was considered right, these passionate men boldly declared that the standard of behavior must be justice and righteousness for all. Their epiphanies, written down in the Old Testament, set the stage, for better or worse, for religion to become a political force. Their proclamation resounds today: If life is not as it should be, radical change is needed.

The prophets were the spiritual antennae of Israel, monitoring its fidelity to the Sacred Covenant Moses made with God at Sinai. In taking their nation to task for its failings, in measuring its realities against sacred ideals, they initiated the tradition of moral critique applied to all, including the highest worldly powers. We now recognize this tradition as an essential element of a just society. For the Jewish prophets, the heart of religion is moral action, not ritual, not mystical ecstasy alone. 'No other sacred scripture,' says the philosopher Walter Kaufman, 'contains books that speak out against social injustice as eloquently, unequivocally, and sensitively.' The Jewish prophets, more fiercely than anyone before them, called the world to recognize that, as Huston Smith wrote, 'Every human being, simply by virtue of his or her humanity, is a child of God and therefore in possession of rights that even kings must respect.' This emphasis on self-transformation through moral faithfulness marks a significant advance in human consciousness.

And with this elevation of monotheism and moral vision, Jewish culture produced another breakthrough in humankind's vision of its place in the world. While the great seers of Asia and most philosophers of Greece saw life on Earth as an endless round, a place from which the liberated soul escaped, the Jews began to see it as a journey toward better things. One day a Messiah would come to set His people free, and bring with Him an age of righteousness. Through this agent of God's will, the world would be redeemed. Time was an arrow, not an endless cycle. The world was headed toward higher ground.

Though a sense of the world's general advance was expressed by a few visionaries in other ancient cultures, the Jews were the first to give it a powerful, culturewide form. Judaism was the first religion to assert that not only the human soul but the world as a whole is on a cosmic journey. This is in sharp contrast with Eastern and ancient Greek notions of cyclical history. The idea that there is a transcendent purpose in world events, which was prevalent in Judaism for the first time among an entire people, was carried forward by Christianity and given new expression, as we shall see, by European philosophers who joined modern ideas of progress with our witness to the Transcendent, thus conceiving the world to be a progressive manifestation of its implicit divinity.

Many prophets, philosophers, mystics, and saints have embodied and shaped the teachings of Judaism, among them: Amos, who emphasized social justice; Hosea, whose overarching message was God's love of his creatures; Isaiah, whose sayings alternate between chastisement for straying from his people's covenant with God and reassurance of His universal love and forgiveness; Jeremiah, who passionately called for social justice and nonviolence; Rabbi Hillel (ca. 60 B.C.E.–first century C.E.) a principal shaper of Judaism at the beginning of the

Christian era who emphasized helping the poor, social justice, the life of the mind, saintly habits, and the intellectual study of the Torah; Philo (ca. 25 B.C.E.–50 C.E.), a philosopher-theologian from Alexandria, Egypt, who was deeply learned in Platonic thought and viewed Jewish life as a mystical practice leading toward union with God; Moses Maimonides (1135–1204 C.E.), often called the greatest figure of medieval Jewry, who was celebrated as both physician and philosopher and taught that religious faith must be rationally justifiable; the Baal Shem Tov (1700–1760 C.E.), the charismatic founder of Eastern European Hasidism celebrated as a healer, teacher, and mystic, who grounded Hasidism both in traditional Jewish law and ecstatic celebration; the Maggid of Mezeritz (1710–72 C.E.), the leader of Hasidism after the death of the Baal Shem Tov, who is generally credited with transforming Hasidism into a mass movement and orienting it toward the mystical, Neo-Platonist teachings of the cabala; and Martin Buber (1878–1965 C.E.), the most well-known interpreter of Hasidism in the twentieth century, who brought many tenets of Judaism into contemporary psychology and religious thought.

CHRISTIANITY

Several centuries later, another prophet arose among the Jews. Like his great predecessors, he spoke God's message to a world in danger of going spiritually deaf. Life's deepest meaning, he claimed, is discovered only in relationship to God and in the establishment of a just society. He was called Jesus of Nazareth.

Six hundred years before Jesus appeared, Jews had begun to hope for a great and holy leader, a Messiah, who would lift His people and mend this spiritually broken world. So moved were the followers of Jesus by their master's spiritual authority that it seemed to them the Messiah had indeed arrived. As that small community spread Jesus' good news through the Roman empire, non-Jews responded, at first in small groups, then in rapidly increasing numbers. Within three hundred years, Christianity had become the dominant religion of the Roman empire, and during the two millennia since, it has become the most populous religion on Earth. It goes without saying that Christianity, like any large-scale social movement, has been involved in its share of inhuman behavior. However, Christian ideas and practices have also been sources of profound individual fulfillment and moral improvement in the world at large.

The teachings of Jesus are dominated by his witness to God's love for humankind and our need to let that love flow through us to others, even to those who attack and torment us. His passionate exhortation – 'But I say to you: Love your enemies and pray for those who persecute you so that you may be children of your Father in heaven' – helps us understand the extraordinary fellowship of early Christians, who lived in a time of terrible oppression. The theologian John Crossan described the Christian utopian dream 'in which material and spiritual goods, political and religious resources, economic and transcendental accesses are equally available to all without interference from brokers, mediators, or intermediaries.' With its emphasis on love and community, early Christianity preserved and extended the Jewish belief in the 'arrow of time,' the promise that the world has direction and purpose. This theology has been framed in many ways during the long course of Christian history.

Saint Paul is often called the second founder of Christianity. His letters are a touchstone for Christian theology, second in importance only to the Gospels. His interpretation of Christ's teaching centers on the transformative powers of love. 'Love is patient,' he wrote.

'Love is kind; love is not envious or arrogant or rude. It does not insist on its own way; it is not irritable or resentful; it does not rejoice in wrongdoing, but rejoices in the truth. It bears all things, believes all things, hopes all things, endures all things. Love never ends.' (I Corinthians 13:4–8)

After Saint Paul, Saint Augustine of Hippo (354–430 C.E.) was the most influential thinker of the early Christian Western Church. In his *Confessions* he declared, 'Understanding follows faith,' and this tenet became a central epistemological underpinning of the Church. But like all world religions, Christianity has nurtured various ways to approach the Transcendent. Its fundamental principles have been embodied, interpreted, and enriched by many thinkers, saints, and mystics, among them: Dionysus the Areopagite (fl. 500 C.E.), a Middle Eastern monk influenced by Neo-platonism, who described the soul's ascent to God in ecstatically mystical terms and influenced subsequent Christian contemplatives; Origen, a contemporary of Plotinus in the third century C.E. and the greatest theologian of the Eastern Christian Church (whom we will turn to in Chapter 15); the fourth- and fifth-century desert fathers of Egypt, Palestine, Arabia, and Persia, whose ecstatic example inspired people throughout the declining Roman empire, including many aristocrats, to adopt an ascetic life of prayer; Saint Benedict, who founded the first great monastery in Western Europe at Monte Casino in the sixth century C.E. and whose rules for monastic life became the template for later monasticism of the Western Christian Church; the Irish monks of the early Middle Ages, who helped preserve Western civilization by copying Greek and Latin manuscripts and bringing their work to the continent; Hildegard of Bingen (1098–1179), a German Benedictine mystic, abbess, poet, painter, playwright, composer, and visionary, who combined spiritual depth with great artistic and practical ability; Saint Francis of Assisi (1182–1226), a universally beloved figure who embodied compassion, simplicity, and love of nature in ways that have captured the world's imagination ever since; Saint Thomas Aquinas (1225–74), the greatest Christian theologian of the middle ages, who addressed humankind's fundamental questions with extraordinary range and depth; Meister Eckhart (1260–1327), who has drawn considerable attention in recent times for his doctrine of the Godhead within ('The eye with which I see God is the same eye with which God sees me'), which accords well with similar ideas in Hinduism, Buddhism, and Sufism; Saint Teresa of Avila (1515–82), a great mystic and abbess who founded a reform of the Carmelites and whose *Autobiography* and other writings are among the world's most influential contemplative manuals; Saint John of the Cross, another mystic of world renown and fellow Carmelite reformer with Saint Teresa; the Protestant mystic layman Jacob Boehme (1575–1624), who influenced the Quakers, William Blake, the philosopher Schelling and other poets and philosophers; Saint Therese de Lisieux (1873–97), a French Carmelite nun who inspired people around the world by her holy simplicity; Padre Pio (1887–1968) a charismatic capuchin monk, healer, and stigmatic who attracted a worldwide following among Catholics and non-Catholics alike; Mother Teresa (1910–98), an Albanian nun who became world famous for helping the poor and won the Nobel Peace Prize in 1979; the twentieth-century theologian Paul Tillich, who pioneered new directions in Christian theology; and Teilhard de Chardin (1881–1955), a French Jesuit priest and paleontologist, whose evolutionary vision of the universe has had a great influence on religious thinkers in the twentieth century.

This honor roll could be greatly enlarged, but it is long enough to suggest Christianity's incalculable richness and depth. Like the other sacred traditions we have noted, it has evoked and nurtured a wide range of ego-transcendent attributes among people from all parts of society. In elaborating Jesus' teaching that God's love channeled through us can save the world, it has dramatized our capacities for transformation and helped set the stage for humankind's further spiritual advance.

ISLAM

Islam is the second most populous and the fastest growing of the world's religions. Though it is customary to date its origins to the birth of Mohammad in sixth-century Arabia, many Muslims see it as a culmination of the wider and older tradition that began with Abraham and produced Judaism and Christianity before it. The first of Islam's two central affirmations is that 'There is no god but God' (*La ilaha illa'llah*). The God referred to here is none other than the One God of the Jews and the Christians, the God who created the universe, revealed His will to Abraham, Moses, and the Jewish prophets, and the God whom Jesus called Father. But according to Islamic doctrine, God's message was often distorted or lost in Jewish and Christian times. Muslims believe that God therefore resolved to fully and clearly disclose Himself to humankind. His chosen instrument was a devout and highly charismatic Arab named Muhammed, whose role as an instrument of Allah is honored in the second of Islam's great affirmations: 'Muhammed is the Prophet of God.' The record of God's revelations is contained in the Qur'an (Koran), the Holy Book of Islam. For Muslims, the Qur'an is the living Word of God, the very presence of God on Earth. The two basic sources for Islamic wisdom are the Qur'an itself and the hadith ('traditions'), which reports the Prophet's sayings and deeds by those who knew him. Through *islam*, or submission, one can surrender to the will of Allah and the Qur'an's teaching.

Devotional persistence is reinforced by Islam in its tradition of daily prayer, which is required five times a day. Muslims can pray at home, work, or a local mosque where, bowing toward Mecca, they pray silently or aloud. However, among Muslims there have always been those who want a deeper and more intimate realization of God than that produced by ordinary religious duties. Sufism, the mystical (and often esoteric) tradition of Islam, nurtures this desire. Whereas ordinary Muslims pray five times a day, the Sufi ideal is to pray without ceasing. If for Muslims there is one God, for Sufis there is only God. We are but rays of the Secret Sun seeking always to know our Source.

Three blessings are given to those who love God with the wholeheartedness of Sufism. They are *islam* (submission), *iman* (faith), and *ihsan* (awareness of God). These blessings were evident in the great Islamic mystic and saint Al-Hallaj (d. 922 C.E.), who declared, 'I am the Truth,' thus testifying to his sense that God is our deepest Self. But for most Sufis, ecstatic union with God does not require monastic life. To paraphrase the modern Sufi teacher Sheikh Muzaffer, we can 'keep our hands busy with our worldly duties while our heart is busy with God.'

Sufism and much Islamic philosophy, like Jewish and Christian mysticism, have been influenced, either directly or indirectly, by the Neoplatonism that began with Plotinus. Notable among those who were thus inspired were Abu Hamid al-Ghazzali (1058–1111 C.E.), a brilliant and learned theologian who came to feel that the quest for direct experience of God was both the crown of religious life and the royal road to truth; Shihabuddin Suhrawardi of Jabal in Persia (ca. 1153–91 C.E.), who connected Platonic ideas with an ecstatic theology of angels and light; Muhyiddin ibn Arabi (1165–1240 C.E.) of Andalusia, one of the greatest mystical visionaries to appear in any religious tradition; and Shaikh Ahmad Ahsai, the seventeenth-century founder of the Shaiki school of Iranian mysticism. These and other philosophers, among them Avicenna of Persia and Samarkand (980–1037 C.E.) and Averroes of Spain (ca. 1126–98 C.E.), helped preserve the philosophy of ancient Greece, in combination with Islamic thought, during Europe's Middle Ages. In doing so they established a luminous interface between philosophy and mystical experience that we can draw upon today in the service of integral transformation.

And with its highly imaginative philosophers, Islam has been graced as well by many great poets. Prominent among them are Rabia al-Adawiyya (d. 801 C.E.), a woman from Basra credited with giving birth to Sufism's great theme of God's all-encompassing love, who wrote: 'I'm going to burn down Heaven/And extinquish the fires of Hell,/So that we may worship God out of love alone'; Abu-Yazid Al-Bistami (d. 874 C.E.) of northwestern Iran; Hafiz (ca. 1320–89 C.E.), one of the most beloved of all Sufi mystic-poets, who is celebrated for his humor, trickster spirit, and his rapturous union with the divine, which he celebrated in more than 5,000 poems; and Kabir (1440–1518 C.E.), a religious visionary celebrated for his great sense of humor, his tolerance, and for preaching a simple love of God.

But the most celebrated Sufi poet is Jalaluddin Rumi (1207–73 C.E.), one of the greatest mystic-writers of all time. He was a devout and learned Muslim and sober Sufi master when in 1244, at the age of thirty-seven, he met Shams of Tabriz and was transformed by their three years of ecstatic conversations. After Shams's death, ecstatic poetry erupted from Rumi, who for the rest of his life dictated thousands of poems, parables, fables, and bawdy teaching stories. His lyric poetry, collected in the twenty-two thousand verses of the *Mathnawi*, forms a long rhapsody on love and its endless surprises, the evolution of consciousness, and ecstatic union with God. It is what he called 'the secret work,' the 'opening of the eyes of the heart,' or 'soul growth.' More than seven hundred years after his death, he is almost certainly the world's bestselling poet. As the eminent translator Coleman Barks put it, verses of Rumi such as these are like explosives on a funeral pyre:

> There is a force within that gives you life—
>   Seek That.
> In your body there lies a priceless jewel—
>   Seek That.
> Oh, wandering Sufi,
>   If you are in search of the greatest treasure,
>   Don't look outside,
> Look within, and seek That.

Since the mid-twentieth century, Sufism has attracted a significant following in Europe and the Americas among people desiring authentic spiritual realization without the constraints of monasticism. Sufism's earthiness, humor, and freedom of expression, as well as the imaginative sweep of its great philosophers, in conjunction with its sophisticated practices, have attracted increasing numbers of men and women. Several pioneering teachers of recent times have adapted Sufi teachings to modern society, among them the Iranian writer Idries Shah and the Indian Sufi Hazrat Inayat Khan with his son Pir Vilayat Khan. These and other teachers who were not Sufis, among them the Russian mystic Gurdjieff and his disciple Ouspensky, have inspired groups devoted to meditation, self-inquiry, and devotional exercises drawn from esoteric Sufi schools.

Though Islam, like many religions, has bred dogmatism, intolerance, hatred, and cruelty, it has elevated the morals and spiritual lives of people in many parts of the world. It has also given richly imaginative expression to the ecstasy of mystical devotion. Its lore of esoteric Sufi practice and the synoptic spirit of its greatest philosophers have much to offer a vision and practice of integral transformation.

THE RENAISSANCE

Europe's Middle Ages, which lasted for nearly one thousand years from the fall of Rome to the Italian Renaissance, brought the institutionalization of Christianity; the glories of Gothic architecture; the luminous wisdom of Meister Eckhart, Ibn al-Arabi, and Moses Maimonides; Dante's great poetry; and the gradual establishment of cities, trade, and social order. But it also brought incalculable miseries of war and poverty, the calamities of the Crusades, and the loss of most high culture from Greco-Roman antiquity. Medieval clerics had preserved some Greek and Roman manuscripts, but most classical learning had been lost when a scholarly young poet in Florence named Petrarch (1304–74 C.E.) was inspired to rediscover it. Often called the first humanist and father of the Renaissance, his love poetry and passion for life anticipated modern society's preference for the natural world over the supernatural and individual expression over pious anonymity.

The love of Greek and Roman culture that Petrarch represented flowered in Florence and other Italian city-states for the next two hundred years. Clerics, scholars, and businesspeople alike embraced classical literature, law, politics, architecture, aesthetics, history, and ethics. This revival intensified when the enlightened aristocrat Cosimo di Medici conceived a Platonic Academy in

Florence that was headed by Marsilio Ficino (1433–99 C.E.), the most influential scholar of his day. There, lecturers and students drew upon the Dialogues of Plato, Persian poetry, Arabic philosophy, and Jewish mysticism, as well as studies in magic, alchemy, and the occult. Ficino produced brilliant translations from Greek of Plato, Plotinus, and other writers of antiquity, and encouraged an integral education of intellect, virtue, and contemplative capacity. From Plato he took the idea that part of the human soul is divine, a concept that was central to the Renaissance. Thus it followed, he wrote to a friend, that man 'could create the heavens and what is in them himself, if he could obtain the tools and heavenly material.'

And the arts blossomed as well. Florence's ruling Medici clan, most notably its patriarch Cosimo and his grandson Lorenzo, who was a celebrated statesman and poet, supported Botticelli, Michelangelo, Leonardo da Vinci, and other men of genius. Leonardo embodied the ideal of the Renaissance man. He was a self-described 'disciple of experiment' who worked on problems in science with extraordinary originality, designed buildings and weapons of war, and produced some of humankind's greatest art.

In all this, the medieval turn toward the supernatural was increasingly complemented by worldly realism and affirmation of the individual. Benvenuto Cellini, a famous craftsman, wrote an autobiography in which he boldly celebrated his own talents and accomplishments; Niccolò Machiavelli, a diplomat and political philosopher, wrote *The Prince*, a darkly realistic analysis of worldly power; and painters such as Giotto, Mantegna, and Masaccio brought naturalism to their depictions of the human figure and face. This new attitude is reflected in an anecdote about the Florentine sculptor Donatello, who was said to have shouted at one of his life-like statues: 'Speak then! Why will you not speak?' In these words can be heard a new consciousness, one with new regard for the distinctive form, beauty, and goodness of the human person. Another cultural breakthrough was underway. The emphasis on transcending the world that had characterized most religious traditions was replaced by a celebration of this world's astonishing possibilities for further development. This consciousness soon spread to other parts of Europe.

In the Renaissance, the high regard for anonymity that marked both medieval and Eastern philosophy was replaced by an emphasis on personal expression, power, and fulfillment. This is evident in the words of the Florentine scholar Pico della Mirandola, who said, 'God the Father endowed man from birth with the seeds of every possibility and every life.' Without appreciation such as this of the individual's potential and essential worth, and without the love of learning and nature released in the Renaissance, we could not fully explore our possibilities for extraordinary life on Earth and the wide range of human capacities described in this book.

THE ENLIGHTENMENT

By the beginning of the eighteenth century, this focus on nature and the individual had spread widely in Western culture. 'We can, by speech and pen,' wrote Voltaire, 'make men more enlightened and better.' With these words the French philosopher and satirist encapsulated the European celebration of reason, revolt against religious oppression, and rejection of kings. Through such proclamations, he helped give a name to the age and became the living embodiment of the Enlightenment.

The debate between faith and reason had its roots in Elizabethan times, being voiced by Shakespeare, the philosopher Francis Bacon, and others, then intensified during the Renaissance and Protestant Reformation, and finally gained increasing momentum with the stunning advances of science. As Richard Tarnas wrote in *The Passion of the Western Mind*, 'The need for a clarifying and unifying vision capable of transcending irresolvable religious conflicts was broadly felt. It was amidst this state of acute metaphysical turmoil that the Scientific Revolution began and finally triumphed in the Western mind.' In the light of increasing scientific discovery, supernatural explanations were no longer needed to understand the world and human nature.

The Enlightenment by definition was a celebration of knowledge. This literary, scientific, and philosophical movement emerged from the discoveries of Copernicus, Kepler, Galileo, Newton, Harvey, Linnaeus, and other scientists; the rationalism of the French philosopher Rene Descartes; the experimental methods of Francis Bacon; the empiricism of the English philosopher John Locke; and the skepticism of the Scottish thinker David Hume. Leaders of the Enlightenment, among them the French thinkers Voltaire, Rousseau, and Diderot, rejected traditional wisdom, whether propounded by church or state, that impeded scientific progress and led to political persecution.

By the end of the eighteenth century, the Enlightenment had exerted enormous influence on European and American life. Emblematic of its ambition was Denis Diderot's *Encylopedié*, a collection of scientific and technological advances that celebrated knowledge as power. The Enlightenment's call for intellectual liberty, tolerance, and the ascendance of reason was embraced in England by the historian Gibbon, in Germany by the philosophers Lessing and Goethe, in America by Benjamin Franklin and Thomas Jefferson, and in Russia by Peter the Great, who had traveled through Europe and was exhilarated by the spirit of discovery he found.

The lasting influence of the Enlightenment was confirmed by the establishment of organizations dedicated to the improvement of scientific work and its protection from interference by church and state. Inspired in part by the Platonic Academy of Florence, the Royal Academy was established in London in 1660, and academies of science were also formed at Paris in 1666, at Berlin in 1700, and at St. Petersburg in 1724. These institutions enshrined the principles of science, which involve the careful observation of nature, the formation of testable hypotheses, controlled experiment, valid predictions of naturally occurring events, and the discovery of natural regularities or 'laws.'

But the advent of science had its shadow side. In its ardor to free itself from the dubious beliefs and dogmas of institutional religion, it increasingly rejected the findings of contemplatives and other explorers of the inner life, even though such discoveries were made through disciplined effort and confirmed by communities of fellow seekers. This is a theme we will emphasize in the pages that follow. In its winnowing of fact from superstitious claims, in its passion to find verifiable data, science increasingly turned away from confirmable facts of the inner life that reveal much about the human potential. In discrediting ancient myths and outmoded practices such as alchemy, philosophers and scientists of the Enlightenment began to reject all spiritual phenomena even though many of them are in principle verifiable. This rejection has grown since, giving rise to a strictly materialist view of the world and human nature. It has also contributed to the exploitation and destruction of the natural world.

But in spite of its excesses, the Enlightenment brought evolutionary liberations of the human spirit. Its rejection of intellectual, moral, social, and political oppression led to the overthrow of despotic regimes. Its cool analyses and satires of churchly stupidities helped religion begin to free itself from superstition and dogma. And its celebration of reason contributed to the wonders of science, the advent of modern technology, the improvement of health, and economic prosperity. Its scientific and social advances have given us more freedom and knowledge for the further development of our human potential.

THE GERMAN IDEALISTS

Before the European Enlightenment, few people had guessed that the world was more than a few thousand years old. In the early 1700s, for example, Isaac Newton, the greatest scientist of his day, supported Archbishop James Ussher's proposal that the Earth had been created in 4004 B.C. But a century later, geologists and paleontologists had shown that our planet had existed for millions of years. And as the Earth's great age was revealed, the idea of progress arose. The new freedoms produced by the French and American revolutions, the stunning successes of science, the marvels of technology, and increasing prosperity gave rise to a new belief that humankind was headed toward better things. The ancient dictum attributed to King Solomon that there is not – and never will be – anything new under the sun was challenged by scientists, philosophers, and laypeople alike.

The French naturalist Georges-Louis Buffon was among the first to dramatize the Earth's great age. In his landmark history of our planet, *Histoire Naturelle*, he audaciously asserted that it had existed for seventy-five thousand years. His daring break with tradition reflected the growing impact of fossil discoveries by naturalists such as the Frenchman Jean-Baptiste Lamarck and Oxford's Sir Charles Lyell, who proposed in his *Principles of Geology* (1803) that earthly transformations had resulted from gradual changes over millions of years. These historic discoveries shook the foundations of traditional thinking that the world was a static place. Not only was our world much older than most people had thought, it was now shown to have given birth to increasingly complex and conscious forms of life. This awakening to the immense panorama of the Earth's development challenged people to ask, 'What is the relation of the evolving universe to God? What is *our* role in the world's advance? Can human nature itself progress?' Like the Jewish prophets two millennia before, more and more people began to sense the great arrow of time. The world had been on a mighty journey. What was impelling it? Where was it trying to go? A historic response to such questions was articulated by the German idealist philosopher Fredrich Schelling in 1801 and his friend Georg Wilhelm Friedrich Hegel in 1806. In summary, their response can be stated like this:

While remaining transcendent to all created things, the divine spirit involved itself in the genesis of the material world and the process that followed, which, though meandering, has produced ever higher levels of existence on Earth. As Schelling wrote: 'I posit God as both the first and the last, as the Alpha and Omega, as the unevolved, *Deus implicitus*, and the fully evolved, *Deus explictus*.' God, who is eternal, was in the beginning. God, eternal, is with us now. God, in eternity, will be with us as the world unfolds.

Evolution, then, follows *involution*. What was implicit is gradually made explicit as the spirit within all things progressively manifests itself. In this, as Schelling put it, the world is a 'slumbering spirit,' waking up as history unfolds. Or, in the words of the twentieth-century Indian visionary Sri Aurobindo, 'Apparent nature is secret God.' This worldview might be called 'evolutionary pantheism,' the doctrine that the divine is *both* immanent

67

in and transcendent to the universe, or 'evolutionary emanationism,' suggesting that the universe emanates from God.

Like Schelling, Hegel saw the world as spirit unfolding. Each stage of human development, he proposed, is both canceled and preserved in the dialectical progress of history. In *The Phenomenology of Spirit* (1806), he traced this ongoing process from the slave of antiquity, who struggled successfully against nature's difficulties, to the stoic's establishment of freedom within himself independent of nature's demands, to the skeptic's development of freedom by dissipating restrictive categories of thought, to the Christian believer's discovery of freedom in a transcendent God, to the modern intellectual's appropriation of reason's highest principles. In this dialectic, successive forms of consciousness subsume the forms that precede them.

Other thinkers have followed in the footsteps of Hegel and Schelling, among them the Russian philosophers Solovyev and Berdyaev, the French Nobel Laureate Henri Bergson, the English philosopher Alfred North Whitehead, the American theologian Charles Hartshorne, the French paleontologist-priest Teilhard de Chardin, the Indian philosopher-mystic Sri Aurobindo, and the American philosopher Ken Wilber. Though there are significant differences in their thought, each has envisioned the developing universe in relation to something ultimate, eternal, or everlasting. In various ways, each of them provides support for a simultaneous embrace of nature and supernature by linking the world's progress to *Geist*, Deity, *Satchitananda*, or some other version of a world-transcending yet imminent reality. The richness of their speculations shows that a promising field for philosophic inquiry appears when the evolving universe is considered in relation to a Supreme Principle or Divinity.

And beyond that, the insights of philosophers such as

these illumine particular processes and specific human conditions that inhibit or facilitate the emergent human capacities we are exploring in this book. The German Idealist's vision of the world as an unfoldment of its essential divinity helps us understand why all of our human attributes – our perception, our knowing, our will, our love – can progress, grow, and rise to higher levels. If we are secretly allied with the source of this ever-astonishing world, we must to some degree share its powers of transformation.

Philosophers such as Schelling, Hegel, Teilhard, and Aurobindo represent an historic shift of perspective from a view that the world as a whole is going nowhere to a belief that it is giving rise in the course of time, through all its setbacks and catastrophes, to new and higher levels of existence. From this perspective, our development as individuals is fundamentally linked with the world's advance. Through the actualization of our latent capacities, we both share and further the progressive manifestation of divinity that comprises the evolving universe. This view of things, which was given its first major expression by the German Idealists, provides the most adequate philosophic support for the vision of evolutionary transformation we are presenting in this book.

THE DISCOVERY OF EVOLUTION

In July 1858, twenty-five years after Sir Charles Lyell published his *Principles of Geology*, the book that dramatically 'redefined geological time,' he and the botanist J. D. Hooker sponsored a joint report to be read to the Linnean Society of London. They reported that the presentation, which would be titled 'On the Tendency of Species to Form Varieties; and on the Perpetuation of Varieties and Species by Natural Means of Selection,' was 'the result of the investigation of two indefatigable naturalists, Mr. Charles Darwin and Mr. Alfred Wallace' They explained how Darwin and Wallace had simultaneously arrived at the theory of natural selection to explain the evolution of species, though they had worked independently half a world apart.

Darwin had begun to develop his theory many years before, but had waited to publish it because he was, as he claimed in his autobiography, 'anxious to avoid prejudice' from the premature exposure of his ideas. He had waited for nearly two decades, marshaling evidence to support his theory, until the fateful day in 1858 when he received Wallace's announcement of his similar discoveries. Ever the gentleman, Darwin submitted Wallace's paper to Lyell, plus his own abstract and a letter substantiating his earlier discovery. With little fanfare, the Darwin-Wallace theory of evolution was first announced to the public.

The revolutionary statement was met with loud silence. But a year later, on November 21, 1859, Darwin's book *On the Origin of Species* was published. It caused an immediate uproar in the scientific community, and the religious community showered it with scorn. Darwin had powerful champions, though, including the eminent biologist Thomas Huxley, who called *Origin* 'the most potent instrument for the extension of natural knowledge, which has come into men's hands since the publication of Newton's *Principia*.' Often called 'the most important publication of the century,' *Origin* boldly announced the theory of evolution and natural selection. From the day the book appeared, many sensitive people were troubled that Darwin did not allow for divine involvement in the unfolding process of living things, yet his establishment of evolution as a fact was embraced by many religious thinkers. Indeed, the long-term influence of Darwinism has been great in both science and religion.

While Darwin is the person most responsible for this

historic event, many pioneers set the stage for it. The paths to evolution, as Daniel Boorstin wrote in *The Discoverers*, were many and varied:

> We would have to recount ancient Greek foreshadowings, Saint Augustine's suggestion that while all species had been created by God in the Beginning, some were mere seeds that would appear at a later time, medieval notions of an organic world, Montesquieu's hints of the multiplication of species from the discovery in Java of flying lemurs, the French mathematician Maupertuis's speculations on the chance combinations of elementary particles, Diderot's suggestions that higher animals may all have descended from 'one primeval animal,' Buffon on the development and 'degeneration' of species, Linnaeus's gnawing doubts that species might not be immutable, the metaphoric fancies of Charles's grandfather Erasmus Darwin on the urges of plants and animals sparked by 'lust, hunger, and danger' to develop into new forms – and countless others.

Two men especially had a powerful influence on Darwin. First was Thomas Malthus, whose work on population theory contained the notion of 'the struggle for existence.' Darwin wrote in his autobiography that Malthus's idea provided him with one of the keys to the mechanism of evolution, saying that natural selection was 'the doctrine of Malthus applied with manifold force to the whole animal and vegetable kingdom.' And of equal importance was Lyell himself, whose friendship and interest in the concept of species strongly influenced Darwin. The French naturalist Jean-Baptiste Lamarck (1744–1829 C.E.) also helped thinking people accept evolutionary ideas. *Transforisme*, as his notion of evolution was called at the time, which was based on the inheritance of acquired characteristics, could not adequately explain the origins of new species, but it helped set the stage for Darwin by bringing the long succession of living things into a developmental perspective.

After Darwin's history-making publication of *The Origin of Species*, more and more people accepted the fact that the Earth had developed for eons, giving rise over enormous stretches of time to single-celled organisms, countless plant and animal species, and eventually to humankind. Darwin's work provided a framework for understanding the development of life, as well as a brilliant theory about its mechanism. 'So why do we believe in evolution?' Sir Peter Medawar asked in his essay, 'The Evidences of Evolution.' Only evolution, he replied, explains the pattern of similarities and differences that turn up in studies of comparative anatomy; only evolution explains vestigial organs, such as the second and forth toes on a horse; only evolution explains the presence of strange creatures such as lung fish, feathered dinosaurs, and mammals that lay eggs.

As we have seen, the facts of evolution have reinforced the strict materialism of many scientists and laypeople, but they also can broaden our vision of the divine immanence. And more than that, they must be addressed by anyone who views the world as a whole and cares about humankind's destiny – which is why they are central to the philosophies of great modern thinkers such as Henri Bergson, Alfred North Whitehead, Teilhard de Chardin, and Sri Aurobindo. Not only are they consonant with a vision of personal and social transformation, but they also lend credence and grandeur to it.

Evolution's discovery confirmed the sense of time's arrow that arose among the Jews and stretched the German Idealist's vision of the world's unfoldment back to the Big Bang. It gives new and compelling significance to our emerging capacities for extraordinary life. No other scientific finding is as important in revealing the astonishing story of our universe and humankind's role in its further advance.

MODERN DISCOVERIES REGARDING THE HUMAN POTENTIAL

Since the early nineteenth century, scientists and scholars have produced a wide range of discoveries, which, taken as a whole, make up the largest body of publicly available knowledge about extraordinary human functioning that has ever existed on Earth. These findings, which have been produced in the spirit of post-Enlightenment science, have come from several sources, including growing acquaintance with once-foreign religious traditions by more and more scholars around the world, increasing numbers of contemplative texts translated into modern languages, a wide range of educational and therapeutic experiments, and numerous empirical studies of human nature's further reaches. The exploration of human potential from which they come is unprecedented in scope, discipline, and variety of method. We will highlight some of them here to indicate the range and creativity of this worldwide process of discovery.

MESMERISM AND HYPNOSIS

Half a century before Darwin's *The Origin of Species* was published, the Austrian healer Franz Anton Mesmer (1734–1815) had started a process of discovery that would eventually inform modern psychiatry and research on the unconscious mind. He believed in a magnetic 'fluid,' or vital force, that flows through all things and can be transmitted directly through physical touch. Beginning in the 1770s, he became famous in Vienna and then Paris, where he became a controversial celebrity while performing spectacular cures. In some respects, Mesmer's therapy resembled methods used by faith healers since antiquity, including hand passes, music, and dramatic incantations, but he framed it in pseudoscientific terms that fit the rationalism of eighteenth-century Europe. By stimulating a self-fulfilling expectation of relief, often through methods that seem bizarre today, he mobilized his subjects' self-restorative abilities through the power of suggestion and demonstrated the human capacity for dramatic change produced by natural rather than supernatural agencies. However, his flamboyant methods and unverified theories about the 'magnetic fluid' caused much consternation in the medical establishment, and he was eventually discredited.

Mesmer's influence grew, however, through the discoveries of his followers and the subsequent development of hypnotism. In spite of their fluctuating reputation during the last two hundred years, mesmerism and hypnotism have been used by therapists and experimenters to demonstrate the power of suggestion, alleviate pain and promote general health, cure phobias and addictions, increase physical energy and strength, retrieve lost memories, improve concentration, establish positive habits, induce experiences that appear to be paranormal, produce exaltations that resemble mystical states, and release a wide range of other untapped capacities. The clinical and educational usefulness of hypnosis has been confirmed by many carefully controlled experiments, and evidence for several of its effects is now overwhelming.

Mesmer's theory of a universal fluid appealed to many German Romantics who conceived the universe to be a living organism unified by a single spiritual presence. Inspired by the spectacular cures and ecstasies that were often produced by mesmerism, German philosophers, poets, and physicians of the 1830s, 1840s, and 1850s studied the connection between trance, clairvoyance, and precognition; the bodily changes and exaltations of religious stigmatics; and the altered states of consciousness they could now produce experimentally. Some of this work was published in two journals devoted to mesmeric phenomena. Meanwhile, in England and India the British doctors John Elliotson and James Esdaile used magnetic sleep to anesthetize patients in surgery, often amputating limbs without causing pain or discomfort, and linked mesmerism to paranormal powers. Eventually, many experimenters found that hand passes and other methods used in mesmerism could be dispensed with, and James Braid, an English doctor, popularized the term 'hypnotism,' which he coined in 1843, to help physicians accept mesmeric phenomena without the sometimes misguided claims of those who produced them. Research on hypnotic effects has continued to this day, augmenting our knowledge about untapped capacities and their release through the power of suggestion.

For two centuries, countless experiments with mesmerism and hypnosis have produced dramatic changes of mind and body without drugs or dependence on supernatural agencies. Such experiments typically evoke transformative experiences and capacities such as sharpened concentration, deep absorption in the task at hand, perceptual acuity and flexibility, improved memory, exceptional bodily strength and control, and access to deep levels of the mind. The extraordinary intelligence, energy, and focused intention that comes into play during hypnosis can be used to foster the emergent capacities described in Part Two.

DYNAMIC PSYCHIATRY

One hundred years after Mesmer dramatized the power of mental suggestion for healing and release of untapped abilities, the Viennese physician Sigmund

75

Freud (1856–1939 C.E.) announced his discovery of the unconscious mind and established the practice of psychoanalysis as a way to uncover hidden dimensions of human nature. His method is based on 'free association,' in which the patient lets his mind run free to reveal its largely unconscious workings; the examination of various 'defense mechanisms' through which we ward off threatening thoughts, feelings, impulses, and social influences; and dream interpretation. Though Freud's focus on sexual repression and infantile sexual trauma led to a break with many psychiatrists, including colleagues such as Carl Jung, Otto Rank, and Alfred Adler, his impact on our views of human nature has been immense. Of this influence, Richard Tarnas wrote, 'Freud radically undermined the entire Enlightenment project by his revelation that below or beyond the rational mind existed an overwhelmingly potent repository of forces which did not readily submit either to rational analysis or to conscious manipulation.'

Freud's student and colleague, the Swiss psychiatrist Carl Jung, who was a student of religion, art, and comparative mythology, left the psychoanalytic movement in 1913 to found analytical psychology, the premise of which is that a person's experience is determined not only by personal history and sexual drives, but also by universal forces of the mind. Jung believed that all humans have access to ancestral memories, or 'archetypes,' that can be understood through the study of myths and close attention to dreams. The goal of Jungian therapy is individuation and the expansion of consciousness, which Jung held to be central tasks of humankind. His lasting innovation in consciousness research was his insistence on exploring the spiritual realms of the unconscious and the latent creativity we all possess, but he also contributed the concepts of the shadow or 'dark side' of the self, introversion-extroversion, and synchronicity.

The Austrian psychoanalyst Otto Rank (1884–1939), another student of Freud, explored the role of the hero in society, the problems of existential anxiety, the creative struggle, and the sacred dimension of human love. Modern people, Rank said, suffer because of their attempt to find cosmic meaning in human love. 'No wonder,' wrote Ernest Becker in *The Denial of Death*, 'Rank could conclude that the love relationship of modern man is a *religious* problem.' The effort to substitute sexual love for divine love is bound to fail and, as Becker writes, 'It produces the sense of utter despair that we see in modern man.' For Rank, one way out of modern neurosis is through creative work. By fashioning a gift to the world we can participate in a self-transcending drama that helps the world advance.

Psychiatrist Wilhelm Reich (1897–1957) conducted the Vienna Seminar for Psychoanalytic Therapy from 1924 until 1930, and some of the papers he wrote at the time have been recommended ever since for students of the analytic method. He also developed theories about the destructiveness of authoritarian social structures, which he outlined in *The Mass Psychology of Fascism* (1933), *The Discovery of the Orgone* (1942), and other writings. Departing from orthodox Freudian theory, Reich rejected symptom analysis in favor of a character analysis, in which the entire personality structure was examined. His views on character analysis anticipated, and often inspired, other psychotherapies, and his insights about the social determinants of neurosis have influenced family counseling, group therapy, and industrial psychology. The basis of Reichian technique is that neuroses and many physical disorders are caused by blockages in the flow of emotional and sexual energy that he called *orgone*, which, like the Hindu *prana*, Chinese *chi*, or Japanese *ki*, pervades the organism and can be transmitted directly through the hands or sexual intercourse.

Such blockages, Reich believed, create various rigidities and malformations of personality, and manifest as 'body armor' (defensive contractions of muscles and ligaments). Reichian analysis aims to eliminate this psychosomatic armor through emotional insight, catharsis, massage, and physical exercises designed to release muscular tensions and promote energetic flow.

In considering our many latent abilities and frequent failure to develop them, we must ask, 'What holds us back?' Dynamic psychiatry gives us important answers. It has shown how social conditioning, repression of child-hood trauma, avoidance of existential anxiety, and other psychological processes limit our feeling, restrict our thought, and reduce our awareness of many higher abilities. It has given us knowledge of human pathologies, destructive cultural conditionings, and unconscious motives that did not exist in former times. We need this knowledge to cultivate the emergent capacities described in this book.

BIOFEEDBACK

Biofeedback training is a method for learning psycho-somatic self-regulation for the promotion of health, the improvement of particular skills, or the attainment of desired mental states. During such training, activity in some body part is detected by sensitive instruments such as the electroencephalograph (for brain waves) or electro-myograph (for muscle activity) and fed back to a subject through sounds or visual displays so that he can learn to modify it. Functioning once considered to be inaccessible by voluntary control is now commonly modified with the help of such feedback. Though the cognitive and somatic processes that make such control possible are not completely understood, the widespread success of bio-feedback training has shown that most, if not all, people can improve their powers of self-regulation. More than ten thousand studies of biofeedback to modify brain waves, heart rate, blood pressure, gastrointestinal activity, and other kinds of bodily functioning have been published in scientific journals. Echoing the belief of many researchers, Alyce and Elmer Green of the Menninger Foundation wrote, 'It may be possible to bring under some degree of voluntary control any physiological process that can be monitored, amplified, and displayed.' Furthermore, numerous studies have shown that self-regulation skills acquired through biofeedback training can be retained after instrumented feedback is discontinued. By 1990, for example, more than two thousand subjects at the Menninger Foundation had learned to modify various bodily processes through a combination of feedback, Autogenic Training, and visualization, so that their new self-control did not depend upon machines. Most biofeedback training programs today emphasize the importance of awareness and volition in the self-regulation and control of autonomic functions.

Though yogis and shamans have often developed extraordinary control of their bodily and mental processes, humankind did not until recent times possess instruments to provide feedback through which we all can modify our autonomic functioning. Such instruments and the biofeedback training they make possible comprise another significant advance of transformative practice. With their help, all of us can cultivate our latent capacities for extraordinary body awareness and control.

IMAGERY RESEARCH

It has long been believed that certain images can help an individual connect with the unconscious mind, heal afflictions, acquire or develop particular skills, expand consciousness, and harness extraordinary energies of body and soul. Such images may be visual, auditory, tactile, olfactory, gustatory, or kinesthetic, and may appear in waking fantasies, visions, dreams, art, or religious symbolism. Since the mid-nineteenth century, many clinical and experimental studies have shown that imagery practice can promote particular virtues, skills, and capacities, and facilitate relief from depression, anxiety, insomnia, obesity, sexual problems, chronic pains, phobias, cancer, and other afflictions. Several thousand studies of this kind have been published in medical journals. A brief survey of disciplines that emphasize imagery can be found in Michael Murphy's *The Future of the Body* (see Chapter Seventeen). Never before have so many imagery practices been available to the general public. Through their power to broaden awareness, strengthen the will, enrich emotions, and facilitate extraordinary physical skills, they can facilitate all of our emergent capacities.

Somatic education is a term now applied to several disciplines developed during the twentieth century in Europe and America. In recent years, the field that comprises these methods has been called Somatics by the American philosopher Thomas Hanna and *Somatotherapie* by French physicians and educators. Philosopher Don Johnson, who has promoted understanding of the field's basic principles more than anyone else, has distinguished somatic education from osteopathy, chiropractic, and standard medical practices that aim primarily or exclusively for symptom relief. In Johnson's words, 'Somatics is legitimately characterized as a field because its many methods share a common focus on relationships between the body and cognition, emotion, volition, and other dimensions of the self. Within that general unity of the field, a particular somatic method can be defined by its concentration on one or more bodily systems.' Among the best known somatic methods are Rolfing, which aims to promote the articulation of knotted muscles and ligaments; the Alexander Method to encourage better carriage and alignment of head, neck, and spine; the Feldendkrais Method to increase kinesthetic awareness, freedom of movement, and spontaneous behavior; the progressive relaxation techniques of Edmund Jacobsen to promote calm, self-aware efficiency in all behavior; the Autogenic Training of Johannes Schultz and Wolfgang Luthe to deepen relaxation and psychosomatic control; the Sensory Awareness of Elsa Gindler and Charlotte Selver to enhance all sensory and kinesthetic modalities; and various neo-Reichian therapies that aim to release psychosomatic tensions and defenses that limit feeling, thought, and behavior. Each of these somatic disciplines can contribute to the integral practices discussed in this book.

Meditation research. Meditation has been central to religious practice since the dawn of human history. In recent decades, though, it has been studied with increasing rigor. This burgeoning research effort was stimulated in part by investigations of yogis and Zen masters that began in the 1930s, and in part by the publication of landmark studies by Herbert Benson and Keith Wallace in *Science, The American Journal of Physiology,* and *Scientific American* between 1970 and 1972. Cardiovascular, cortical, hormonal, and metabolic changes, as well as several behavioral effects and alterations of consciousness produced by meditation, have been explored in recent years. Though modern studies give us only a first picture of meditation's foothills with a few glimpses of its peaks, what they give us corresponds in several ways with traditional accounts of contemplative experience. New sophistication of method is gradually improving our understanding of meditation in ways that complement the insights contained in the contemplative literature, and the results of meditation research are accumulating in the manner of scientific knowledge generally, forming a publicly accessible body of empirical data that can serve generations to come. In Part Two, we discuss some of these research findings.

Comparative studies of extraordinary experience. Many accounts of supernormal experience have appeared in the *Proceedings*, *Journals*, and archives of the British and American Societies for Psychical Research; in publications of the Alister Hardy Research Center at Oxford University (originally called the Religious Experience Research Unit; in Frederic Myers's *Human Personality*, Edmund Gurney's *Phantasms of the Living*, William James's *Varieties of Religious Experience*, Herbert Thurston's *The Physical Phenomena of Mysticism*, Marghanita Laski's *Ecstasy*, Raynor Johnson's *Watcher on the Hill*, Michael Murphy's *The Future of the Body*, and other journals and books. Taken as a whole, these accounts make up a natural history of sorts, not of rocks or animal specimens but of extraordinary human experience. They go beyond catalogues of supernormal experience in contemplative texts such as Patanjali's *Yoga Sutras* and Theravada Buddhism's *Visuddhimagga* in that they include evidence for supernormal capacities produced by types of empirical research that did not exist in earlier cultures. This book draws upon them all, either directly or indirectly.

HUMANIST AND TRANSPERSONAL PSYCHOLOGY

The therapeutic engagement with spiritual experience initiated by Rank, Jung, and other psychiatrists has been developed by a loosely affiliated group of humanistic and transpersonal psychologists in the Americas, Europe, Japan, and Australia. No single figure governs their thinking, nor does any unified approach command their allegiance, but they frequently turn to Jung, William James, Abraham Maslow, Carl Rogers, Rollo May, and other psychologists and psychiatrists who have focused on human nature's potential for growth as well as its disabilities. Hypotheses and empirical studies arising from the humanistic and transpersonal orientations have been presented in the *Journal of Humanistic Psychology* and the *Journal of Transpersonal Psychology* since the 1960s. Philosopher Ken Wilber has proposed a model of human growth that integrates the humanistic and transpersonal perspectives with the findings of many developmental psychologists, the moral development theories of Lawrence Kohlberg, and numerous contemplative teachings. In arguing that contemporary discoveries in psychology can be joined with religious insights, the transpersonal orientation points the way toward the integral psychology we need to explore our greater potentials.

THE DIFFUSION OF PRACTICES AND IDEAS REGARDING THE HUMAN POTENTIAL

The discoveries we have just reviewed have broadened understanding of the human potential, directly or indirectly, in ways no sociologist or cultural historian has adequately traced. Yet their influence continues to grow in contemporary personality theory, psychotherapy, education, and religious thought. In recent decades, they have been supplemented by the worldwide diffusion of Eastern philosophies, yogas, and martial arts; Christian mystical practices, Sufism, Neoplatonism, and Jewish cabalism; and the insights and disciplines of modern teachers such as Gurdjieff, Rudolph Steiner, Ramakrishna, Ramana Maharshi, and Sri Aurobindo. This diffusion of ideas and practices, many of which were once reserved for religious initiates, is evident in programs at mainstream temples and churches, YMCAs, and University extension programs, and organizations such as California's Esalen Institute and Institute of

Noetic Sciences. At Esalen, for example, some ten thousand people a year since 1962 have attended seminars and workshops to explore various aspects of the human potential. Centers modeled largely on Esalen are active in many parts of the world.

This diffusion of ideas, research findings, and transformative practices has given rise to – and been furthered by – a burgeoning number of books, journals, television programs, audiotapes, videotapes, and newspaper articles. These vary greatly in taste, depth, and quality, ranging from brilliant translations of the upanishads and luminous Buddhist texts to moronic tracts about lost continents and UFOs and the messianic proclamations of cult leaders. Seminars and workshops on these subjects, too, range from the ridiculous to the sublime. But discernment is growing about the relative strengths and weaknesses of such programs, and about the qualities of teachers associated with them. A quiet winnowing of methods is underway among people around the world who are exploring the human potential. As countless men and women explore new ways of growth, they are learning through direct experience to discriminate good teachers from bad, valid data from unsupported claims, wholesome from destructive practices. Such learning, which is discussed in several books listed in our bibliography, constitutes a folk wisdom of sorts that complements what has been learned in the sacred traditions and through scientific discoveries of modern times about our greater potentials.

Though this growing knowledge has not yet been appreciated in all its ramifications, nor perceived by most historians, it is here to stay. It comes from many domains of inquiry and a growing synthesis of their various findings. It is empirically based, having been tested again and again by disciplined communities, whether scientific or contemplative. If we need a term for this approach, we might call it a synoptic, multidisciplinary, or integral empiricism (bearing in mind that *empiricism* usually refers to data acquisition and verification limited to sensory experience).

This comprehensive science of the human potential has been developing for more than a century and a half, rendering debates about the antagonisms between science and religion, or between body, mind, and soul, increasingly out of date. Powerful evidence of our latent capacities has been gathered, studied, and incorporated into more and more programs for human growth. In the words of playwright Christopher Fry, 'The enterprise now is exploration into God, where no nation's foot has trodden yet.'

THE CONTINUING STORY

Long ago, humans learned to use fire, move in small groups across the continents in search of better living conditions, and follow shamans to the spirit world. Today, we use atomic power, send explorers to the moon, and follow spiritual leaders of many kinds to newly discovered regions of mind and soul. During the past three thousand years, this long journey from the Stone Age has accelerated. In the great awakenings we have reviewed, humankind has quickened its knowledge of the world, the self, and things Transcendent. The religious traditions have given us visions of moral excellence, a lore of extraordinary human attributes, and countless transformative practices. The Renaissance and Enlightenment gave us new appreciation of the individual and liberated the powers of reason. Modern science has shown that evolution is a fact. And several modern philosophers beginning with the German Idealists have given us a first vision of the evolving universe in relation to the divine.

This general advance has been marked by setbacks and monstrous distortions of the human spirit. Women, for example, are notably absent from many of the chronicles of history because in most societies they typically have been denied basic human rights and equal status with men in human affairs. That has been the case because they generally have been regarded by men as inferior in dealing with matters of the mind and have consequently been denied education and vocational opportunities. Nevertheless, our species is emerging in spite of its regressions and meanderings from much of its ignorance and incapacity. It is an astonishing story, this advance from Paleolithic culture to the wonders of modern life. And it seems more marvelous still when viewed as a further advance of the evolving universe. Like the cosmos itself, humankind will not stay fixed within its apparent limits. With each historic turn we have noted, its possibilities for further development have increased: All of these awakenings, we believe, point the way to another evolutionary leap and have helped prepare us for it.

Part Two

The Emerging
Human Being

The great human awakenings reviewed in Part One have laid a foundation for what we foresee as a next great step in evolution. Building on what those awakenings have given us, we can begin to picture a future that will include further expression of our latent abilities. Our capacity for luminous perception and mystical knowing; our powers of volition; our abilities to communicate; our vitality; and our very identity can blossom into the greater life many of us sense in moments of inspiration. It is our deep conviction that we can cultivate these emergent capacities so that they will manifest in our lives with a deeper love, purpose, and synchronistic flow.

In the chapters that follow we will explore these kinds of extraordinary human experience, with descriptions of how they make their appearance and practices to establish them more consistently in our everyday life. To appreciate the kind of change we envision here, you might think about ancient Egypt when ordinary people could not read or write because these abilities were reserved for a small group of privileged scribes and priests. Similarly, until recently only an elite group could operate computers whereas today second-graders use them to do their homework. In this sense, the extraordinary abilities we discuss in the pages that follow, though fully evident now in relatively few people, are accessible to us all. They reflect a part of human nature not yet actualized, which, we believe, can become the norm for every human being.

3

OUR EXPANDING PERCEPTION

Do you know how far your perceptions can reach into the world around you? Do you believe that your awareness can reveal dimensions beyond the immediate physical world? Numerous studies of extraordinary experience and transformative practice show that we can vastly improve our vision, refine our hearing, develop our ability to sense things through touch, enhance our sense of smell, refine our internal body awareness, and cultivate extrasensory abilities. We believe that most of us glimpse these capacities from time to time and that all of them can be developed.

Certain wine tasters, for example, can discriminate between many thousands of vintages. Some perfume experts can distinguish up to thirty-thousand scents. There are 'cloth feelers' who can judge the quality of fabrics even if their fingers are covered with wax.

One's sense of balance can also be developed, as we see in great dancers, divers, bridge workers, and gymnasts. And we can experience and develop clairvoyance and the perception of subtle energy. As you consider these experiences, we recommend that you try to recall moments when your ordinary perceptual abilities have been stretched, when one or more of your senses came newly alive.

THE ART OF SEEING

Many athletes report dramatic enhancements of their visual powers. John Brodie, one of the National Football League's best quarterbacks for several years, described occasions when, as he said in an interview with one of the authors, 'Time seems to slow way down, in an uncanny way, as if everyone were moving in slow motion. It seems as if I have all the time in the world to watch the receivers run their patterns, and yet I know the defensive line is coming at me as fast as ever.'

Similarly, the golfer Jack Fleck claimed that during his playoff victory over Ben Hogan during the 1955 U.S. Open Golf Championship, 'The hole looked as big as a wash-tub. I suddenly became convinced I couldn't miss. All I tried to do was keep the sensation by not questioning it.' And even more dramatically, running back MacArthur Lane said that at times he saw the football field as if with an 'extra eye,' at times from a point above his head.

These experiences, like artistic and religious illumi-nations, frequently seem to be freely given, as if by a higher power, though they are typically triggered by disciplined effort. They also involve a new level of func-tioning ('an extra eye' or a 'point above the head' as Lane described it). Often, they require a discriminating surrender, a disciplined letting go, as in Fleck's 'not questioning.'

In his book *The Art of Seeing*, Aldous Huxley described his recovery from near-blindness as a kind of modern parable. He writes of urban boredom, fear, and over-anxiety as psychological obstacles to good vision, and recommends the development of memory and imagin-

92

ation, and relaxation techniques such as palming, sunning, and alertness, to heighten our capacity for vision. 'We spend too much time staring at one thing and thinking of another,' he says.

Can vision be developed? To explore this question we can look to certain people whose work and livelihood depends on their ability to cultivate seeing. These include surgeons, artists, explorers, race car drivers, police officers, firefighters, and baseball players who have less than half a second to hit a pitch traveling up to one hundred miles per hour.

During Mark McGwire's chase of the home-run record in baseball one of his teammates was asked if he knew the slugger's secret. The player told the interviewer that before every game McGwire sat for a half an hour staring into the darkness of his locker, visualizing every pitch he anticipated during the game. Such practice helped him see with greater clarity and improve his chances of hitting the ball.

In mid-career the Japanese baseball star Sadaharu Oh was mired in a terrible batting slump. To regain his focus as well as his self-confidence, he began to practice Kendo, the martial art of swordmanship. One of the techniques was called *metsuke*, which refers to focus or a point of observation. In his autobiography he writes:

In this exercise the swordsman is required to deeply observe his opponent and to do so in a flash – because in battle one can't count on an excess of time. The student is taught to make this observation as though with two sets of eyes: one that will take in his opponent's eyes – the eyes mirroring what is in the spirit – the other paying attention to the opponent's body. Because this two-layered vision is seemingly imposs- ible (it is very hard to perfect, the instruction most often is to look at the opponent as though he were a distant mountain. Musashi [the great samurai] called it a 'distanced view of close things.'

Some cultures have developed enhanced visual abilities, as we learn from Laurens van der Post's observations of the Kalahari bushmen, who train themselves to see game more than a mile away. We can also learn from the rigorous attention practice that photographers such as Henri Cartier-Bresson have developed to see 'the decisive moment' that can capture history. The French writer Jacques Reda's walked the streets of Paris with the intention of seeing one new thing each day, knowing that the practice renewed his love for the city.

Think about your own experience. You may have found yourself involved in some sporting activity when a moment of extraordinary vision gave new beauty and mystery to your surroundings. Perhaps the light seemed brighter than before or you were surprised by the marvelous textures of the grass. Or perhaps your vision suddenly improved in a moment of unexpected danger.

Many kinds of experience today teach us that we have the ability to see at times with a range and acuity beyond our ordinary expectations. Distant objects can seem closer, allowing us to perceive them in greater detail. Time can seem to slow down so that we are able to perceive events that ordinarily would be imperceptible. Colors, shapes, and peripheral details can be perceived in a way that fills us with awe and appreciation. The world comes alive in such moments, and we see all things transfigured. In his *Long Day's Journey Into Night*, the American playwright Eugene O'Neill dramatizes such experience in these words of his character Edmund:

I lay on the bowsprit, facing astern, with the water foaming into spume under me, the masts with every sail within the moonlight, towering high above me. I became drunk with the beauty and singing rhythm of it, and for a moment I lost myself – actually lost my life. I was set free! I dissolved in the sea, became white sails and flying spray, became beauty and rhythm, became moonlight and the ship and the high dim-starred sky! I belonged, without past or future, within peace and unity and a wild joy, within something greater than my own life, or the life of Man, to Life itself! To God, if you want to put it that way.

In such moments it is usually the case that more than vision is filled with beatitude. Our other senses, too, are often lifted up as if they are inextricably linked to one another.

SUPERNORMAL HEARING

In his bestselling book *The Mozart Effect*, author and musician Don Campbell reminds us that the word 'heal' is related to 'making a sound.' In music, then, is our healing – if only we listen, if only we hear it. Intuitively we know that music and other sounds affect our mood. A cooing dove outside our window can make us feel happy, a distant church bell can enchant us, and a faraway train whistle can evoke childhood memories long forgotten – but only if we truly hear them. The poet David Wright described the magic of listening in his autobiography *Deafness: A Personal Account:*

Suppose it is a calm day, absolutely still, not a twig or leaf stirring. To me it will seem quiet as a tomb though hedgerows are full of noisy but invisible birds. Then comes a breath of air, enough to unsettle a leaf; I will see and hear that movement like an exclamation. The illusory soundlessness has been interrupted. I see, as if

I heard, a visionary noise of wind in a disturbance of foliage . . . I have sometimes to make a deliberate effort to remember I am not 'hearing' anything, because there is nothing to hear. Such non-sounds include the flight and movement of birds, even fish swimming in clear water or the tank of an aquarium. I take it that the flight of most birds, at least at a distance, must be silent . . . Yet it *appears* audible, each species creating a different 'eye-music' from the nonchalant melancholy of sea-gulls to the staccato of flitting swallows . . .

In moments such as Wright describes, physical sounds are perceived with new acuity, depth, and richness. However, there is another kind of hearing that includes the perception of sounds that have no apparent physical cause. Such perceptions were described by the pioneering psychical researcher Edmund Gurney in his *Phantasms of the Living*. Gurney presented the following account by Professor Ernesto Bozzano:

On the 22nd day of March, 1832, about 10:00 in the evening, two hours before Goethe's death, a carriage stopped outside the great poet's house. A lady got out and hastened to enter, asking the servant in a trembling voice, 'Is he still alive?' It was Countess V, an enthusiastic admirer of the poet, who always received her with pleasure because of the comforting vivacity of her conversation. While she was going up the stairs she suddenly stopped, listening to something, then she questioned the servant, 'What! Music in this house? Good heavens, how can anyone play music here on such a day as this?' The man listened in turn, but he had become pale and trembling, and made no reply. Meanwhile, the Countess had crossed the drawing room and gone into the study, where only she had the privilege of entry. Frau von Goethe, the poet's sister-in-law, went to meet her [and] the two women fell into each other's arms, bursting into tears. Presently the Countess asked, 'Tell me, Ottilie, while I was coming upstairs I heard music in the house. Why? Why? Or perhaps was I mistaken?'

'So you have heard it too?' replied Frau von Goethe. 'It's inexplicable! Since dawn yesterday a mysterious music has resounded from time to time, getting into our ears, our bones.' At this very instant there resounded from above, as if they came from a higher world, sweet and prolonged chords of music which weakened little by little until they faded away.

Beautiful and informative sounds that are not attributable to ordinary causes have often been reported by religious figures. The Christian Saint Guthlac heard angelic songs as he died, and Saint Therese de Lisieux heard celestial music on her deathbed, as did the poet William Blake. Saint Joseph of Cupertino heard a bell calling him to God on the day before his passing. In his essay 'The Fire of Love,' the English contemplative Richard Rolle (1290–1349 described music revealed to him by prayer:

When I was sitting in [chapel] reciting psalms as well as I might before supper, I heard above me the noise of harpers, or rather of singers. And when with all my heart I attended to heavenly things in prayer, I perceived within me, I know not how, a melody and a most delightful harmony from heaven, which abode in my mind. For my thought was straightaway changed into a song, and even when praying and singing psalms I gave forth the selfsame sound.

Supraphysical or 'celestial' music like Rolle's, called *nad* in Sanskrit, has long been celebrated in Hindu-Buddhist spiritual lore. According to this tradition, the rhythms and harmonies of *nad*, which religious devotion can reveal, rise to greater and greater levels during intense contemplative practice. It is said that we all can contact this transcendent harmony as if it were a constant background music. Joy, anger, sadness – indeed all our moods – are unconsciously amplified by it. This doctrine is summarized in the Nada-Bindu Upanishad of the Rig Veda, in which we are instructed to concentrate upon *nad* to lift ourselves beyond ordinary consciousness. The secret is a discipline of intense listening.

Have you ever practiced hearing this way? Think back to moments when listening was suffused with extraordinary meaning. As a child, did you ever listen intently for one of your parents to come home? In such moments of quiet anticipation we often hear sounds we've never heard before, perhaps the house settling or a distant train or the quiet movement of crickets and frogs outside. Such listening, if practiced with care, can become a practice through which your hearing abilities expand in ways that greatly surprise you.

LUMINOSITIES

The Irish have long testified to 'second sight,' the ability to see things beyond the range of the ordinary senses, claiming in their songs and poetry that there are 'thin places' where it is easier for the extraordinary or the sacred to rise. Among such places are sacred sites and sweeping vistas, and special times such as dawn and dusk, the time of 'Celtic Twilight.' Similarly, Hindus and Buddhists have developed an extensive lore about the 'third eye' and other suprasensory abilities, and Jewish, Islamic, and Christian mystics have described different kinds of 'spiritual senses.'

One such ability involves the perception of auras or

halos around animals, plants, and humans, sparks that fill the air, or unexplained lights in temples and ceremonial caves. In modern times, such perceptions have been deemed important by the psychiatrists Carl Jung and Wilhelm Reich. Jung equated such experiences with the opintheres, or luminous points, of alchemical texts, with the 'world-pervading soul-sparks' of cabalistic lore, with the 'atoms of light' reported by ancient gnostics, and with the 'sparks of stellar essence' discussed by the Greek philosophers Heraclitus and Democritus.

In the journal *Quadrant*, physicist-businessman Edward Russell described several episodes during which he perceived luminosities of this kind:

> Discussing a difficult task with an employee, I must have asked the impossible, because a look of desperate, forlorn hopelessness came over him. Then his entire aura lit up with hundreds of little sparks.
>
> Sometimes a bright spark exactly between and slightly above two persons precedes intimate rapport based on a shared idea. I have observed lovers who appear to be contained in a common 'cloud of affection,' which I see as a mist or haze enveloping and flowing around and between them. Or during an animated discussion (when the sparks fly!) I have seen luminosities literally flowing between the participants . . .

In the lore of virtually every sacred tradition, auras, unexplained lights, and divine sparks are said to be objectively real. Each of us, it is said, can learn to apprehend them through prayer, meditation, or other disciplines. You may have noticed auras around charismatic public speakers, or around the love of your life. Many people describe luminosities around their newly born child, or surrounding a book, art object, or stranger that seems to beckon from across a room.

CLAIRVOYANT PERCEPTION

There is considerable evidence that clairvoyance, or 'remote viewing,' is a common though largely unappreciated human ability. Some anthropologists believe that shamans of Stone-Age cultures used it for hunting and other purposes; it is considered to be a real power in most Hindu, Buddhist, Sufi, and Taoist contemplative traditions; and it has often been attributed to Jewish and Christian mystics.

Over the last few decades, several scientific experiments on clairvoyance were conducted with U.S. government grants at the well-known research and consulting organization SRI International. A director of this research, physicist Russell Targ, has described clairvoyant spying techniques and has presented his work at the Soviet Academy of Sciences. Research on remote viewing has also been conducted at other research centers. In the Soviet Union, as in the United States, various government agencies sponsored such work in the hope it would be useful as a way of detecting enemy weapons systems and military activity.

In 1995, the CIA commissioned a review of this government-sponsored research. The review committee's primary task was to evaluate the remote viewing experiments conducted at the Science Applications International Corporation (SAIC) as well as the SRI studies. The committee included a Nobel Laureate physicist, internationally known experts in statistics, psychology, neuroscience, and astronomy, and a retired U.S. Army major general who was also a physician. Because the SRI studies had previously established the existence of remote viewing to the satisfaction of most of the government sponsors, the SAIC experiments were not conducted as 'proof-oriented' studies, but rather as a means of learning how psi perception worked.

In one of these experiments, a remote viewer given only latitude and longitude coordinates of a location somewhere in the United States successfully described a secret facility in Virginia whose very existence was highly classified. He was able to describe the facility's interior and could identify the names of secret code words written on folders inside locked file cabinets. A skeptical newspaper reporter later heard this astonishing story and decided to check it out for himself. He drove to the location specified by the map coordinates, some one hundred thirty-five miles west-southwest of Washington, D.C., expecting to find 'the base camp of an extraterrestrial scouting party or, at the very least, the command center for World War III.' Instead, he found 'just a spare hillside, a few flocks of sheep, and lots of droppings.' No secret military outpost, no armed personnel, no buildings. He didn't realize that he had seen exactly what he was supposed to see – flocks of sheep on a hillside. The secret military facility was indeed at that very spot, hidden deep underground.

The American parapsychologist Rhea White has described the reports of 'saintly psi' recorded in Alban Butler's *Lives of the Saints*, an encyclopedic multi-volume collection of stories about the holy people of Christendom. Have you had such an experience, perhaps when someone you knew was in trouble? Have you sensed who is calling when the phone rang? You might consider taking such moments more seriously and listening more closely to the nudges of intuition they involve.

ADVANCED BODY AWARENESS

As we expand our perception of the worlds outside us, we can also develop awareness of the worlds inside our skin. This can be done through meditation, yoga, biofeedback, martial arts, sports, and other activities. Great distance runners, for example, learn to change their racing stride by responding to subtle changes of muscle tone. Accomplished yachtsmen can track their boats' courses through tiny alterations of balance. Rodeo riders can stay on bucking bulls by means of extraordinary muscular feel.

Body awareness, however, is not limited to muscular feel and sense of balance. It is also made possible by means of visual imagery, sounds, tastes, and smells. Some highly conditioned athletes monitor their levels of stress by the taste of their saliva or the smell of their sweat. Certain runners and martial artists describe visual images that seem to represent their organs, tissues, and cells.

But bodily sensitivity, it seems, can go beyond the ordinary range of our nervous system. Many people feel that they can connect with the innermost workings of their organs and cells in ways that medical science has difficulty explaining. In this, such people are supported by yogis, Zen masters, Sufis, and other spiritual adepts who have developed extraordinary somatic awareness. In every religious tradition, there is a richly detailed lore about this.

For example, among the hundreds of extraordinary powers, or *siddhis*, produced by Hindu-Buddhist yoga, it is said that there are some by which an adept can perceive the smallest particles of matter. The *anudrishti siddhi* – a term derived from *anu*, atom, and *drishti*, insight – refers to the perception of small, hidden, or remote things, including bodily structures. The *antara drishti siddhi* is said to produce an X-ray look into our own insides. And the *animan siddhi*, one of eight famous powers that are referred to in several yoga texts, enables one to see one's bodily cells and the atoms of which they are composed. It is striking that this ability was discovered thousands of years before the advent of microscopes and other instruments of modern science.

However, recent experiments as well as long-standing contemplative experience have shown that habitual psychological habits and associations, whether conscious or unconscious, influence the imagery associated with clairvoyance, whether of things inside or outside the body, sometimes distorting what appears to be accurate information. The Targ–Puthoff experiments cited above, as well as testimony from the Hindu, Buddhist, and Taoist yogic traditions, suggest that internal clairvoyance – like every other type of extraordinary functioning – is shaped by the mind–body complex in which it occurs, with all its genetic and cultural history. This is a theme to which we will return: All of our capacities, whether normal or supernormal, somatic or extrasomatic, are subject to the limitations and distortions produced by our inherited and socially conditioned nature.

Nevertheless, it is possible through wise discipline to learn how to scan our bodily structures and processes, developing a microscope with zoom lens as it were, by means of which we can focus on particular organs, tissues, and cells for healing or transformation. A cooperative dialogue might then ensue in which our bodies could communicate needs and early warnings to us. And perhaps we can go even further. According to countless seers and sages, we can undertake extraordinary journeys into the normally invisible spaces of our bodily architecture and detect, as we might in outer space, extraordinary secrets of matter.

You might have had similar moments of extraordinary perception. If you have, we would suggest that you think of them not as isolated events but as the birth of a new way of apprehending the world. Suddenly seeing remarkable beauty, hearing new levels of sound, or clairvoyantly perceiving the details of a remote location are all experiences widely reported around the world.

There is overwhelming evidence that systematic long-term practice can facilitate the actualization of all our emergent abilities. In Chapter Sixteen we suggest specific exercises that can help you develop the capacities described in this and subsequent chapters.

4

THE MYSTERY OF MOVEMENT

As he left the courtroom after his trial for claiming that the Earth orbited the sun, Galileo muttered three of the most famous words in history:

Eppur si muove, 'Still, it moves.' He was defiantly referring to the motion of the planets, but his words also symbolized the human fascination with the phenomenon of movement in general. We move; therefore we live.

The centrality of movement in human experience is evident in the lore of extraordinary human feats, whether in sport, everyday life, shamanism, the martial arts, or the sacred traditions. The Japanese swordmaster Yagyu, for example, said that swordsmanship can become an activity in which one's greater self, or Original Mind, can 'grasp with human hands, walk with human feet, and see with human eyes.' Similarly, shamanically influenced traditions in certain Native-American groups celebrate higher powers that help initiates run in ways that transcend normal human abilities. And in the lore of Tibetan Buddhism, so-called *lung-gom* practices are said to transform ordinary movement into something superhuman. Lama Govinda, a European scholar of Tibetan yogic practice, wrote that by means of such practices:

. . . a direct influence is possible upon the bodily functions and their respective organs, so that a psycho-physical cooperation is established, a parallelism of thought and movement, a rhythm that gathers all available forces into its service. If one has reached the point where the transformation of one force or state of materialization into another one is possible, one may produce various effects of an apparently miraculous nature, as, for instance, the transformation of psychic energy into bodily movement (a miracle that we perform on a smaller scale every moment, without being conscious of it), or the transformation of matter into an active state of energy, resulting at the same time in a reduction of weight or the apparent elimination or reduction of the power of gravitation.

The pioneering student of Tibetan mysticism, Alexandra David-Neel, claimed to have seen a yogic adept on the northern plain of Tibet. The man proceeded with an unusual gait, she wrote, his gaze fixed on the distant horizon. '[He] did not run [but] seemed to lift himself from the ground as if he had been endowed with the elasticity of a ball. His steps had the regularity of a pendulum.' The Tibetans in David-Neel's party immediately identified the man as a *lama long-gom pa*, a monk endowed with supernormal powers, and bowed in respect as he passed. Four days later when herdsmen told the party that they had seen the lama, David-Neel was able to estimate the speed at which he had been traveling. To have reached the herdsmen when he did, he had moved with unbelievable speed for two days without stopping.

At a gathering of members of the Native American Church in the mountains of northern Mexico in the early 1990s, six Tarahumara Indians arrived after running two hundred and fifty miles – fifty miles a day for five days –

fueled only by salt tablets. When they arrived they told the gathering that they didn't need to eat or drink on their long run because they were 'full of the gods' and because they 'prayed all along the road.'

In seeking to capture the experience of moving with such power and grace, the Buddhists have offered the idea of 'non-doing in action.' This occurs when action is effortless and there is nothing forced. There is only the natural rhythm of things, as in the Japanese expression. 'Spring comes; grass grows of itself.'

'Out of body' or 'traveling clairvoyance' can be thought of as another type of extraordinary movement ability. That our spirit-body can travel outside the physical body to which it is normally attached has been testified to in virtually every culture and has been studied by reputable modern researchers. Dr. Brian Weiss relates the story told to him by a surgeon. While visiting a patient after surgery, his patient inquired whether he had found the valuable pen that had rolled out of his pocket during the operation. The patient then told him exactly where to locate the missing pen. What was remarkable about this was that the patient was under general anesthesia and unconscious during the entire procedure. To make matters more amazing, the patient was totally blind in everyday life and could not possibly have seen the pen fall.

Stories of such experience have been well documented since the nineteenth century. In his monumental book *Human Personality and Its Survival of Bodily Death*, Frederic Myers, one of the principal founders of modern psychical research, told this story involving out-of-body movement:

On October 3rd, 1863, [Mr. Wilmot wrote] I sailed from Liverpool for New York, on the steamer *City of Limerick*, of the Inman line, Captain Jones commanding. On the evening of the second day out, soon after leaving

107

Kinsale Head, a severe storm began, which lasted for nine days. During this time we saw neither sun nor stars nor any vessel; but bulwarks on the weather bow were carried away, one of the anchors broke loose from its lashing and did considerable damage before it could be secured, and several stout storm sails, though closely reefed, were carried away, and the booms broken.

Upon the night following the eighth day of the storm the tempest moderated a little, and for the first time since leaving port I enjoyed refreshing sleep. Toward morning I dreamed that I saw my wife, whom I had left in the United States, come to the door of my state-room, clad in her night-dress. At the door she seemed to discover that I was not the only occupant of the room, hesitated a little, then advanced to my side, stooped down and kissed me, and after gently caressing me for a few moments, quietly withdrew.

Upon waking I was surprised to see my fellow-passenger . . . leaning upon his elbow, and looking fixedly at me. 'You're a pretty fellow,' said he at length, 'to have a lady come and visit you in this way.' I pressed him for an explanation, which he at first declined to give, but at length related what he had seen while wide awake, lying in his berth. It exactly corresponded with my dream.

This gentleman's name was William J. Tait, and he had been my roommate in the passage out, in the preceding July, on the Cunard steamer *Olympus*; a native of England, and son of a clergyman of the Established Church. He had for a number of years lived in Cleveland, in the State of Ohio, where he held the position of librarian of the Associated Library. He was at this time perhaps fifty years of age, by no means in the habit of practical joking, but a sedate and very

108

religious man, whose testimony upon any subject could be taken unhesitatingly.

The incident seemed so strange to me that I questioned him about it, and upon three separate occasions, the last one shortly before reaching port, Mr. Tait repeated to me the same account of what he had witnessed. On reaching New York we parted, and I never saw him afterward.

The day after landing I went by rail to Watertown, Connecticut, where my children and my wife had been for some time visiting her parents. Almost her first question when we were alone together was, 'Did you receive a visit from me a week ago Tuesday?' 'A visit from you?' said I, 'we were more than a thousand miles at sea.' 'I know it,' she replied, 'but it seemed to me that I visited you.'

My wife then told me that on account of the severity of the weather and the reported loss of the *Africa*, which sailed for Boston on the same day that we left Liverpool for New York, and had gone ashore at Cape Race, she had been extremely anxious about me. On the night previous, the same night when, as mentioned above, the storm had just begun to abate, she had lain awake for a long time thinking of me, and about four o'clock in the morning it seemed to her that she went out to seek me. Crossing the wide and stormy sea, she came at length to a low, black steamship, whose side she went up, and then descending into the cabin, passed through it to the stern until she came to my state-room. 'Tell me,' said she, 'do they ever have state-rooms like the one I saw, where the upper berth extends further back than the under one? A man was in the upper berth, looking right at me, and for a moment I was afraid to go in, but soon I went up to the side of your berth, bent down and kissed you, and embraced you, and then went away.'

The description given by my wife of the steamship was correct in all particulars, though she had never seen it. I find by my sister's diary that we sailed October 4th; the day we reached New York, 22nd; home, 23rd.

Such experiences of so-called 'bilocation,' simultaneously being in more than one location, have been described at length in Catholic tradition. In *The New Catholic Encyclopedia*, it is listed among the principal phenomena of Christian devotion. It is also described as a development of the *akasha* and *moksha* siddhis of Indian yoga and in the lore of Taoism, Tibetan Buddhism, and Sufism. But such events are not limited to religious adepts. They frequently occur spontaneously, during erotic and other ecstatic experience, illness, near-death episodes, vivid dreams, crisis, and intense adventure. A rock climber, for example, testified that:

... about 15 or 20 feet above the ground, I slipped and fell. As I fell, I seemed to be about 5 or so feet out from the face, looking at my body falling. I vaguely recollect moving around to the other side of my body to look at it. Once I hit the ground, I was immediately preoccupied with my pain and came into my body.

Like other supernormal capacities discussed in this book, out-of-body experience powerfully suggests that we are not confined to the worlds revealed by our ordinary sensorimotor capacities. Not only can we perceive dimensions beyond ordinary hearing and sight, but it seems at times that we can actually move through them in some sort of spirit-body.

You might have noticed these things happening to you. Perhaps you were running and you were overwhelmed with 'runner's high,' when the endorphins began to pump in your body and you felt a kind of ecstasy. Or maybe it occurred when you were in a paddleboat with your child pumping your legs in time with hers and noticed how extraordinary it was to move your legs in synch, together, marveling at the connection of pumping legs and a moving boat. Or you could have been walking through the woods when it dawned on you that the common euphoria you often feel while walking often leads to your best ideas.

With that in mind, we encourage you to remember moments when you moved in some extraordinary way and build on them intentionally, exploring the practices related to this emerging ability detailed in Chapter Sixteen. All transformative change begins with awareness and intention.

ENHANCING
COMMUNICATION

As cultures have evolved, human communication has progressed from the first sounds and gestures of Paleolithic tribes to the wonders of modern language. Our ability to communicate has developed not only through the growing richness and precision of speech but also through the elaboration of gestures and facial expressions. And in addition to these ways of communicating, which have been studied in depth by anthropologists and psychologists, we at times connect with each other in more mysterious ways. As the sacred traditions teach us and modern researchers such as William James have maintained, we reach out to our fellows telepathically. Most important for the vision of human possibility we are presenting here, all of these communication modalities can be cultivated and enriched.

Most of us have experienced being touched, or 'met,' in ways that seem to transcend our physical senses. Yet when we experience such connections they feel like a natural part of our perceptual field. This is the case, we believe, because such experiences are part of the cultural socialization each of us undergoes from childhood. Sigmund Freud, Carl Jung, and other prominent psychiatrists, as well as modern parapsychologists, have given us compelling evidence that we communicate all our lives through both sensory and extrasensory means.

From the day we are born we notice and then imitate words, gestures, postures, and facial expressions. Our abilities to interact with others are constantly shaped, for better or worse, by family, friends, and teachers, as well as by passing acquaintances and by people we identify with through poems, movies, or books. We learn how to form new words and phrases, alter our responses, and broaden our range of expressive movement to convey our feelings, intentions, and thoughts.

In what would be a new step in this socialization and evolutionary process, modern people, we believe, can move consciously toward the level of communication exemplified by certain mystics and saints. According to his friends, Saint Francis of Assisi spoke with creatures of the forest. Yogis, it is said, influence those around them with their contagious serenity. According to the celebrated history of the desert fathers *Historia Monachorum*, Christian contemplatives reach out through extrasensory means to nurture and communicate with others.

Furthermore, there is evidence that certain yogis and saints transmit ecstatic states by extrasensory influence. In the lore of Hinduism, such transmission, or *diksha*, can be effected by a glance, a gaze, a touch, a word, an embrace, or other gesture. And it can occur when the recipient is physically distant or unaware it is happening. Scripture asserts that Jesus could heal others through a mere touch.

In recent decades, science has turned its attention to telepathic, or 'non-local,' communication. One landmark set of such experiments was conducted by psychologist William Braud and anthropologist Marilyn Schlitz of the Mind Science Foundation in San Antonio, Texas. Braud and Schlitz conducted thirteen studies involving sixty-two 'influencers,' two hundred seventy-one subjects, and four experimenters in which one person influenced another's skin activity – even though they were in separate rooms – through visualization exercises and biofeedback from their targets. In these thirteen experiments, the 'influencers' were presented with polygraph records of their distant subjects' electrodermal activity, which they tried either to quiet or to excite by employing one or more of the following strategies:

- Imagery and self-regulation techniques to induce the intended condition (either relaxation or arousal) in *oneself* while imaging and intending a corresponding change in the distant subject
- Imaging the *other person* in appropriate relaxing or activating settings
- Imaging the desired outcomes of the polygraph pen tracings, i.e., few and small pen deflections for calming periods, many and large pen deflections for activation periods

Taken together, these thirteen studies yielded significant evidence for the experimental effect ($p = 0.000023$, $Z = 4.08$, and mean effect size = 0.29). The Braud-Schlitz research design was extremely well controlled and ruled out coincidence, common external stimuli (because influencers and their subjects were housed at separate locations), and common physiological rhythms. These studies demonstrated reliable and relatively robust interactions between living systems at a distance. According to Braud and Schlitz, the experiments' effects may be interpreted 'as instances of causal influence by one person directly upon the physiological activity of another person, or as an anomalous informational process combined with unconscious physiological self-regulation on the part of the influenced person.' The Braud-Schlitz experimental design guaranteed that the effect could not be attributed to conventional sensorimotor cues, common external stimulation, common internal rhythms, or coincidence.

But these experiments produced more than physiological effects. The subjects in them often reported emotional or mental responses that corresponded to the influencers' experience. For example, one subject reported a vivid impression of the influences coming into his room, walking behind him, and vigorously shaking his chair. The impression was so strong that he found it difficult to believe that the event hadn't happened – and indeed, in this session, the influences had employed such an image!

During another session, an experimenter remarked to an influencer that his subject's electrodermal tracings reminded him of the German techno-pop instrumental musical group Kraftwerk, and when the experimenter went to the subject's room, the subject's first comment was that early in the session, for some unknown reason, thoughts of the group Kraftwerk had come into her mind. The subject could not have overheard the experimenter's earlier comment to the influences.

The results of these experiments support the experience of extrasensory rapport long claimed by members of sports teams, orchestras, and jazz groups that are suddenly inspired; by participants in mass healings at shrines or revivalist meetings; and by observers of hypnotic experiments during which most of the subjects enjoy special success. It can be argued, of course, that the contagious aspects of group behavior are mediated entirely by sensory cues, but the experiments noted here provide further evidence that extrasensory influences also help to convey moods and intentions.

Every day, it seems, we experience or hear about some sort of extraordinary communication. You may have sensed that someone was about to call just before that telephone rang, and you may have intuited the message the caller was about to deliver. Or you have mysteriously sensed that a friend needs to reach you and then have them say when you call, 'I've been wanting to talk with you!'

But a note of caution here. Everyday experience, as well as the religious traditions, teaches us that extraordinary communication abilities can be employed for destructive purposes. This ancient observation has been confirmed by psychotherapists and research psychologists. Sigmund Freud, Wilhelm Stekel, Jule Eisenbud, Jan Ehrenwald, and other psychoanalysts, for example, have argued from their own therapeutic experience that telepathic interaction, like any other human ability, must be developed and used with the same consideration of ethics that we demand of ordinary communication.

Again we remind you that certain practices are designed to cultivate our experience of higher communication. Suggested exercises on this ability are included in Chapter Sixteen.

OPENING TO A GREATER ENERGY

From the beginnings of recorded history, shamans, saints, and mystics have described their experience of extraordinary energy. This remarkable life force, which is often associated with enhanced perception of the world as well as a capacity for freer physical movement and new powers of communication, rises from the core of transcendent experience. Its appearance brings a greater vitality into mind, body, and soul and lifts all our perceptions and abilities.

Dancer and choreographer Martha Graham put it this way:

> There is a life force, a quickening that is translated through you into action, and because there is only *one of you in all time*, this expression is unique. But if you block it, it will never exist through any other medium and be lost . . . It is your business to keep it yours clearly and directly, to keep the channel open.

From time immemorial people have sought this life force, whether in physical activity, erotic love, religious ritual, the healing arts, prayer, meditation, or yoga. We instantly recognize those who have it. We say they have 'charisma,' or that they are 'highly charged,' or that they have a mysterious focus or sense of destiny about them. 'So what is it?' asked the legendary French dance teacher Nadia Boulanger, 'this force which makes saints, heroes, geniuses, which makes men pursue their destinies to the end? It seems to me that . . . it is a form of vision experienced by the great mystics, on days when they were granted a profound concentration.'

There have been innumerable examples throughout history of this extraordinary energy, among them:

- The ability of certain shamans to endure great environmental extremes
- The *incendium amoris*, or 'fire of love,' evident in some Catholic mystics such as Philip Neri
- The 'boiling *n/um*' (production of exceptional bodily heat and vitality) of the Kalahari bushmen
- The resistance to cold, or *tumo*, generated by Tibetan yogis
- The so-called 'kundalini' effects triggered by some forms of Hindu and Buddhist yoga

The increases of vital capacity evident in these phenomena result in part from processes understood by mainstream science. The Tibetan yogis' resistance to cold, for example, is caused partly by vasodilation. The bodily heat of Kalahari bushmen is produced to some extent by the energy expended in their dancing. However, to close observers of such experience it seems that something else is involved. Given the fact that these extraordinary phenomena are typically associated with religious ecstasies and mystical insight, it is plausible that they are powered by energies beyond those presently understood by mainstream science and, indeed, that is what shamans, yogis, Catholic saints, and even some sports-people say.

'A man's spiritual consciousness is not awakened,' said Sri Ra-makrishna, 'unless his kundalini is aroused.' Kung bushmen told anthropologist Richard Katz that *n/um* is 'given by the gods.' For numerous Catholic saints, the *incendium amoris* is a gift of the Holy Spirit. Many athletes say that in their greatest feats they are carried by 'a connection with energies beyond themselves.'

According to numerous witnesses, the Catholic saint Philip Neri often felt a burning love of God that heated his entire body. The Catholic scholar Herbert Thurston wrote:

> [I]t sometimes extended over his whole body, and for all his age, thinness and spare diet, in the coldest days of winter it was necessary, even in the midst of the night, to open the windows, to cool the bed, to fan him while in bed, and in various ways to moderate the great heat. Sometimes it burned his throat, and in all his medicines something cooling was generally mixed to relieve him. Cardinal Crescenzi said that sometimes when he touched his hand, it burned as if the saint was suffering from a raging fever . . . Even in winter he almost always had his clothes open from the girdle upwards, and sometimes when they told him to fasten them lest he should do himself some injury, he used to say he really could not because of the excessive heat he felt. One day, at Rome, when a great quantity of snow had fallen, he was walking in the streets with his cassock unbuttoned; and when some of his penitents who were with him were hardly able to endure the cold, he laughed at them and said it was a shame for young men to feel cold when old men did not.

The boiling *n/um* of the Kalahari bushmen resembles the Catholic *incendim amoris* in many ways. 'You dance,

dance, dance,' a Kung healer told anthropologist Richard Katz. 'Then *n/um* lifts you up in your belly and lifts you in your back, and then you start to shiver. [It] makes you tremble, it's hot. *N/um* enters every part of your body right to the tip of your feet and even your hair.'

Experiences of this kind, which have been reported in many cultures throughout history, are too charged with a special energy, excitement, and vision to be dismissed simply as products of exercise, vasodilation, or social suggestion. They have an autonomous and highly contagious power, a relentless and overwhelming intensity that alters the body, induces ecstasy, and confers special abilities. All of these phenomena are sharply differentiated by those who experience them from ordinary mental or somatic events, and in their respective traditions are ascribed to forces beyond ordinary functioning.

You may have experienced moments of this life force yourself. One can become aware of it while swinging a tennis racket, giving a speech, dancing, making love, working in a laboratory, writing a poem, or doing manual labor. We can recognize it in an athlete who seems to get a second wind when the pressure is on his or her team, in an orator who has enough energy to lift an entire audience, in a mother who rises in the middle of the night to care for a sick child – for days, weeks, or years on end.

Many techniques are available now to help us increase our energy for both mental and physical activity. Research with somatic education, for example, has shown us how to free disabling constrictions in our body. Fitness research has shown that all of us can raise our level of available energy through regular and intelligent exercise. And various kinds of psychotherapy, by resolving internal conflicts, removing defenses against past traumas, and reducing chronic muscular tensions, can open us to new levels and kinds of vitality.

And as we have said, spiritual practice can help move us toward a transcendent awareness that includes the supernormal life force we have just described. As with our other extraordinary attributes, such experience can be integrated with our entire being.

ECSTASY

In the fall of 1987 the world-famous scholar of mythology Joseph Campbell was asked by Bill Moyers on the television series, *The Power of Myth*, what someone in a midlife crisis should do if they have lost their way.

'I have always told my students to follow their bliss,' Campbell replied, 'and if you follow your bliss, doors will open where there were no doors before.'

Campbell's idea of bliss was rooted in the ancient Hindu notion of *ananda*, the divine joy that underlies the universe. In *ananda*, God's eternal delight, one finds a powerful and lasting inspiration to serve the world. What Campbell did not mean by bliss was mere 'fun.' This was no recommendation for instant gratification or self-indulgence. As he said in a documentary about his life and work, 'By bliss I mean the deep sense of being totally engaged in life.' This sense of immersion in what you are doing, as in moments of deeply absorbing work or feeling that you are on the right course in your life, can provide a glimpse of *ananda*, the transcendent ecstasy. As with the other emerging human attributes we are discussing, joy is a fundamental aspect of higher human functioning.

In knowing the bliss Campbell referred to, one feels congruent with a higher state of being, a greater calling, a larger life, whether in work, love, play, worship, or meditation. It is a state in which what we do reflects who we are fundamentally and who we are becoming. If these moments sometimes feel as if they are gifts from the gods, one might remember that that is how the ancient Greeks felt about it. They believed that the ecstatic experience raised human beings from ordinary reality to a higher realm, and they personified that sense of elevation in the god Dionysus.

Throughout history the power of ecstasy has been demonstrated in the human need to celebrate and is reflected in carnivals and fairs such as Mardi Gras and May Day. Certain people have become known as 'ecstatics' for their sense of being 'intoxicated with God.' Think of Saint Francis of Assisi, Rumi, Hildegard of Bingen, William Blake, or the great Indian mystic Sri Ramakrishna. But not only spiritual adepts experience transcendent joy. So do soldiers writing home from war, mothers after childbirth, scientists after an unexpected discovery, and artists in the throes of creative work. There are countless forms of joy.

There is the joy of ecstatic discovery in one's own writing, beautifully discribed by the Chilean writer Pablo Neruda in his *Memoirs*:

> In my poems I could not shut the door to the street, just as I could not shut the door to love, life, joy, or sadness in my young poet's heart . . .
>
> *You can say anything you want, yessir, but it's the words that sing, they soar and descend . . . I bow to them . . . I love them, I cling to them, I run them down, I bit into them, I melt them . . . I love words so much . . .*

And there is the joy of lovers. In her book *A Natural History of the Senses*, Diane Ackerman wrote:

Perhaps the most famous kiss in the world is represented by Rodin's sculpture *The Kiss*, in which two lovers, sitting on a rocky ledge embrace tenderly with radiant energy, and kiss forever. Her left hand wrapped around his neck, she seems almost to be swooning, or to be singing into his mouth. As he rests his open right hand on her thigh, a thigh he knows well and adores, he seems to be ready to play her leg as if it were a musical instrument . . . His calves and knees are beautiful, her ankles are strong and firmly feminine, and her buttocks, waist, and breasts are all heavily fleshed and curvy. Ecstasy pours off every inch of them. Touching in only a few places, they seem to be touching in every cell . . . It is as if they have fallen down the well of each other; they are not only self-absorbed, but actually absorbing one another.

In his book *Ecstasy*, psychologist Robert Johnson wrote, 'It was once considered a favor of the gods, a divine gift that could lift mortals out of ordinary reality into a higher world. The transformative fire of ecstasy would burn away the barriers between ourselves and our souls . . .'

Through such practices as active imagination, working with dreams, ritual, prayer, and meditation, ecstasy can enter every dimension of life, including challenge and pain.

Indeed, long human experience as well as much scientific research has shown that our capacity for joy can help us redefine and move past the most trying circumstances.

Through athletic or martial-arts training, for instance, many people come to enjoy strenuous exercise and environmental extremes.

Through ascetic practices, shamans and yogis learn to endure wounds with complete equanimity and even turn them into occasions of joy.

And many clinical and experimental studies have

shown that pain can be diminished or eliminated and pleasure increased by hypnotic, psychotherapeutic, meditative, athletic, yogic, or other exercises.

Modern studies of pain control support the contention to be found in all sacred traditions that suffering can be overcome through certain virtues and disciplines. The Indian philosopher Sri Aurobindo reflected the teaching of saints and philosophers in many lands when he wrote:

> We feel pleasure or pain in a particular contact because that is the habit our nature has formed, because that is the constant relation the recipient has established with [it]. But it is within our competence to return quite the opposite response, pleasure where we used to have pain, pain where we used to have pleasure.
>
> The nervous being in us, indeed, is accustomed to a certain fixedness, a false impression of absoluteness in these things. [However] there is something in us which takes delight impartially in all external being and enables us to persevere through all labors, suffering and ordeals.
>
> In our ordinary life this truth is hidden from us or only glimpsed at times or imperfectly held or conceived. But if we learn to live within, we infallibly awaken to this presence which is our more real self, a presence profound, calm, joyous, of which the world is not the master.

As Michael Murphy notes in *The Future of the Body*:

> For mystics of the Christian tradition, ordinary pains and pleasures are transcended through . . . contact with Christ's living presence. For Buddhists, suffering is rooted in desire, which can be dissolved in nirvana. For Vedantists, unhappiness is overcome by the experience of ananda, self-existent delight. In spite of their

differing metaphysics, religious teachers East and West have asserted that we can realize a joy that subsumes ordinary pains and pleasures. 'From delight all these creatures are born,' says the Taittiriya Upanishad. 'By delight they exist and grow. To delight they return. For who could live or breathe if there were not this delight of existence as the ether in which we dwell?' [But] the acknowledgment of such blessedness does not release us from our biologically inherited and culturally conditioned responses to potentially painful stimuli. Only through transformative practice can we transform our habitual pains and pleasures into the lasting enjoyment described in the Taittiriya Upanishad.

However, such fulfillment does not always require formal discipline. On a sunny morning as we walk down a long familiar street thinking about nothing in particular, or through the glance of someone we love, or in a field at sunset, a sudden unaccountable gladness, something free and untouchable, is given to us. Or a redeeming buoyancy arises in the midst of our suffering, pervading our pain like a subtle presence, lifting us into its merciful sustenance, spreading to others with a life of its own. At such times we know, deeply and beyond all doubt, that there is a truth and a goodness, a redeeming joy in which this world rests. In these unexpected, unguarded moments, we experience that gift mystics describe, a delight that passes understanding.

8

LOVE

Of all our attributes, love points most surely toward the greater life that is latent in us. The primacy of love among human capacities has been celebrated in story and myth since the dawn of history.

In the Greek myth of Crete's great labyrinth there is a word for the magical gift that allows the princess Ariadne to save the life of Theseus, the Athenian prince with whom she has fallen in love. The gift is a ball of golden string from Daedalus, the labyrinth's inventor, with the instructions that she give it to Theseus and that he unroll it as he proceeds to the center of the maze. In the labyrinth he must defeat the terrible Minotaur – then follow the string out again into the arms of his lover.

The name of the golden ball is 'clew,' the origin of our modern word 'clue,' as in the sign that a detective must find in order to solve a mystery. The ancient authors of the myth, it seems, were saying that love is the thread that leads us through the labyrinth of life and that this thread is the 'clue' for a greater existence. Love is an abiding pointer to the greater life that beckons to us.

Among the kinds of love with which most of us are familiar, one is the fellow feeling and often-joyous solidarity evident in great friendships. Such love was evident among Martin Luther King, Jr., and his fellow civil rights crusaders. It is apparent in the long-suffering tenderness of nuns toward one another and the shared sense of destiny felt on great sports teams. It arises in times of civic danger, when neighbors rally to sandbag the banks of a raging river or when mothers stand arm-in-arm against drug lords to help keep their kids drug-free.

We feel such camaraderie in movies like *Saving Private Ryan*, in which a troop of GIs in World War II are ordered to find a soldier in France. The fate of Private Ryan has suddenly become symbolically important because it has become public knowledge in the States that his four brothers have been killed in action. That several soldiers must risk their life for the symbolic value of one private's life is remindful of the famous question raised by the German philosopher Arthur Schopenhauer. How is it, he asked, that a soldier can throw himself on a hand grenade to save his fellows? From whence comes his love and courage? Schopenhauer's answer cuts to the quick. That soldier, he wrote, has the sudden realization that *he and his fellow soldiers are one.*

What these displays of feeling have in common is the implicit knowledge that love can rise in groups as well as individuals and thus transform communities, cultures, and ultimately the world. We know this is true because we have witnessed the effects on great numbers of people when a single leader felt such love. Think of Nelson Mandela or the mothers for peace in Northern Ireland who helped bring an end to sectarian violence. These inspired souls showed that love can transform a culture and send ripples of change everywhere.

Yet just as quickly, the love involved in group action and mission can disappear when the group's goals are accomplished, or the comrades are gone. This love is typically connected with an objective time and place and among a certain group and, as the situation changes, it can lose the connection with the transcendent that is its source.

Erotic love, too, often loses its way, even though it carries the golden thread of the transcendent. The sixteenth-century Jewish mystic the Baal Shem Tov celebrated the connection of erotic love with God when he wrote, 'From every human being there rises a light that reaches straight to heaven, and when two souls that are destined to be together find each other, the streams of light flow together and a single brighter light goes forth from that united being.' Such love can reflect the transcendent, but we know that in practice it often does not.

The search for Eros is replayed every day in romance novels, love songs, plays, and movies. The plots are instantly recognizable in the pain surrounding the pursuit of a lover, the jealousy and rage of the spurned, and the sometimes-disastrous end of once-promising romance, as well as the intoxicated melding with the one we think is our soul mate. However, while stories and songs tell us that ultimate joy lies at the heart of romance, they don't always say for how long such love's union might live. The perennial problem with the erotic is that 'desire perishes because it tries to be love,' as poet Jack Gilbert writes in 'The Great Fires.' Erotic love ends, or sometimes never really begins, because the rush of romance is mistaken for the deeper love that is trying to come through it.

The pressing question for all who search for true love is: How do we know the real thing from the spurious? How can we separate our projections of true love from true love itself? For romantic love to last, it must be infused with a higher love that makes one's destiny with a lover clear. The philosopher Jacob Needleman cites Søren Kierkegaard in his book, *A Little Book on Love:*

. . . the power to intentionally love another human being . . . comes to us only as a *result* of our ability to open to the Higher (the eternal or God) within and above . . . It is a grave error, says Kierkegaard, to imagine one can love another person intentionally without at the same time – and *more fundamentally* – loving the Highest within oneself and above oneself.

In his book *Sex, Ecology, Spirituality*, the philosopher Ken Wilber sheds light on how love seeks expression in our spiritual development. Drawing on the distinction made by the ancient Greeks, he distinguishes *eros* from *agape*, a higher and more disciplined love that can lift romance to a greater expression. Through *agape*, *eros* can be transformed into a deeper and more lasting love. And the same is true for camaraderie. Like *eros*, it carries the seed of lasting love. It, too, can grow beyond the call of mission or a historic moment into a lasting transcendent unity.

The transformative power of love has been celebrated since antiquity. In Plato's *Symposium*, for example, Socrates describes its progress from devotion to a single body to beauty in all bodies, and from devotion to bodies to beauty in laws, institutions, and wisdom:

He who has been instructed thus far in the things of love and who has learned to see the beautiful in due order and succession, when he comes toward the end will suddenly perceive a nature of wondrous beauty, a nature which in the first place is everlasting, not growing and decaying, or waxing and waning . . . remember how in that communion only, beholding beauty with the eye of the mind, he will be enabled to bring forth, not images of beauty, but realities . . .

Saints and mystics such as Saint Francis of Assisi and Sri Ramakrishna embodied this universal and transcendent love. Saint Francis loved lepers, animals, and the poor, the ugly and the beautiful, the high and the low, the sun and the moon. Legend tells us that in the dead of winter he spoke to an almond tree, saying, 'Speak to me of God!' and the tree responded by breaking into bloom.

And married love can blossom in extraordinary ways. Psychiatrist Rudolph von Urban, a student of Freud, described many examples of this. One couple told him that during moments of physical intimacy the wife was sometimes enveloped by 'a nimbus of greenish-blue light that radiated from her whole body,' imbuing their relationship with a transcendent joy. Another man and woman experienced an electrical flow through their skin, 'A million sources of delight merged into one.'

Commenting upon a similar experience related to him by a friend, the British poet Peter Redgrove wrote:

> [The man] slept, and then woke a short time afterwards with a beautiful feeling from love-making, as though [his skin] were open and enlarged and no longer a barrier, and through it he could feel his wife sleeping by him and inter-penetrating his skin, as though their bodies had intermingled . . After lying there and enjoying this afterglow, he opened his eyes and found that the room was full of a golden-colored gossamer arranged in a webwork that emanated from . . . centres of gold, and this webwork extended, as if in care, to the small bed of their daughter.

The man's experience resembles the ecstatic condition described by the Indian mystic Sri Ramakrishna. 'In the course of spiritual discipline,' he said, 'one gets a "love body" endowed with "love eyes" and "love ears." One sees God with those love eyes. One hears the voice of God with those love ears. One even gets a sexual organ made of love . . . and with this love body the soul communes with God.'

In his own devotion, Ramakrishna exhibited a remarkable physical radiance and highly contagious energy. During the initiation of his disciple Narendra, and in the course of other meetings, people near him felt a presence or force that had immediate physical effects. In his celebrated diary, Ramakrishna's follower 'M.' recorded several instances of such transmission, which appeared to involve something substantial materialized by Ramakrishna's love of God. People saw lights around the Indian saint, or felt a liberating power near him, or were enveloped by a palpable spiritual substance, just as the persons noted above felt a new energy and presence around their lovers. Returning to the imagery of Socrates's speech, Ramakrishna brought forth not images of goodness and beauty but physical expressions of them.

Indeed, religious ecstasies have been associated with various physical signs in virtually every sacred tradition. Such signs include great beauty of voice and countenance, extraordinary luminosity, superabundant vitality, and a sense that the ecstatic inhabited a new kind of flesh. Holy persons in every culture have, through their love of God, regenerated their bodies, their associates, and even the physical spaces around them.

Agape can transform all relationships. Think of a struggling student who exhibited new talent through a teacher's interest, or a normally depressed acquaintance who was filled with new life by performing some generous deed, or a dispirited friend who was given new purpose by someone who appreciated his special gifts. Love takes many forms and has many kinds of effects but always gives birth to new life.

Our experience of love takes many forms in everyday life. It may come suddenly in a glance between two people, in a wild fantasy about our dream lover, in a moment of closeness between friends or within a group dedicated to an important cause, or during spiritual devotion. Our challenge is to lift these moments toward their highest expression. Each moment of love is a first expression of the ever-present love waiting to be born in us. How much love can we express? How free are we from the projections or unconscious needs that cut us off from it? How deep are our spiritual experiences? The level of our love is our best gauge of this.

Love grows through intention and practice. It is our conviction that beyond the passion of personal desire or the grace of divine love bestowed upon us at times spontaneously, it is possible and desirable for all of us to practice the kind of attention and intention that we have already described in the previous chapters. Jacob Needleman calls this 'intermediate love,' and concludes in his book that it answers the need for a form of love that includes both the personal and the impersonal. 'In fact,' he writes, 'the *practical* teachings of wisdom point to a love that is just that – a love that carries both the personal intensity of subjective desire *and* the selfless wish for another's well-being.' The philosopher's ideal love is mutually beneficial and transcendental: 'The work of love is the work of presupposing the wish for awakening in the other.'

9

TRANSCENDENT
IDENTITY

Taken as a whole, the extraordinary experiences described in this book seem to form a pattern. When viewed in their entirety, they appear to be attributes of a single but many-sided nature pressing to be born in us. Each of them, it seems, points toward – and carries the seed of – a greater integration. The expanded perceptions, movement-abilities, energies, and other capacities described in this book call us toward a more inclusive and abundant nature overflowing with joy, meaning, and purpose.

Each of us begins this life in a circumscribed world of parents and friends, then gradually begins to expand our sense of self. If our development is reasonably healthy, we begin to embrace the details of our social context and differentiate our personal identity from the sea of others around us. If we are fortunate, we begin to know ourselves as unique people, with particular families, communities, nations, and histories. As our experience broadens, our sense of self grows into a unique biographical identity.

At times, however, many of us are introduced to the prospect of another identity, a being that transcends the ordinary self. Poets and philosophers have long celebrated this awakening, and every sacred tradition is based largely upon it. Saints and sages since antiquity have claimed that we can realize an identity beyond our personal history, a being that spiritual teachers have called by such names as *atman* (in the Indian Upanishads), Big Mind (in Zen Buddhism), 'the soul at one with God,' or the 'true self.' In this transcendent identity, which is connected it seems with the essence and divine source of the universe, we feel as though we have discovered who we really are.

An American woman known as 'Peace Pilgrim,' who for many years made long pilgrimages for world peace, gave up her name, home, and former life after an experience of this kind. This is how she described her awakening, which brought a new calling to serve the world, and a new identity:

I became increasingly uncomfortable about having so much while my brothers and sisters were starving. Finally I had to find another way. The turning point came when, in desperation and out of a very deep seeking for a meaningful life, I walked all one night through the woods. I came to a moonlit glade and prayed.

I felt a complete willingness, without any reservations, to give my life – to dedicate my life – to service. 'Please use me!' I prayed to God. And a great peace came over me. From that time on, I have known that my work would be for peace – peace among nations, peace among groups, peace among individuals, and inner peace. However, there's a great deal of difference between being willing to give your life and actually [doing it], and for me fifteen years of preparation and inner seeking lay between.

[Then one day] I was walking in the early morning. All of a sudden I felt very uplifted, more uplifted than I had ever been. I knew *timelessness* and *spacelessness* and *lightness*. I did not seem to be walking on the earth. There were no people or even animals around, but every flower, every bush, every tree seemed to wear a halo. There was an emanation around everything and flecks of gold fell like slanted rain through the air.

[But] the most important part of it was not the phenomena: the important part of it was the realization of the oneness of all creation. I knew before that all human beings are one. But now I knew also a oneness with the rest of creation. The creatures that walk the earth, and the growing things of the earth. The air, the water, the earth itself. And, most wonderful of all, *a oneness with that which permeates all and binds all together and gives life to all.* A oneness with that which many would call God.

The inspiration for the pilgrimage came at this time . . . I saw, in my mind's eye, myself walking along . . . I saw a map of the United States with the large cities marked – and it was as though someone had taken a colored crayon and marked a zigzag line across, coast to coast and border to border, from Los Angeles to New York City. I knew what I was to do. And that was a vision of my first year's pilgrimage route in 1953!

I entered a new and wonderful world. My life was blessed with a meaningful purpose.

Many of the world's great philosophers, poets, and religious figures have described the experience of a greater calling and self. The Greek philosophers Pythagoras, Socrates, and Plato; the Sufi poet Jalaluddin Rumi; the Christian mystic Meister Eckhart; the English poets William Blake and William Wordsworth; the American sage Ralph Waldo Emerson; the American poet Walt Whitman; the modern Indian mystics Ramana Maharshi, Sri Ramakrishna, and Sri Aurobindo; and countless others have created a lore and literature of ego-transcending identity. The young Siddhartha, destined to become the Buddha, fell restless with the materialism of his father's palace; the young Jesus was grieved by the temple's money-changers; the young Saint Francis grew weary of his wastrel ways. All sensed a greater calling that inspired a transcendence of their old identities, a break with their former life, and new connection with a deeper level of reality. Ralph Waldo Emerson described such realization in this way:

All goes to show that the soul in man is not an organ, but animates and exercises all the organs; is not a function, like the power of memory, of calculation, or comparison, but uses these as hands and feet; is not a faculty, but a light; is not the intellect or the will, but the master of the intellect and the will; is the background of our being, in which they lie – an immensity not possessed and that cannot be possessed. From within or from behind, a light shines through us upon things and makes us aware that that we are nothing, but the light is all.

The Indian mystic Sri Ramakrishna initiated his famous disciple Narendra (later Swami Vivekananda) into an experience of the transcendent identity Emerson described. In his introduction to *The Gospel of Sri Ramakrishna*, Swami Nikhilananda described Narendra's experience:

Narendra, because of his Brahmin upbringing, considered it wholly blasphemous to look on man as one with his Creator. One day at the temple garden he said to a friend: 'How silly. This jug is God? This cup is God? Whatever we see is God? And we too are God? Nothing could be more absurd.' Sri Ramakrishna came out of his room and gently touched him. Spellbound [Narendra] immediately perceived that everything in the world was indeed God. A new universe opened around him. Returning home in a dazed state, he found there too that the food, the plate, the eater himself, the people around him, were all God. When he walked in the street, he saw that the cabs, the horses, the streams of people, the buildings, were Brahman. He could hardly go about his day's business . . . And when the intensity of the experience abated a little, he saw the world as a dream. It took him a number of days to recover his normal self. He had a foretaste of the great experiences yet to come . . .

Once again, we hear of new worlds opening up in an ego-transcendent experience. The experience of transcendent selfhood is built on this overwhelming realization. A greater being, it seems, is seeking to emerge in us, a being that knows at once that it is fundamentally connected with the great field of creation around us. This is not merely an intellectual idea but a direct realization. It carries a greater sense of certainty than our biographical identity.

In the Bhagavad Gita, Krishna, the Lord of Existence, says, 'It is an eternal portion of Me that has become the living being in a world of living things.' Commentators upon the Gita have interpreted this line to mean that a supreme personhood, a Self beyond the ordinary self (*purushottoma*), supports the individual's action in the everyday world. Krishna, by this interpretation, symbolizes ultimate selfhood, immanent in the world while transcending created things. A similar doctrine can be found in every sacred tradition. According to the Japanese Buddhist scholar Gadjin Nagao, there is in Buddhism:

. . . the expression 'great self' (mahatmya), a term which undoubtedly had affinity to the Universal Soul of

[Hindu] atman-theory. Real awakening, or attainment of Buddhahood, is explained as the annihilation of the 'mean self' and the realization of 'great self.'

According to Plato, the soul communes with the divine archetypes before it takes birth in this limiting world of the senses, but through the practice of virtue and pursuit of the Good, it can rise toward its higher life. Describing his own experience of a higher self, the great Neoplatonist philosopher Plotinus wrote:

Often I have woken up out of the body to myself and have entered into myself, going out from all other things. I have seen a beauty wonderfully great and felt assurance that then most of all I belonged to the better part. I have lived to the full the best life and come to identify with the Divine.

The realization of an identity that transcends the constraints of ordinary selfhood has been celebrated by countless Jewish, Christian, and Islamic seers. 'My Me is God, nor do I recognize any other Me except my God himself,' wrote Saint Catherine of Genoa. 'To gauge the soul we must gauge it with God,' wrote the German mystic Meister Eckhart, 'for the Ground of God and the Ground of the Soul are one and the same ... The eye with which I see God is the same eye with which God sees me.'

The supreme identity represented in these statements is recognized by those who experience it to be the secret basis and fulfillment of human nature. That is why mystics in disparate cultures have described 'a most real I' or 'truest self.' Alan Watts described such experience as a shift from seeing the world as fragmented entities to a basic wholeness, to a sense that *all of existence is seeing through our eyes.*

People have described experiences of a larger identity,

'personhood,' or being since the dawn of recorded history. Some of these revelations happen during religious rituals, prayer, or meditation. Others occur spontaneously, while caring for the sick, traveling in the wilderness, during high moments of artistic creation, working in a garden, or cleaning house. Yet though their circumstances differ, these experiences are similar in that they point toward an ego-transcendent identity. In this identity, we believe, all the extraordinary attributes we have described assume their greatest power and significance.

In this experience of our most fundamental self, we don't *think* we have connected with the divine within, we *know* that we have. Everything around us is seen to be part of a supremely creative unfoldment, a divine purpose in which we know ourselves to be deeply involved. But there is a paradox here. In this realization of profound solidarity with the world we also realize our fundamental uniqueness. We see both our oneness with all things and our unique place in the evolving universe.

The saints and sages who have most famously celebrated such awakening have also exhibited a unique sense of calling and unmistakable personality. No one stood out in their culture more than Jesus, Buddha, Muhammed, or Saint Francis. All the philosophers and poets we have cited were vivid unforgettable characters. In Chapter Twelve, we will return to this paradox.

10

TRANSCENDENT KNOWING

Like the transcendent identity we have just described, transcendent knowing involves a recognition that we are essentially one with God and the evolving universe. But as we are using the term here, it also involves access to life-giving inspirations, memories, and intuitions beyond those with which we are normally acquainted. Through these extraordinary kinds of knowing we can serve the world with greater creativity and power.

'Although similar to states of feeling,' wrote the philosopher William James, 'mystical states seem to those who experience them to be also states of knowledge. They are states of insight into depths of truth unplumbed by the discursive intellect. They are illuminations, revelations, full of significance and importance; all inarticulate though they remain.'

Though such illuminations are most typically associated with mystics and saints of the sacred traditions, they happen to people in all walks of life. In his autobiography *The World As I See It*, Albert Einstein characterized such knowing in this way:

The most beautiful and most profound emotion we can experience is the sensation of the mystical. It is the

141

sower of all true science. He to whom this emotion is a stranger, who can no longer wonder and stand rapt in awe, is as good as dead. To know what is impenetrable to us really exists, manifesting itself as the highest wisdom and the most radiant beauty which our dull faculties can comprehend only in the most primitive form – this knowledge, this feeling is at the center of true religiousness.

In *The Varieties of Religious Experience*, William James presented this firsthand account of such knowing by the Canadian psychiatrist Richard Bucke:

All at once, without warning of any kind, I found myself wrapped in a flame-colored cloud. For an instant I thought of fire, an immense conflagration somewhere close by in that great city; (then) I knew that the fire was within myself. Directly afterward there came upon me a sense of exultation, of immense joyousness accompanied or immediately followed by an intellectual illumination impossible to describe.

Among other things, I did not merely come to believe, but I saw that the universe is not composed of dead matter, but is, on the contrary, a living Presence; I became conscious in myself of eternal life. It was not a conviction that I would have eternal life, but a consciousness that I possessed eternal life then; I saw that all men are immortal; that the cosmic order is such that without any peradventure all things work together for the good of each and all . . .

In certain rare moments such as Bucke described, when mystical knowing is joined with a sense of transcendent identity, we see that from a place beyond the ordinary self we can receive information and creative impulses that help enrich the world. As is the case with the other extraordinary attributes we are discussing in this book, knowledge and identity merge in a higher unity. Such integration is typically marked by a burst – or flood – of inspiration.

INSPIRATION

'And then there is inspiration,' the visionary dancer and choreographer Martha Graham remarked. 'Where does it come from? Each of us have moments where we are swept away by an inner sense of excitement about something we are doing or want to do. In this state, whatever we are working on seems to come alive with significance and even necessity, and our contribution seems to validate who we are or, perhaps more accurately, who we can be. In that instant we know that something transcendent is moving within us. But such inspiration cannot be forced, or demanded. In some sense, it must be received.'

The following passage in a letter attributed to Mozart describes this self-transcending process:

When I am, as it were, completely myself, entirely alone, and of good cheer . . . It is on such occasions that my ideas flow best and most abundantly. Whence and how they come, I know not; nor can I force them. Those ideas that please me I retain in memory, and am accustomed, as I have been told, to hum them to myself. If I continue in this way, it soon occurs to me how I may turn this or that morsel to account, so as to make a good dish of it, that is to say, agreeably to the rules of counterpoint, to the peculiarities of the various instruments, etc.

All this fires my soul . . . My subject enlarges itself, becomes methodized and defined, and the whole, though it be long, stands almost complete and finished in my mind so that I can survey it, like a picture, at a glance. Nor do I hear in my imagination the parts

143

successively, but I hear them, as it were, all at once (*gleich alles zusammen*) ... What has thus been produced I do not easily forget, and this is perhaps the best gift I have my Divine Maker to thank for.

Whether given to artists such as Mozart, to mystics who claim divine guidance, or to a mother caring for a child in need, such inspirations share a number of features, among them their speed and spontaneity, their joy, their exceeding of ordinary cognitive processes, and their seeming to come 'all at once' and 'all together.' And at times, they also involve memories that seem to come from beyond our normal processes of mental recall.

SUPERNORMAL MEMORY

Through the ages, and in virtually all cultures, certain people have been known for great feats of memory. In Celtic Ireland, bards were required to memorize a different poem, chant, riddle, or song for every day of the year, some of which required eight or more hours to recite. In ancient Greece it was common for school children, as well as poets, to memorize great stretches of Homer's *Iliad* and *Odyssey*. In her masterful study *The Art of Memory*, Francis Yates explores the 'inner gymnastics and invisible labors of concentration' that comprise such feats of recall in ancient Greece, the Middle Ages, and the Renaissance. Among the athletes of memory she describes, the Roman philosopher and orator Seneca 'could repeat two thousand names in the order in which they had been given; and when a class of two hundred students or more spoke each in turn a line of poetry, he could recite all the lines in reverse order.'

Such feats show that ordinary memory can be greatly expanded through intention and practice. For example, the psychiatrist Viktor Frankl, in *Man's Search for Meaning*, told how he helped keep prisoners alive during their incarceration at Auschwitz during World War II by challenging them to keep images of their loved ones alive in their mind or, if they were writers or musicians, to finish their incomplete books or compositions, without writing materials, *in their minds*. Describing this activity, he wrote:

> This intensification of inner life helped the prisoner find a refuge from the emptiness, desolation and spiritual poverty of his existence by letting him escape into the past. When given free rein, his imagination played with past events, often not important ones, but minor happenings and trifling things. His nostalgic memory glorified them and they assumed a strange character. In my mind I took bus rides, unlocked the front door of my apartment, answered my telephone, switched on the electric lights. Our thoughts often centered on such details, and these memories could reduce one to tears.

Memory can expand even further when we look for meaning in our lives. At times, it can take on the nature of inspiration when we seem to 'remember' a greater existence, a higher realm, and what we are meant or destined to become. Such experience can be initiated by a flood of memories about long-forgotten events that, once recalled, show how they have prepared us for the greater things we are meant to do.

INTUITION

But transcendent knowing is not limited to artistic or scientific work. At times it comes as immediate knowledge about how we should proceed in the everyday conduct of our lives. We might call this 'precognitive' or 'anticipatory' intuition. It might come as a hunch, 'gut feeling,' or image of our doing something at a particular time or place that ultimately leads – as if by 'synchronicity' – to new information, connections, or situations that enrich our lives and allow us to actualize larger projects. With intention and practice, we can learn to recognize such intuition more quickly and follow its lead.

Transcendent knowing, then, like the other extraordinary attributes described in this book, seems to come from a being or nature beyond the ordinary self. And when it is cultivated, it increasingly reveals a higher Presence calling us toward greater life and action in this ever-evolving world.

11

A WILL
BEYOND EGO

Everything flows and nothing stays,' said Heraclitus, the fifth-century Greek philosopher. He was speaking of the way time moves on, and how change is the only constant in life. However, the word 'flow' is also evocative of another kind of experience, the one that feels 'just so,' 'just right,' or in sync.

The ability to act in such flow, unburdened by self-defeating habits, is another attribute of our emerging nature. Experiences of transcendent identity and knowing help us act in this way. They can form the basis for it. For it is the case that from a less egobound self and consciousness, we have a stronger and more skillful will, a greater power of volition. Through such will, we can serve the world more creatively. In everything we do, we can find access to energies beyond our usual motives and impulses. According to religious teaching through the ages, extraordinary willpower occurs when we move past egocentricity into a stream of action that seems to come from a higher part of ourselves. In India's great scripture the Bhagavad Gita, the warrior Arjuna becomes a powerful instrument of God by transcending his selfish needs and his attachment to immediate results. In Taoist teaching, it is said that by concentrating vital energies, quieting thoughts, and disregarding external rewards, we can realize mastery in everyday work and thus express our deeper nature, which is identical with the Tao. According to the Taoist sage Chuang-Tzu:

Ch'ing, the chief carpenter, was carving wood into a stand for musical instruments. When finished, the work appeared to those who saw it as though of supernatural execution; and the Prince of LU asked him, 'What mystery is there in your art?'

'No mystery, Your Highness,' replied Ch'ing. 'And yet there is something. When I am about to make such a stand, I guard against any diminution of my vital power. I first reduce my mind to absolute quiescence. Three days in this condition, and I become oblivious of any reward to be gained. Five days, and I become oblivious of any fame to be acquired. Seven days, and I become unconscious of my four limbs and my physical frame. Then, with no thought of the Court present in my mind, my skill becomes concentrated, and all disturbing elements from without are gone. I enter some mountain forest, I search for a suitable tree. It contains the form required, which is afterwards elaborated. I see the stand in my mind's eye, and then set to work. Beyond that there is nothing. I bring my own native capacity into relation with that of the wood. What was suspected to be of supernatural execution in my work was due solely to this.'

If we examine firsthand accounts of such volition from sports, the martial arts, and other disciplines – or indeed from any walk of life – we find that it is marked by intense focus and heightened involvement in the action at hand. The American psychologist Mihaly Csikszentmihalyi has studied such activity, which he calls 'flow,' for several decades. He characterizes it as a 'breakthrough to new

148

levels of thought and behavior that occurs without social reinforcement and immediate rewards.'

Research on flow has been conducted with elderly Korean women, Indian and Thai adults, Tokyo teenagers, Navaho shepherds, farmers of the Italian Alps, and workers on assembly lines in Chicago. According to Csikszentmihalyi, the main dimensions of flow include 'deep concentration, clarity of goals, loss of a sense of time, lack of self-consciousness, and transcendence of the sense of self. . . . (These characteristics of flow) are recognized in more or less the same form by people the world over.' Csikszentmihalyi has found that flow can be practiced. His findings resonate with the claim of sages through the ages that while extraordinary willpower can come spontaneously, as a matter of grace, to recapture and develop it we must become aware of its possibility and decide to cultivate it.

'The winds of grace are always blowing,' said the Indian mystic Sri Ramakrishna, 'but to catch them we have to raise our sails.' Through surrender to a power beyond our normal impulses, we can realize new strengths and act with more than our usual willpower. This possibility is reflected in the prayer, 'Thy will, not mine, be done.'

George Leonard coined the term 'focused surrender' to describe the paradox of achieving flow. In his book with Michael Murphy, *The Life We Are Given*, he described the Zenlike results of his research on the phenomenon. He noted that exceptional moments of grace, or 'perfect rhythm,' involve the unlikely marriage of trying and not trying, of zeroing-in and letting go. It appears that both focused intentionality and the surrender of ego are necessary to experience existence at such a fundamental level and create what often seems miraculous.

Through the ages, volition arid prayer have been closely linked. For Homer, we pray because 'all men need

149

help from the gods.' In Islam, prayer is a ladder or journey reaching to heaven, where greater powers for life are given to us. Saint Therese of Lisieux called prayer 'an uplifting of the heart' through which we help lift up the world. Philosopher William James called it 'real work.' The Dakota Sioux medicine man Ohiyesa wrote, 'In the life of the Indian there was only one inevitable duty – the duty of prayer.' And in recent years, researchers such as Elizabeth Targ and Marilyn Schlitz and physicians such as Larry Dossey have produced experimental evidence that prayer is a real force that can heal bodies, moods, and mental suffering.

Yet if prayerful intention and focused surrender are ways to create a will beyond ego and state of flow in our lives, the question arises: How do we get started? One answer comes from our sense of the call, the summons from the beyond. We are often guided to this by subtle clues, by impulses or hunches we can easily overlook. If we pay attention to them, we can open to a higher part of ourselves. 'When a moment knocks on the door of your life,' wrote the Russian novelist and poet Boris Pasternak, 'it is often no louder than the beating of your heart, and it is very easy to miss.'

12

THE EXPERIENCE OF INTEGRATION AND SYNCHRONISTIC FLOW

The extraordinary experiences described in previous chapters have been testified to in virtually all cultures since the dawn of human history. As we have seen, they become evident among men and women young and old, in many types of activity, from the common to the sublime. Many of them have been tested and confirmed in scientific experiments, and all of them have been celebrated in the sacred traditions. Indeed, the justification and power of all religion comes in large part from experiences of this kind, not only among mystics and saints but also among people with little or no religious calling. The enhanced perceptual and communication abilities, moments of higher identity and knowing, crowning experiences of joy, and embracing love that grace our life point again and again to possibilities for transformation that all of us harbor.

When such experiences are viewed in their entirety, they appear to reveal a greater nature pressing to be born in us. Taken as a whole, they seem to be the various attributes of a greater self, a larger personhood, which we can open into through intention and practice.

A HIGHER INTEGRATION

Until now, we have mainly discussed our emergent attributes as discrete experiences because this is usually the way they first come to us. But we believe that something more than their separate activity can grace our lives. As we have said, each seems to be intrinsically related to the others, which suggests that as our greater nature comes forth it will include them all in a higher unity. Though this all-embracing integration lies in our distant future, men and women around the world are having glimpses and first experiences of it.

For example, many contemporary studies have shown that people in various cultures experience the flowing, ego-transcendent action discussed in the previous chapter. As we have seen, such activity is not unlike the 'non-doing' celebrated in Taoism, the 'action without attachment to results' advocated in Buddhist and Hindu scriptures, or the transcendence of egocentric striving described in the Christian, Jewish, and Islamic faiths. Such action is also related to Carl Jung's notion of synchronicity. The famous Swiss psychiatrist defined this phenomenon as the appearance of 'meaningful co-incidences,' events that dramatize and reinforce certain turns in our lives in a manner that seems governed by something beyond mere chance. Such events, Jung believed, point to a principle or quality of the world that leads individuals toward further personal growth and their deepest calling.

There is reason to believe that as we integrate our greater capacities, we tend to experience more moments that can be called synchronistic. In such moments, which often seem uncanny, events conspire to push or attract us in ways that feel purposeful – or even destined. We discover a book and coincidentally hear of a workshop about it. We think of a new career move and meet someone who has just accomplished one like it. We think of an old friend and soon she calls with something important to tell us. Such moments often have a numinous and revelatory quality. They seem to point to something important, something with great consequence for us. We are turned – at least for a moment – beyond our usual thought and behavior toward a greater identity where, as we have seen, we rise beyond ordinary biography into a greater calling, a larger self that appears to be joined with the creative force that animates the world at large.

OVERCOMING OBSTACLES

For most of us, these moments are fleeting and sometimes disappointing. We meet someone new in a way that feels important but the relationship sours or leads us to a seeming failure. The once-numinous flow suddenly stops. What seemed to have been meaningful synchronicity appears to have been illusion. Many of us have experienced such events, during which we were misled by false hopes or faulty conclusions. However, a case can be made that some synchronicities do not bear fruit because we do not sufficiently embrace the other attributes of our emergent nature. Here is where practice is needed. To maintain the transcendent flow that synchronicities promise, we must cultivate all of the extraordinary attributes pressing to be born in us.

The higher perspective, for example, that characterizes the transcendent identity and knowing described in previous chapters involves awareness of our usual psychological patterns. Understanding our largely unconscious scripts, motivations, and behavioral tendencies is crucial because they often lead us to misinterpretations of potentially creative events and frequently limit our responses to them. Through counseling, meditation, and other practices, we can better respond to the creative opportunities life gives us. As our self-knowledge grows, our discernment about people and events improves so that special moments of opportunity can be perceived with growing wisdom.

We want to emphasize this. The cultivation of our greater attributes is not an easy task. At this step in our integration of extraordinary experience, the way can be difficult and full of dead ends. Synchronistic flow requires our transcendence of limiting habits and scripts, narrow desires, and mechanical responses to life's graces.

AN INTEGRATED, SYNCHRONISTIC FLOW

To repeat: As they are cultivated, all of our extraordinary attributes contribute to the realization of our greater nature, and are necessary for the experience of an integrated flow. Among the thousands of people we have spoken to who are engaged in transformative practice, we observe this principle at work. The cultivation of transcendent identity, for example, can create a higher perspective and detachment through which we can more wisely embrace new challenges and opportunities. Similarly, the cultivation of the luminous intelligence we have called 'transcendent knowing' can help us experience our higher calling and lead us to remember 'who we really are' or 'what we are secretly meant to do,' often triggering images of what to do next.

We can, in other words, work through our habitual dramas and begin to engage the world with what we have called 'precognitive' or 'anticipatory' intuition. Such intuition, if followed, can move us into the right circumstances for a meaningful event to occur. This event, if interpreted wisely from a perspective beyond our normal scripts and desires, can then yield a further development of our life mission.

However, as we have said, interpretations of synchronistic events can be tricky. An apparent synchronicity, for example, might suggest to us wrongly that we abandon a promising but now-difficult project. It might prompt us to avoid a situation that should be faced, or end a relationship still filled with creative potential. We need both patience and discernment here. When a magical moment seems to call, we must wait, without jumping to conclusions, until we have enough information to see where it can most creatively take us. We can look for its 'silver lining,' the meaning in it that rings true to our highest intuition, with both caution and hope.

This first integration and consequent flow, which are sensed and discussed by more and more people now, have the potential to create a society more conscious of how the transcendent operates in daily life. As we propose in Part Three, it could begin to fulfill our greatest dreams and help human culture flourish. Eventually, we believe, it could help evolution advance and lead us toward forms of embodiment not yet seen on Earth.

Part Three

Participating

13

TRANSFORMING CULTURE

For millennia, poets have envisioned times and places in which people lived with joyous accord. Philosophers have long dreamt of good societies. And activists in many fields have embodied such dreams in programs for creative cultural change. We believe that the aspiration for social transformation implicit in such visions and activities is essential to the greater life pressing to be born in us. Our ego-transcendent nature, our larger self, has a fundamental urge to help further the world's advance. This drive, this call, has long been expressed in the dreams of humankind.

Sumerians carved visions of paradise from the epic of Gilgamesh. The Greek poet Hesiod wrote about the Blessed Isles, an enchanted world with buildings of gold encircled by perfumed waters. And Tibetans dreamt of Shambhala, a land of jeweled palaces and emerald walls where lamas live in an ascended state. In Europe during the Middle Ages, visions of this kind were expressed in quest stories such as the search for Avalon or El Dorado. Travelers told tales of magical islands such as Hyperborea off the Scottish coast and Hy Brasil to the west of Ireland.

Such visions, which were long embedded in legend, myth, and poetry, have also been given more reasoned form by philosophers of various persuasions. In his dialogue *The Republic*, for example, Plato envisioned a city-state ruled by philosopher-kings, in which people were given roles to fit their abilities as guardians, soldiers, or workers; and some two thousand years later, in 1516, Sir Thomas More described an imaginary island called *Utopia*, meaning 'noplace' or 'nowhere,' that was governed with justice and regard for all. Though the name *Utopia*, or 'noplace,' suggested the idea's allegorical or even satirical nature, More's vision is regarded as a catalyst for later visions of human perfectibility.

With the advent of the Renaissance and the Enlightenment, visions of human betterment were given novelistic form. In 1627 the philosopher Francis Bacon published *New Atlantis*, a novel that celebrates science as the tool to build utopia. Daniel Defoe wrote *Robinson Crusoe*, a story of solitude on a paradisiacal island. And in the late nineteenth century, Edward Bellamy's *Looking Backward* appeared, giving rise to passionate utopianism in America and Great Britain (which was embodied in 'looking backward' clubs).

In the twentieth century, however, an ever-growing awareness of human perversity made such literature seem dangerously naïve. Against the background of Hitler, Stalin, and the Holocaust, ideas of human perfectibility, which had been expressed by the Nazis' 'superman,' seemed to be prescriptions for evil. Two dystopian novels, Aldous Huxley's *Brave New World* and George Orwell's *1984*, expressed a widely held suspicion about utopian visions. By the end of World War 11, most people thought that the notion of utopia had been extinguished.

Nevertheless, in direct response to twentieth-century social ills, many intentional communities sprang up in the 1960s. The behavioral psychologist B. F. Skinner wrote *Walden Two*, which, while controversial for its theories of human behavior, inspired several groups of this kind.

But few of these experiments lasted long. Most were hampered – or destroyed – by destructive relations among their participants, and some turned into dangerous cults. But do the naïveté of utopian dreams and the widespread failure of intentional communities prove that social progress is impossible?

The answer, clearly, is no. Many social reforms, among them the civil rights, environmental, and women's movements, have produced historic cultural advances. The Cold War ended with little bloodshed. Apartheid was eliminated in South Africa. With all our social ills, many of which continue to horrify us, people are finding creative ways to renew institutions and cultures. There are countless places to express the impulse behind our humanitarian dreams, and that impulse is intrinsic to our greater nature. Deep down, we want to serve the world, and there are innumerable ways to do so. This becomes increasingly evident as we cultivate the empathy, sense of mission, capacity for love, and other life-giving attributes described in this book. We believe that the integration of these attributes, and the sense of inspired flow they produce, can make our efforts of reform more heartfelt and effective.

And, as we have seen, a broad view of evolution can help us join our aspirations for personal and social transformation. A sense of the world's stupendous advance can inspire and lend perspective to all our works, especially when they are supported by transformative disciplines. We have seen what prodigies of body and soul such practices give rise to, and we have described the life-enriching activity they can produce. In this chapter, we will suggest some ways in which the realization of our greater capacities and the perspective it gives us can contribute to the world's evolutionary progress. Our aim is not to be comprehensive but to list a few fields that can be furthered by the development of our higher attributes.

Science is a good place to start. It is a central place to work for human advance because it is crucial to our acquisition of knowledge about the human potential.

TOWARD A SCIENCE OF EXTRAORDINARY HUMAN ATTRIBUTES

Today, there exists more publicly available knowledge about our transformative capacities than has ever existed in human history. Unfortunately, though, philosophic prejudices of various kinds, competition between scientific specialists, and the sheer size of the information explosion make it difficult to view this knowledge as a whole. That this is the case is expressed in the saying, 'We seem to know more and more about less and less.'

The tremendous pressure to specialize makes it difficult for scientists and scholars in any field to recognize the wide range of extraordinary experiences outlined in this book. In spite of such fragmentation, though, such experiences can be viewed as a whole to find patterns that connect them. It is possible now to gather verified data about our greater capacities from medical research, anthropology, psychology, sociology, psychical research, religious studies, sports, the arts, and other fields. As we have seen, psychologists such as William James and Abraham Maslow, pioneering scholars of supernormal experience such as Frederic Myers and Marghanita Laski, research physicians such as Larry Dossey, parapsychologists such as Marilyn Schlitz and William Braud, anthropologists such as Michael Harrier, and other scientists and scholars we have referred to are exemplars of this bold, broadminded approach. They have helped show us the way toward a greater science of the human potential.

These men and women have answered a passionate calling, had love of their fields and joy in their work. Most have described self-transcendent experiences that empowered their creative acts. And all of them have been highly disciplined, which is one reason why they were well regarded by their associates. We want to emphasize this. Self-transcendent experience and disciplined work – in science or any field – are deeply compatible. Abraham Maslow claimed that the self-actualizing people he studied typically *become* their work, not in a negatively addictive way, but in a manner that enriches the world.

One reason why scholars and scientists such as those we've just named were esteemed by their colleagues was that they employed methods appropriate to their sometimes-controversial subject matter. Each was empirical in their methods, depending upon controlled experiments, the observation of naturally occurring events, or comparisons of subjective reports and reliable testimonies to unusual phenomena. They maintained critical distance from their data while bringing boldness and imagination to their observations and theories. All of them, in short, have shown that it is possible to bring the revelatory methods of science to the further reaches of human nature.

More than ever before, humankind has the means to build a science of the human potential. Researchers in many fields have taught us to winnow accurate information from distorted perceptions of extraordinary events and to discriminate good data from bad. Psychical researchers, for example, have learned how to supplement anecdotal accounts of telepathic, clairvoyant, and other paranormal events with well-controlled studies of them, and the sacred traditions have established rigorous tests to confirm the validity of supernormal experience. Though the fact is not widely appreciated by mainstream scientists, contemplatives East and West have long had their extraordinary insights and powers tested by peers and teachers who have a disciplined acquaintance with such experience. Philosophers Ken Wilber and Stephen Phillips, among other contemporary thinkers, have argued that there is a fundamental similarity between scientific and contemplative empiricism.

Nevertheless, many scientists and philosophers today reject the evidence for supernormal phenomena and automatically associate reports of it with outmoded or superstitious beliefs. The pioneering scientists we have mentioned, though, have not dismissed such evidence of our greater nature. They have shown us how to approach it with imagination and care, sympathy and precision. In doing this, they have often needed to rise above their prejudices and predispositions. They have sometimes been graced by intuitions that lifted them past their blind spots and were frequently led to their discoveries by hunches that seemed to come from beyond. For them, science itself became a transformative discipline. Those of us called to the study of human nature in its further reaches can take inspiration from their work.

THE TRANSFORMATION OF EDUCATION

No institution has more reason than does education to embrace our growing knowledge about human nature's emergent capacities. Our schools should identify possibilities for growth in every child, promote interest in lifelong learning, and cultivate body, heart, and soul as well as strictly cognitive abilities. Given our increasing access to the many transformative practices described in this book, all of which facilitate health, creativity, and a sense of vocation, it is our belief that education must transcend current debates about the relative worth of intellectual skills and attributes such as empathy, integrity, and self-awareness. As philosophers have held since ancient times, the fundamental purpose of education is to bring forth our best and deepest qualities. From Plato to the present day, leading educators have called our schools to address the whole person.

Fortunately, certain schools support this holistic approach, some of them in response to contemporary proposals for educational reform. An influential proposal of this kind was put forth by George Leonard, who covered education for *Look* magazine in the 1950s and 1960s and won more awards for education reporting than any other journalist of his day. Leonard visited hundreds of schools, often spending several days in a single classroom to evaluate the educational system from the students' and teacher's points of view. At first he was favorably impressed, but he eventually was troubled by what he found. He was increasingly disturbed by the high ratio of students to teachers, the boredom among students and certain teachers alike, the absence of passion, and the general dreariness evident in many schools. His disillusionment with America's educational system led him to recommend a broader and deeper schooling. In magazine articles and his eloquent book *Education and Ecstasy* (1968), Leonard has proposed daring and creative ways in which schools at every level can simultaneously cultivate our physical, emotional, cognitive, and spiritual capacities. In such schools, he writes, students can:

- learn the commonly agreed upon skills and knowledge of the ongoing culture (reading, writing, figuring, history, and the like), and to learn them joyfully
- learn how to ring creative changes on all that is currently agreed upon
- learn delight, not aggression; sharing, not excessive acquisition; and uniqueness, not narrow competition
- learn heightened awareness of emotional, sensory,

and bodily states and, through this, increased empathy for other people
- learn how to enter and enjoy varying states of consciousness in preparation for a life of change
- learn how to explore and enjoy relations between people – learn how to learn, because learning-a word that includes singing, dancing, interacting, and much more – is the main purpose of life

Leonard believes that every educator, parent, and student must become involved in transforming the current educational system. He suggests starting with these three assumptions: first, that the human potential is much greater than we have been led to believe; second, that education without joy is a mere shadow of education; and third, that learning is life's ultimate purpose. Someday, the ability to learn with joy will become a central measure of social life. Leonard wrote:

The master teacher pursues delight, shameless in his use of spells and enchantments. Great men, as every schoolboy knows, have greeted their moments of learning with crazy joy. We learn how Archimedes leaped, crying 'Eureka!' from his bathtub; how Handel, on finishing the Hallelujah Chorus, told his servant, 'I think I did see all Heaven before me, and the Great God himself.' But we fail to acknowledge that every child starts out as an Archimedes, a Handel. The eight-month-old who succeeds in balancing one block on another has made a connection no less momentous for him than Archimedes's . . . Much of his life at that age, in fact, is learning. Explaining why he was unable to think about scientific problems for a year after his final exams, Albert Einstein said: 'It is in fact nothing short of a miracle that the modern methods of instruction have not yet entirely strangled the holy curiosity of inquiry . . . It is a grave mistake to think that the enjoyment of seeing and searching can be promoted by means of coercion and a sense of duty.'

And yet, life and joy cannot be subdued. The blade of grass shatters the concrete. An Einstein emerges from the European academies. Those who would reduce, control, quell must lose in the end. The ecstatic forces of life, growth, and change are too numerous, too various, too tumultuous.

Education reflects our most basic views of the human potential. If we do not recognize our greater possibilities, we are unlikely to conceive an education that encourages them. The enhanced perceptual and communication abilities, intuitive knowing, and capacities for love we've described, which lead us toward a greater calling and mission, can and must be nurtured. An education that did so would bring forth virtues of heart and soul as well as skills such as reading and writing.

Today, unfortunately, most U.S. schools are caught in a tide of standardized achievement testing, which tends to work against creativity, originality, and the joy of learning. Highest priority is given not to learning in a broad sense, but to learning how to make good grades on paper-and-pencil multiple-choice tests. Increasingly, subjects not included on the tests are cut back or simply dropped from the curriculum. Such integrative subjects as drama, physical education, and the arts are replaced by practice sessions in test-taking, which, at best, ensure that as many test-takers as possible come up with the same answers-and perhaps eventually learn to think like everyone else.

However, there are signs the victims are rebelling. All across California, for example, teachers who in 2001 won bonuses of $591 for raising their students' test scores by a specified amount are protesting by donating their prizes to innovative programs, scholarships, and charities. And there are numerous schools and educational groups doing their best to reverse this movement toward human standardization.

One such organization is The George Lucas Educational Foundation (GLEF). Founded by the creator of *Star Wars*, the foundation is headed by Dr. Milton Chen, a distinguished educator who holds an A.B. from Harvard and a doctorate from Stanford. Dr. Chen and his staff seek out schools throughout the United States that are dedicated to innovation and the joy of learning, and tell their stories through a handsome semiannual newsletter called *Edutopia*, videotapes, a website (*www.glef org*), pamphlets, CDs, and a speakers' bureau. The schools they choose to showcase feature strong community involvement, imaginative use of technology, cooperative learning, and project orientation, along with an approach to education that involves mind, body, spirit, and emotion.

In the Sherman Oaks Community Charter School in San Jose, California, for example, principal Peggy Bryan went so far as to sacrifice a cafeteria in favor of a spacious learning center where students can move about freely in creating projects, aided by informational technology, as in George Leonard's book, *Education and Ecstasy*. At the Benjamin Franklin Middle School in Ridgewood, New Jersey, eighth-graders produce a daily news and public service show on BFBN (Ben Franklin Broadcast News), broadcast live on their local cable station. But the school's major emphasis is on social and emotional intelligence and a physical education program in which all students can participate. 'If we can create an environment where we feel good and care for each other,' says Benjamin Franklin principal Tony Bencivenga, 'everything else falls into place.'

We believe that education's greatest mandate is to inspire in students a sense of our potential greatness in this stupendous, ever-evolving universe. In doing this, it can help them find their deepest vocation as well as powers through which they can contribute to the world's advance.

RESHAPING BUSINESS

Business, too, can become an arena of learning and growth. As many business leaders and consultants have seen, organizations can facilitate self-discovery and our call to serve the world at large while promoting greater efficiencies of production and service.

Warren Bennis, a business professor, presidential adviser, and expert on leadership, has studied the links between personal and organizational development. Through long acquaintance with politicians and businessmen, he has identified various abilities that typify good leaders, among them persistence, self-knowledge, capacity for risk, commitment, and love of learning. 'The learning person looks forward to failure or mistakes,' he writes. 'The worst problem in leadership is early success. There's no opportunity to learn from problems. I suspect that we learn the most while facing adversity.'

The attributes of good leaders that Bennis has identified correspond in many ways to the emergent capacities described in this book. Leaders, he says, typically have 'emotional wisdom,' which is characterized by an ability to accept people as they are, to meet events in the here and now, to trust others even when it seems risky, and to act without constant approval and recognition. Bennis asks us to remember 'that learning to be an effective leader is no different than learning to be an effective person . . . When we talk about "growing leaders," we're inevitably involved in personal transformation.'

Success in business, says Bennis, is often best facilitated

by what he calls 'Great Groups.' Many problems, he writes, are:

> ... too complex to be solved by any one person or any one discipline. Our only chance is to bring people together from a variety of backgrounds and disciplines. I call such collections of talent Great Groups. The genius of Great Groups is that they get remarkable people – strong individual achievers – to work together. But these groups serve a second and equally important function: they provide psychic support and personal fellowship. They help generate courage. Without a sounding board for outrageous ideas, without personal encouragement and perspective when we hit a roadblock, we'd all lose our way. Great Groups remind us how much we can really accomplish by working toward a shared purpose. To be sure, Great Groups rely on many long-established practices of good management-effective communication, exceptional recruitment, genuine empowerment, personal commitment. But they also remind us of author Luciano de Crescanzo's observation that 'we are all angels with only one wing; we can only fly while embracing one another.' In the end, these groups cannot be managed, only led in flight.

Bennis is not alone in the connection he makes between personal and organizational transformation. According to many psychologists who have studied the modern workplace, there is an inescapable link between the philosophy a business adheres to and the morale of its participants. Numerous studies have shown that all organizations can increase their creativity and efficiency at once by nurturing their members' capacities for learning and growth. If they facilitate what we have called 'integrated flow,' they can increase their chances of success. As one's well-being in work increases, a magnetic attractiveness often occurs, bringing people together to produce 'predictable miracles.'

Like Bennis, Peter Senge is a leading thinker today on the topic of organizational development. In his widely read book *The Fifth Discipline: The Art and Practice of the Learning Organization*, he discusses organizations in which new patterns of thought are nurtured, collective aspiration is set free, and people are encouraged to learn together. Businesses can become learning organizations by encouraging flexible, creative, and holistic thinking: the embrace of complexity, personal mastery, clarification of vision, focusing of personal energies, high regard for objectivity, the uncovering of subconscious mental pictures, shared 'pictures of the future' that foster commitment and enrollment rather than compliance, and dialogue that helps team members suspend assumptions and enter into creative alliances. Senge has learned through his research that meditation and other transformative practices can facilitate the development of these abilities.

Like Bennis and Senge, many business leaders have affirmed a vision of organizational life that affirms the human potential. Business for them improves products and services with increasing efficiency while helping to improve the world at large. Many studies have shown that this happens most when workers find meaning in their work and when their organization is infused with a sense of purpose and devotion to their welfare.

Business, in short, seems to work best when it joins a commitment to both personal and social transformation. Like education, environmentalism, and the other fields we are briefly examining here, it relies upon a synergy of the individual and the group to realize its highest ends. With this synergy, it can become a vehicle for humankind's further advance.

A DEEPER ENVIRONMENTALISM

The clearest way into the Universe is through a forest wilderness.

JOHN MUIR

Live in the fields, and God will give you lectures on natural philosophy every day.

RALPH WALDO EMERSON,
Nature

Re-enchantment with the Earth as a living reality is the condition for its rescue from the destruction we are imposing on it. To carry this out effectively, we must now, in a sense, reinvent the human as a species within the community of life species.

FATHER THOMAS BERRY,
The Dream of the Earth

Care for the environment is one of our greatest imperatives. Plant and animal species are disappearing rapidly. Rivers and seas are increasingly polluted. Global warming is a fact. Realizing this, more and more people today are working to preserve and restore the world's natural beauty and dwindling resources.

We believe that this environmental activism is deeply consonant with the development of our greater capacities. The ego-transcending experiences we have described, which lift us toward a higher, more embracing identity, make us more deeply aware of our relationship with the world around us. They do this not in intellectual terms, but with a compelling perception of life's unity. Our drive to preserve the Earth's unspoiled places and rejuvenate those that have been degraded is made even stronger when we experience our fundamental solidarity with them.

The American naturalists John Muir and Henry David Thoreau, who as much as anyone else have helped inspire environmentalism in the United States, were led to their work by a spiritual affinity with the natural world. 'Shall I not have intelligence with the Earth?' wrote Thoreau. 'Am I not partly leaves and vegetable mould myself?' Muir described a similar feeling when he wrote:

> I used to envy the father of our race, dwelling as he did in contact with the new-made fields and plants of Eden; but I do so no more, because I have discovered that I also live in 'creation's dawn.' The morning stars still sing together, and the world, not yet half made, becomes more beautiful every day.

Muir, who founded the Sierra Club, spent many years in California's Yosemite Valley and Sierra Nevada mountains. That he experienced a mystical oneness with nature is evident in these passages:

Heaven and earth are one –
    Part of the vesture of God,
Around all the earth the deep Heaven lies and is
    Part of it.
The dark bodeful night
Becomes divine and glows transfigured in light,
Puts on the garment of Eternity
That comes from no earthly sun – a sight to be
    Worshipped.

. . . as the warmth and beauty of fire are more enjoyed by those who, knowing something of the origin of wood and coal, see the dancing flames and are able to contemplate the grand show as having come from the sun ages ago . . . so also are those Yosemite temples the more enjoyed by those who have traced the Divine Mind in their making.

In their journals and other writings, Muir and Thoreau often described the numinous presence they encountered in the natural world. Many of us have felt what they described. Such enchantment is waiting for us all and can inspire works such as theirs to nurture the Earth, which, as Muir wrote, is 'one with heaven.' Here again, our emergent nature moves to enrich the world at large. Respect and care for the natural world flows from our feeling of connection with it.

But to be effective, work to preserve the environment also requires practicality. We can, for example, work with business in our efforts to restore the world's natural resources. The social innovator Paul Hawken advocated this approach in his book *The Ecology of Commerce*. Business, he wrote:

> . . . is not just a reasonable agent for such change; it is the *only* mechanism powerful enough to reverse global environmental and social degradation. Every commercial act in today's industrial society, regardless of intention, degrades the environment. We need a system where the opposite is true, where the everyday acts of work and production accumulate in a better world as a matter of course.

Hawken and his colleagues Amory and Hunter Lovins, in their book *Natural Capitalism*, have proposed that natural resources are a form of capital. By realizing this, businesses can, with their money, financial acumen, and organizational skills, use this 'natural capital' for both financial and environmental profit. Organizations such as Greenpeace and the Sierra Club, they write:

174

... have now become the real capitalists. By addressing such issues as greenhouse gases, chemical contamination, and the loss of fisheries, wildlife corridors, and primary forests, they are doing more to preserve a viable business future than are all the chambers of commerce put together. While business leaders hotly contest the idea of resource shortages, there are few credible scientists or corporations who argue that we are not losing the living systems that provide us with trillions of dollars of natural capital: our soil, forest cover, aquifers, oceans, grasslands, and rivers. Moreover, these systems are diminishing at a time when the world's population and the demand for services are growing exponentially.

Hawken and the Lovinses describe many ways in which commerce can profit through environmental awareness. Many businessmen and environmentalists agree with them, arguing that through the wise use of resources businesses can simultaneously create jobs and lessen their impact on the natural world. Many people now believe that we can at the same time grow our economy, use fewer resources, and begin to restore our damaged environments.

Practicality, then, becomes an ally to our love of nature. Here again we observe the interdependence of our emergent capacities. The empathy and perceptual sensitivity produced by transformative practice tend to strengthen our feelings for the environment. We can follow their call not only by protesting against those who pollute, but by working from within the system of commerce that looks away from environmental degradation. The heightened perception of beauty, the joy in things of the natural world, and the sense of the sacred inherent in our greater nature can empower all our efforts to nurture the world around us.

175

INTIATIVES FOR PEACE AND ECONOMIC DEVELOPMENT

Whether we work to improve education, business, or care for the environment – indeed if we work in any field for creative social change – transformative practice can help us. The emergence of our greater capacities can facilitate all our projects for the public good. Many heroes of social reform have shown us that this is the case.

In his book *Eyes of the Heart*, for example, Haiti's first democratically elected president, Jean-Bertrand Aristide, described a 'path for the poor in the age of globalization.' This visionary former head of state has put his vision into action, helping to empower many people in need in Haiti and other parts of the world. He has catalyzed some of this work through the Aristide Foundation for Democracy, which brings rich and poor together to explore a wide range of social concerns. The foundation has organized a cooperative of small vendors and day laborers, most of whom are women, that offers credit at low interest, provides transportation and a community store for those in need, sells schoolbooks at half price, runs a radio and television station staffed partly by children, and invests in food production. Aristide also started Lafanmi Selvai, a center for street children. The salt for his people, he has said, is *learning*. To learn is to wake up. 'But this kind of struggle,' says Aristide, 'requires a connection to the Transcendent.' In his view, ordinary people can better serve the world when they find a higher mission and purpose.

While attending the 1996 State of the World Forum in San Francisco, journalist-photographer Michael Collopy's life was changed when he heard Marian Wright Edelman, founder of the Children's Defense Fund, call the audience to creative social action. Inspired by her words and example, Collopy interviewed and made photographic portraits of seventy-five influential peacemakers – among them spiritual leaders, politicians, scientists, artists, and activists – and authored the inspirational book *Architects of Peace*. Among those he interviewed was General Lee Butler, a former Commander in Chief of the Strategic Air Command who later headed the Second Chance Foundation, the purpose of which is the reduction of nuclear danger. Butler described the evolution of his views after he was 'chilled to the depth of his strategic soul' by the inherent flaws of nuclear strategy.

Collophy also interviewed the ex-president of the Soviet Union, Mikhail Gorbachev, who described his 'Damascus moment,' an illumination like General Butler's that transformed his attitude toward the arms race. It came while he was riding a helicopter with former U. S. President George Bush to Camp David. 'Near President Bush sat a military aide,' he said, 'with the nuclear codes enabling him to destroy the Soviet Union. Near me sat my military aide with the codes to destroy the United States. Yet President Bush and I sat together on that small helicopter talking about peace.' This sudden recognition inspired him to change directions in the Soviet conflict with the United States and steered him toward a new paradigm of international relations. In his interview with Collopy, he said:

I am committed to a nuclear-free world . . . The twentieth century must be seen as a *century of warning*, a call to humankind for the necessity of developing a new consciousness and new ways of living and acting.

In 1974 Muhammad Yunus was teaching at the Chittagong University in Bangladesh and feeling the agony of his newly independent homeland. He asked himself why the people in a nearby village had to die of hunger. 'Was there anything I could do,' he asked, 'to delay the process or stop it, even for one person?' On a visit to the village in question to experience its misery firsthand, he encountered a woman making bamboo stools. The encounter changed his life and eventually the lives of countless people in Bangladesh and beyond. He found that it cost the woman only twenty cents to buy the bamboo for a stool, but that she had to borrow the money from the supplier who then kept her in an indentured relationship. Yunus thought about giving her pennies to buy the wood – but then had a better idea, which reverberates to this day. Together with one of his students, he created a list of forty-two villagers who needed a small amount of money to liberate themselves from their virtual slavery. This is how he described his sudden resolution:

> When I added up the total dollars they needed I experienced the biggest shock of my life: It added up to twenty-seven dollars! I felt ashamed to be a member of a society that could not provide twenty-seven dollars to forty-two hardworking, skilled human beings. To escape my shame, I took the twenty-seven dollars out of my pocket, and gave it to my student and said, 'Take this money. Give it to those forty-two people we met and tell them this a loan, which they can pay back whenever they are ready.'

The villagers were shocked that anyone would trust them with money, and local bankers were derisive when Yunus asked them to advance some more. But Yunus was undeterred. In 1983 he set up the Grameen Bank as an alternative to conventional banking and began to loan village women a few cents or dollars at a time with the understanding that they make small but regular weekly repayments. 'By the time the loans are paid off,' Yunus reported, 'the women are completely different people. They have explored themselves, found themselves.'

As of this writing, Grameen Bank works in thirty-six thousand villages in Bangladesh; has 2.1 million borrowers, 94 percent of them women; and employs twelve thousand people. The bank completed its first billion dollars in loans several years ago and the recovery rate of loans is about 98 percent.

'Grameen-type programs are now popping up in many countries,' Yunus told an interviewer. 'To my knowledge, fifty-six countries – including the United States – are involved in such endeavors. But the effort doesn't have the momentum it needs. More than a billion people on this planet earn the equivalent of one American dollar or less a day. If we create institutions capable of providing business loans to the poor for self-employment, we will see the same success we have seen in Bangladesh. I see no reason why anyone in the world should be poor.'

The Grameen Bank provides a shining example of what inspired individuals can accomplish when they evolve from selfcenteredness to a recognition that the web of life connects us all. Often, the prospect of seemingly insurmountable problems around stifles our urge to act, yet what is important is to commit to whatever cause moves us. What is needed is a new awareness, a new alertness, and an ability to care. The Australian nuclear activist Dr. Helen Caldicott summarized her philosophy in this regard: 'The only cure is love,' she wrote. 'Love, learn, live, legislate.'

ENERGIZING OUR CHURCHES

In this chapter, we have suggested some ways in which we can bring the gifts of transformative practice to the world at large. Churches, of course, have always been a first place to do this because they are meant to embody our call to service in the light of a higher power.

179

Unfortunately, though, many religious groups lose their spiritual depth in stultifying rituals or engage in fruitless social conflicts caused by dogmatic conceptions of the good. As we all know, religious conflicts large and small have brought suffering to millions of people.

Any institution's failure to embody its highest purposes is disappointing – or tragic – and this is the case with many religious groups. When a religion causes misunderstanding among different peoples, or when it inhibits the development of its members' ego-transcending capacities, it becomes a travesty of its stated purposes. When it promotes a narrow conception of the good, it becomes an enemy rather than a friend to the noblest aspirations of humankind, to our capacities for love and enlightened service. But there is an antidote to this in the human awakenings we are celebrating here.

In the growing capacities for love and knowing, with which we are graced through transformative practice, we find an antidote to the narrowness and deadness evident in some religious groups. Inspired by our awakening to the Transcendent, each of us can help to rejuvenate the church, temple, or other spiritual institution to which we belong. We can find strength in this by remembering that every enduring religion has stood witness to our ego-transcending capacities for knowledge, love, and world service. As we have seen, extraordinary human attributes have been nurtured in every sacred tradition, even if given different names and different degrees of import-ance. The siddhis of Hindu–Buddhist lore, the 'adornments' of Sufism, the charisms of Catholic saints and mystics, and the 'gifts of spirit' celebrated in Judaism and Protestant Christianity have an unmistakable simi-larity. Indeed, it seems to us that they are the very same attributes of our emergent human nature. Every sacred tradition has borne witness to these attributes and to the spiritual energies with which they seem to be connected.

We will discuss their connection with higher spiritual realms in the next two chapters.

In essence, all religions point to the extraordinary in us, to the greater life that is pressing to make its appearance on Earth. Recognition of this, we believe, is spreading in the global village. As more and more people appreciate the possibilities for growth that we are discussing in this book, they will demand that their churches and temples focus to a greater extent on direct experience and less on dogma and religious competition.

As our deeper nature becomes more apparent, and as our dedication to practice and integration proceeds, the world of religion must move toward a recognition of our common spiritual ground, our shared humanity, and our prospects for extraordinary life. Such developments will deepen our sense of the Transcendent in everyday existence and open us to worlds formerly unseen.

THE AFTERLIFE AND ANGELIC REALMS

No matter what spiritual beliefs we hold, all of us are 'wounded,' as certain philosophers say, by our seemingly irrepressible questions about immortality. As we face life's brevity, mysteries, and misfortunes, few of us can help but wonder what really waits beyond the grave. Since the Stone Age, humans have sensed that physical death might not be the end but instead a transition – that some part of us, a spirit or soul, survives the body's passing.

The intuition that an afterlife actually exists is often dismissed as wishful thinking or attributed simply to a childlike hope for better things in worlds to come. But there has always been evidence to support it. Indeed, as we explore the phenomena described in this book, we are moved closer to perceptions of worlds beyond. In this chapter we will review the evidence for postmortem existence and explore some ways in which transformative practice might place us in better alignment with it.

But first we must remind ourselves that there are different beliefs about the soul's survival. Hindus, Tibetan Buddhists, and Neo-platonists believe in reincarnation. Taoist sages and numerous shamans have claimed that just a few advanced spirits survive. Jews, Christians, and Muslims typically hold that we live a single life on earth but exist as souls in the afterlife. Given these various beliefs, each of them attested to by spiritual adepts deeply acquainted with the inner life, there is good reason for caution in trying to specify the nature of postmortem existence.

Nevertheless, certain types of experience that point to some sort of afterlife are common across cultures among people with divergent religious beliefs. As we saw in Chapter Eight, individuals in many times and places – among them mystics and sages who are central to religious history – have claimed that they directly experienced an immortal self, or soul, that journeys from one earthly life to the next, or in worlds beyond our planet. As we saw in Chapter Four, people have out-of-body experiences during intense athletic endeavors, sleep, great pain, or crisis, and men and women young and old have said they entered or perceived other worlds during prayer, meditation, or near-death episodes. Apparitions of the dead have been reported by modern as well as ancient peoples, even by hardheaded individuals who disdain religious superstition. And as we shall see, children in various parts of the world report memories of a past life that researchers are now verifying with apparent success. These and other kinds of experience give us reason to believe that there are worlds beyond the range of our senses with which many of us have occasional contact and into which, conceivably, we will pass.

But most important for our proposals in this book, virtually all doctrines of postmortem existence hold that the soul can develop in the afterlife. That is the main point we want to emphasize here. Most doctrines and lore of the afterlife are consonant with our belief that the evolutionary advance of human nature can continue in realms beyond this one. The Christian doctrine of Purgatory, for example, holds that through surrender to God we can after death ascend by stages to Paradise. The Tibetan Book of the Dead is a manual to guide the soul after its release from the flesh toward the clear light of nirvana. Shamanic teachings in many parts of the world point the departed to ecstasies beyond the grave. In spite of their differing metaphysics, such teachings share the premise that our spiritual journey continues after the body's demise. This premise has been inspired by a variety of transpersonal events that happen in every culture, among them out-of-body episodes, near-death experiences, and mystical ecstasies produced by contemplative practice.

EXPERIENCES OF EGO-TRANSCENDENT IDENTITY

The experience of an identity, an immortal being beyond one's ordinary sense of self, is described in much the same way by people with divergent backgrounds, temperaments, and religious beliefs. This greater, or higher, self is said to eliminate one's sense of separateness from others while at the same time conferring a greater personhood. It typically brings both freedom and security, neither of which depends on one's habitual ideas or behaviors. And paradoxically, while it lifts one beyond familiar reminders of the ordinary self, it seems to reveal something remembered. It is immediately recognizable to such an extent that some people claim that it is their true and eternal self, their ultimate identity, their original nature or 'face.'

This experience – or recognition – has been reported since the beginnings of recorded history. It was symbolized in the hymns of ancient India, among the oldest religious scriptures, as for example in these lines from the Rig Veda (1.164.20):

184

Two birds, beautiful of wing, friends and comrades, cling to a common tree, and one eats the sweet fruit, while the other regards him and eats not.

According to religious scholars, this famous verse refers to an essential unity between a worldly self (eating the sweet fruit) and its world-transcending identity (that eats not). Similar images exist in later Indian scriptures such as the Swetaswatara and Mundaka Upanishads.

As we saw in Chapter Eight, the experience of transcendent identity occurs in traditions with different philosophies. This is evident, for example, in its recognition by Buddhists who espouse the doctrine of *anatta*, or no-self, which holds that all sense of self is illusory. Certain Buddhists, in short, have been led by their direct experience of a greater self, or 'big mind,' to use language that their metaphysics tends to disfavor. In short, like the other extraordinary experiences we have described, the realization of ego-surpassing identity is common to individuals and traditions with differing ideas and predispositions. It has been reported by Platonist and Neoplatonist philosophers of ancient times, by Christians of the Middle Ages such as Meister Eckhart, by Sufis and Jewish seers, and by modern Hindu mystics such as Sri Ramakrishna and Sri Aurobindo (again, see Chapter Eight).

These various testimonies, given for more than three millennia, provide the deepest basis for our recognition of an afterlife. An identity, or self, that transcends our body, emotions, and patterns of thought must be better able to survive death than an ego attached to its immediate surroundings. According to the philosophers we have cited, it causes death to lose its sting. It is the surest, most pervasive ground of a greater life, both in this world and the next.

OUT-OF-BODY EXPERIENCE

In Chapter Four, we classified out-of-body experience as a type of supernormal movement. As we have seen, it happens in sports, contemplative trance, crisis, and other circumstances when a person's energies and volitional powers are gathered for extraordinary effort, and it typically seems to occur in some sort of spirit-body. Charles Lindbergh had such an experience. He told an interviewer that during his famous transatlantic flight of 1927, in which he was taxed beyond his ordinary limits:

> ... I felt myself departing from my body as I imagine a spirit would depart – emanating into the cockpit, extending through the fuselage as though no frame or fabric walls were there, angling upward, outward, until I reformed in an awareness far distant from the human form I left in a fast-flying transatlantic plane. But I remained connected to my body through a long-extended strand so tenuous that it could have been severed by a breath.

While fighting on the Italian front during World War 1, the young Ernest Hemingway was wounded by shrapnel and thought he would die. He later told a confidante that he believed his soul had left his body. Many people near death have had the same feeling. A man, for example, who had struggled desperately to escape a strong undertow suddenly felt too tired to care. A peace settled over him and then it seemed:

> ... that a wonderful transition occurred. I was high above the water looking down. The sky, that had been so grey, was iridescent with indescribable beauty. There was music that I seemed to feel rather than hear. Waves of ecstatic and delicate color vibrated around

me and lulled me into a sense of peace beyond comprehension.

In the water beneath me, a boat came into view, with two men and a girl in it. Then I saw a blob in the water. A wave tossed it and rolled it over. I found myself looking into my own distorted face. What a relief, I thought, that that ungainly thing was no longer needed by me. Then men lifted the form into the boat, and my vision faded. The next thing I knew, it was dark and I was lying on the beach, cold and sick and sore. Men were working over me. I was told later that they worked over me for more than two hours.

Experiences of this kind have been collected by Sylvan Muldoon, Oliver Fox, Robert Crookall, Robert Monroe, and other students of out-of-body episodes. Such studies show that the traveling subject typically feels as if he or she has traveled in some sort of spirit-body that can perceive and move in the physical world. Evidence for such a body resides in the fact that nearly every sacred tradition has given it a name. Ancient Egyptians called it the *ka*, Greeks the *ochema*, and Hindus the *kosha*, *deha*, or *sarira*.

The Dutch philosopher J. J. Poortman has catalogued doctrines and firsthand accounts of the spirit-body in his monumental four-volume work *Vehicles of Consciousness*, which demonstrates the great wealth of evidence for it, to be found in the Vedic hymns and other scriptures of Hinduism, the Old and New Testaments, pre-Socratic philosophers, Plato, Aristotle, Plotinus, Saint Paul, Saint Thomas Aquinas, Swedenborg, and several modern novelists, scientists, and philosophers. The great detail and beauty to be found in descriptions of the spirit-body, and the affirmations of its existence by great saints and mystics since antiquity, will impress most readers of Poortman's study. Such accounts provide further evidence that our consciousness inhabits a spirit-body during both out-of-body experience in this life and post-mortem existence.

NEAR-DEATH EXPERIENCE

Since the publication of Raymond Moody's *Life After Life* in 1975, several thousand cases of near-death experience have been examined by physicians, neurophysiologists, psychologists, psychiatrists, and parapsychologists. For several years, *The Journal of Near Death Studies* has provided a forum for studies of the phenomenon, and pioneering books on the subject have been written by Kenneth Ring, Steven Sabom, and other researchers. This field of study has been catalyzed in part by new resuscitation techniques through which many people are revived after heart attacks, accidents, and other events that take them to the edge of death. Increasing numbers of people today survive medical catastrophes that once would have killed them, and when they are resuscitated, many of them describe out-of-body episodes, a passage into another world, joyous meetings with departed loved ones, encounters with angelic figures, merging with a higher light, and other experiences that convince them that they glimpsed the life to come. The sheer volume of such experiences, their unmistakable similarities, and the sense of conviction with which they are reported impress most who examine them.

Contemporary research with dying people supplements the near-death literature. A systematic study by psychologists Karlis Osis and Erlander Haraldsson, for example, revealed several striking correspondences between the death-bed experiences of people in different cultures, including visions of other worlds and people long dead, redemptive elevations of mood, and a higher light and joy that promised a greater life to come. The results of their study can be found in their book *At the Hour of Death.*

Studies of this kind show that men and women young and old with a wide range of religious beliefs glimpse what seem to be angelic realms and a luminous postmortem existence. It is indisputable that such experiences resemble perceptions of the afterlife reported not only by visionaries but also by people in all walks of life since the dawn of human history. It is a fact that countless people have had revelations of this kind, among them many who had previously doubted that there is a life to come. This cumulative witness through the centuries is an enduring centerpiece of human literature, philosophy, and religion. Its persistence strongly suggests that it is based on valid perceptions. People glimpse worlds beyond the grave, we propose, because they have latent powers to do so and because the afterlife they see reminds them of the greater existence they harbor.

APPARITIONS OF THE DEAD

In their study of dying persons, Osis and Haraldsson found that many people near death have visions of departed friends, relatives, or religious figures who come to 'take the patient away,' helping them pass to another mode of existence. The two psychologists, like various psychical researchers of the past one hundred twenty years, tried to distinguish hallucinations produced by drugs, high fever, or disturbing emotions from visions that occurred to people in a clear state of mind. Their analyses, they wrote:

> . . . clearly indicated that the majority of apparition cases cannot be readily explained by such medical

factors as high temperature, hallucinogenic diseases, the administration of drugs that could produce hallucinations (such as morphine or Demerol, or by hallucinogenic factors in the patient's history. The phenomenon of seeing apparitions shortly before death seems to cut across differences of age, sex, education, and religion. However, involvement in religion, regardless of the denomination, seems slightly to facilitate such experience.

We recommend the Osis-Haraldsson study to readers interested in otherworldly phenomena associated with dying people. Over the course of many years, through patient, sympathetic, and careful research, the two found that the approach of death produces many extraordinary experiences that resemble those we have described in this book. Their study supports our proposal that the soul continues its evolutionary journey after the body's passing.

However, apparitions of the dead are not limited to dying people. Many surveys by pollsters, psychologists, and psychical researchers have shown that they appear to healthy people as well, sometimes bringing worldly information beneficial to those who perceive them, sometimes imparting inspiration or comfort, and sometimes bringing new insights about higher things and the life to come. Among the many reviews of such research, we recommend *Apparitions* by G. N. M. Tyrell. The book includes: a description of the pioneering 'census of hallucinations' conducted by the British Society for Psychical Research in the late nineteenth century, the theories proposed by Edmund Gurney and Frederic Myers to account for apparitional phenomena, a summary of characteristics that apparitions exhibit, various theories regarding the agencies behind apparitions, and various speculations about the role of apparitions in the human adventure.

Surveys such as Tyrell's and research such as the Osis–Haraldsson study, as well as literature and scripture since ancient times, show that apparitions have appeared to people since antiquity. Some are friendly; some are not. Some appear to be departed souls, some entities from worlds beyond. In the founding scriptures of Hinduism, Homer, Plato, the Old and New Testaments, the Qur'an, Shakespeare, Blake, Coleridge, and countless testimonies of modern times, we find accounts of phantom figures that threaten, inspire, guide, or support those who encounter them. Apparitions have long reminded humankind that there is more to life than our senses perceive, more than our immediate desires reach for, more than the ordinary self conceives.

THE CASE FOR REINCARNATION

Indians and other Asian peoples, as well as prominent Western philosophers such as Plato, Pythagoras, Origen, and Plotinus, have taken reincarnation to be a fact. Though it is not widely known, many famous artists and writers of recent times have also believed in reincarnation, among them the French novelists Victor Hugo and Honore Balzac, the German poets Heine and Rilke, the English poets Wordworth and Shelley, and the American novelist Jack London. In his *Human Personality and Its Survival of Bodily Death*, Frederic Myers wrote:

> The simple fact that [reincarnation] was probably the opinion both of Plato and Virgil shows that there is nothing here which is alien to the best reason or to the highest instincts of men. Nor, indeed, is it easy to realize any theory of the *direct creation* of spirits at such different stages of advancement as those which enter upon the earth in the guise of mortal man. There

191

must, one feels, be some kind of continuity – some form of spiritual Past . . .

Dr. Ian Stevenson, a psychiatrist at the University of Virginia Medical School, and a number of his colleagues have studied more than two thousand seven hundred subjects, most of them children, who have claimed to remember past lives. Stevenson's research started in the mid–1960s and continues among his colleagues today, taking them to India, Turkey, Lebanon, Southeast Asia, Western Europe, and across North and South America. His method, briefly, is to search for evidence that a life was lived in accordance with a particular subject's memories. He and his colleagues have collected well-documented birth records, photographs, and firsthand accounts of people who resembled those remembered by their subjects. Since 1965, the Stevenson group has assembled a body of case studies that strongly suggests that reincarnation is a fact.

Many of these subjects have a deformity or birthmark that corresponds in some way with an event in the remembered life or a feature of the remembered person. A Turkish boy with several birthmarks, for example, remembered being killed by bullet wounds, and indeed a man had been killed in the approximate time and place the boy named and photographs showed that he had suffered bullet wounds in locations close to those of the marks on the subject's body. Stevenson's monumental two-volume work *Reincarnation and Biology* presents many case histories of this kind with a compelling array of photographs showing correspondences between marks or deformities on the subjects' bodies and wounds or features of the remembered people.

This work might prove to be a landmark of scientific discovery related to postmortem survival. Bruce Greyson, Emily Kelly, Antonia Mills, and other colleagues continue to collect and confirm past-life memories, adding new statistical analyses, new methods for uncovering evidence, and new subjects. Though their work is still little-known, it may prove to be historic. Ian Stevenson, conceivably, might be remembered as the Charles Darwin of reincarnation.

ANGELIC REALMS

Encounters with disembodied entities are a common feature of deathbed and near-death experiences. Some are with departed loved ones, others with beings that appear to be angles or guardian spirits who assist the dying person's passage to the afterlife. Such beings also appear in other circumstances, for example, to sailors at sea and other adventurers who are in crisis.

Joshua Slocum, the first person to circumnavigate the globe alone, described his encounter with a phantom sailor in his book *Sailing Alone Around the World*. Slocum described a dream and then a vision on the following day of a 'tall sailor' who claimed to have helped him steer his ship through a dangerous storm while he was sick. And Charles Lindbergh, too, encountered phantom figures during his pioneering flight across the Atlantic. In his book *The Spirit of St. Louis*, he wrote:

> While I'm staring at the instruments, during an unearthly age of time, both conscious and asleep, the fuselage behind me becomes filled with ghostly presences – vaguely outlined forms, transparent, moving, riding weightless with me in the plane. I feel no surprise at their coming. . . . Without turning my head, I see them as clearly as though in my normal field of vision. There is no limit to my sight – my skull is one great eye, seeing everywhere at once.

These phantoms speak with human voices – friendly, vaporlike shapes, without substance, able to vanish or appear at will, to pass in and out through the walls of the fuselage as though no walls were there. Now, many are crowded behind me. Now, only a few remain. First one and then another presses forward to my shoulder to speak above the engine's noise, and then draws back among the group behind. At times, voices come out of the air itself, clear yet far away, traveling through distances that can't be measured by the scale of human miles; familiar voices, conversing and advising on my flight, discussing problems of my navigation, reassuring me, giving me messages of importance unattainable in ordinary life.

I'm on the borderline of life and a greater realm beyond as though caught in the field of gravitation between two planets, acted on by forces I can't control, forces too weak to be measured by any means at my command, yet representing powers incomparably stronger than I've ever known.

Lindbergh and Slocum, like other adventurers who have reported perceptions of disembodied entities, had been taxed to the edge of endurance before their strange encounters and, though exhausted, had struggled to maintain alertness. Conceivably, this stress-induced vigilance focused their perception to an extraordinary degree while their ordinary perceptual barriers were lowered through fatigue so that they were open to psychic visitations. Certain entities that adventurers and others perceive appear to be menacing. Others are friendly. Sometimes, like Slocum's tall sailor, they provide guidance or bring reassurance. For some people, these mysterious presences challenge assumptions, bring joy and strength, and suggest that life has dimensions beyond the range of the ordinary senses. Often they seem to be messengers, pointing us toward the greater life for which we are ultimately destined.

Indeed, the word 'angel' derives from an ancient Greek word for 'messenger.' In Christianity, Judaism, and Islam, such beings are intermediaries between the higher and lower worlds, their wings symbolizing their freedom and their luminous bodies the light they bring from God. Since ancient times, they have inspired awe and affection as they fly back and forth between heaven and Earth, carrying messages from one realm to the other.

Angels and their native realms are celebrated in all religions. The Hindu *apsaras* are heavenly dispensers of love and delight, wrapping the dead in their voluptuous breasts while carrying them in ecstasy to paradise. In the Qur'an it is said that the tears of the archangel Michael, which were shed for the transgressions of the faithful, gave rise to the cherubim. Early Hebrew writers believed that angels were born afresh each day like the morning dew. In the Talmud it is claimed that every Jew is assigned eleven thousand of them.

But angels bring more than love and light. They can be warriors for the good and initiate spiritual struggle. Jacob wrestled with an angel and was then called Israel. Cherubim guarded the Ark of the Covenant. Saint George and the archangel Michael were portrayed as winged heroes who killed dragons. Indeed, representations of angels can be immensely complex. The fifth-century mystic known as 'pseudo-Dionysius' arranged the angelic order in three triads, from the seraphim, cherubim, and thrones nearest God, through the dominions, virtues, and powers of the second heavenly circle, to the principalities, archangels, and angels of the third. This vision of the angelic realms has been held by many Christians since.

The hours of the day, the days of the week, the months of the year, the seasons of the year, the signs of the zodiac, and each of the planets have been represented by angels.

By the fourteenth century it was said that there were 301,655,722 angels hovering at the borders of our temporal universe, 133,306,668 of them fallen from God. A similar complexity can be found in Hindu visions of the spiritual hierarchies, in Buddhist lore of the 'middle realms,' and in the teeming spirit-worlds of popular Taoist belief.

But our purpose in stating these facts is not to argue for a particular hierarchy or picture of angels. For us, the importance of these complex symbols lies in their witness to humankind's long-standing sense that there are beings beyond the physical world with whom we sometimes interact. Angels have not been forgotten in modern times – witness the many books, plays, and movies that now celebrate them. The fact that people in all walks of life today, including many who dismiss religious superstition, have encounters with disembodied entities reminds us that such experience is an enduring feature of human nature. It is not limited to certain cultures or periods of history. It has not been eliminated by modern science. Given that fact, and because such experience seems central for many people in their openings to a greater life, we think it must be acknowledged. Today, as always before in human history, people are guided, consoled, and inspired by presences that seem to come from other dimensions of existence.

Those of us seeking a comprehensive understanding of humankind's larger potentials must at least consider those leadings attributed to guardian spirits or angels. It is important to remember that all knowledge advances, whether in high science or practical affairs, at least in part through acceptance of things that once seemed strange or unlikely. Worlds beyond ours, after all, are no stranger than the weird features of many earthly creatures, certain odd turns of the human mind, or the bizarre behavior of quarks and other subatomic particles. Beings that inhabit extraphysical worlds might indeed interact with us, in ways we do not understand, perhaps at times to our detriment, but also for our greater good.

Indeed, transformative disciplines already point many people toward worlds they equate with a greater life to come. The luminous knowing and identity, the indescribable joy, and the ego-surpassing love they experience seem to thin the veils between them and worlds beyond. If through the integration of our greater attributes we are indeed helping evolution advance, then we must consider the possibility that this process can lead us as physical beings toward an ever-greater alignment with higher realms. If evolution has brought us, as we have seen, from inorganic matter to life and embodied consciousness, then in its next stages it might bring us further yet-to a condition perhaps that joins this world with those beyond it, in which our bodies increasingly manifest the glories of spirit.

15

LUMINOUS EMBODIMENT

We have explored the mysterious trajectory of evolution from the fiery furnaces of ancient stars to the appearance of our human ancestors and onward through a wide range of human attributes that point toward extraordinary life on Earth. We have suggested ways in which our emerging capacities can be integrated through intention and practice into a transcendent, synchronistic flow – a condition of body, mind, and soul that can help to enrich institutions and cultures and produce ever greater alignment with higher dimensions of existence.

In doing this, we have viewed the long story of evolution as a fulfillment of the world's inherent potential. The tiny seed from which our universe sprang had within it the ability to produce billions of galaxies. Within the primordial seas of the cooling Earth were possibilities for life. In our planet's first organisms there existed the potential for consciousness. And our earliest human ancestors carried seeds of the self-surpassing capacities we have described in this book. Here we want to propose yet another potential that would, if actualized, carry forward evolution's stupendous advance. We have already had a few glimpses of it. It is inherent in the mysterious relations between our soul, our mind, and our flesh.

In short, we propose that our emergent capacities, which alter our physical functioning to some degree whenever they make their appearance, can gradually give rise to a new and more luminous embodiment. We know that this is a radical idea. We are aware that to many it will seem far-fetched. But there have long been intuitions of it, as well as evidence that it has begun to manifest in certain people.

THE COEVOLUTION OF MIND AND BODY

New abilities among our animal ancestors were made possible by changes, whether large or small, of their bodily structures and processes, and we can suppose that analogous changes in us – developed through practice rather than natural selection – will accompany and support a lasting realization of our emergent attributes. This supposition is supported by recent scientific discoveries and by contemplative lore regarding the bodily changes involved in the expansion of consciousness.

Drawing upon both modern findings and contemplative teachings, we can begin to picture bodily changes that might accompany the further development of our greater attributes, supposing: first, that esoteric accounts of bodily transformation, though frequently fanciful, reflect actual developments of physical structures as yet unrecognized by science; second, that supernormal capacities, like their normal counterparts, require distinctive types of supporting structure and process; and third, that we can extrapolate from physiological changes already revealed by modern research in imagining bodily developments required for high-level change. Modern meditation, hypnosis, and biofeedback research, for example, have revealed a large number of somatic changes that facilitate the enrichment of behavior and consciousness (for more information, see the Guided Readings for Part Two), and recent research has shown that neurogenesis, the creation of new brain cells in adults, does indeed happen, either to facilitate new kinds of functioning or to support the restoration of capacities lost by injury or disease.

The extraordinary flexibility exhibited by certain yogis, athletes, and saints, and the astonishing agility of certain dancers and shamans, indicate that muscles, tendons, and ligaments are, under some conditions, capable of extraordinary power and elasticity. Might such capacities be taken to new levels still? The 'kundalini-type' experience of Hindu-Buddhist lore, the *incendium amoris* of Catholic saints, the *tumo* of Tibetan yogis – indeed many of the energetic mutations we described in Part Two – may well involve the release of bodily forces that science does not yet understand. Indeed, it is conceivable that such experience involves energies that arise from a repatterning of the body's most basic elements. Supernormal restructuring of the body might entail atomic and molecular reformations that transform the look, feel, and capacities of tissues and cells. If this is the case, there is no telling what bodily breakthroughs transformative practice might eventually produce. That such mutations might occur has long been prefigured in legend and myth and in religious doctrines such as the Roman Catholic belief in the body's glorification.

CHRISTIAN DOCTRINES OF THE GLORIFIED BODY

As ratified by the Fourth Lateran Council in 1215, the resurrection and glorification of the body is a dogma of the Roman Catholic Church. It has been formally defined by the Church in this way: 'All will rise with their own bodies which they now have so that they may receive according to their works, whether good or bad.' This means that the bodies of those people whose works have been good will be glorified and share the soul's beatific vision of God. In spite of its seeming absurdities, this doctrine has fascinated theologians and philosophers since antiquity. Its hold on these prominent thinkers, we propose, indicates its resonance with the long-enduring intuition that the body is capable of transfiguration.

Here we will quote Saint Paul; Origen, who lived two centuries later; Saint Thomas Aquinas, who lived in the Middle Ages; and the twentieth-century Catholic writer Romano Guardini to indicate the prominence of the idea through the long course of Christian history. The prime reference for most subsequent discussions of glorification is Saint Paul's epistle I Corinthians 15:39–44. This much-quoted passage reads:

> All flesh is not the same flesh: but there is one kind of flesh of men, another flesh of beasts, another of fishes, and another of birds.
>
> There are also celestial bodies, and bodies terrestrial: but the glory of the celestial is one, and the glory of the terrestrial is another.
>
> There is one glory of the sun, and another glory of the moon, and another glory of the stars: for one star differs from another star in glory.
>
> So also is the resurrection of the dead. It is sown in corruption; it is raised in incorruption;
>
> It is sown in dishonor; it is raised in glory; it is sown in weakness; it is raised in power:
>
> It is sown a natural body; it is raised a spiritual body. There is a natural body, and there is a spiritual body.

Christian theologians have frequently commented upon the four characteristics Saint Paul attributed to the glorified body, namely *impassibility* ('what is sown in corruption rises in incorruption'), *clarity* ('what is sown in dishonor rises in glory'), *agility* ('what is sown in weakness rises in power'), and *subtility* ('what is sown a natural body rises a spiritual body'). Saint Thomas Aquinas described these four aspects of glorification in *Summa Contra Gentiles* 4.86. Following the Greek philosopher Aristotle, he regarded soul to be the body's 'form,' the agency that gives life and shape to human flesh. As a thought experiment, read the following passages while keeping in mind the extraordinary capacities described in Part Two. Notice the similarities between them and the attributes of glorification Saint Thomas describes.

The glory and power of the soul elevated to the divine vision will add something more amply to the body united to itself. For this body will be entirely subject to the soul – the divine power will achieve this – not only in regard to its being, but also in regard to action, passion, movements, and bodily qualities.

Therefore, just as the soul which enjoys the divine vision will be filled with a kind of spiritual lightsomeness, so by a certain overflow from the soul to the body, the body will in its own way put on the lightsomeness of glory. Hence, the Apostle says: 'It is sown in dishonor. It shall rise in glory.' (I Corinthians 15:43)

Moreover, the soul which will enjoy the divine vision, united to its ultimate end, will in all matters experience the fulfillment of desire. And since it is out of the soul's desire that the body is moved, the consequence will be the body's utter obedience to the spirit's slightest wish. Hence, the bodies of the blessed when they rise are going to have agility. That is what the Apostle says in the same place: 'It is sown in weakness, it shall rise in power.' For weakness is what we experience in a body found wanting in the strength to satisfy the desire of the soul in the movements and actions which the soul commands, and this weakness will be entirely taken away then, when power is overflowing into the body from a soul united to God.

They will not be able to suffer anything which is harmful to them. For this reason they will be incapable of suffering. Nonetheless, this incapability of suffering will not cut them off from the modification essential to sense knowledge, for they will use their senses for pleasure in the measure in which this is not incompatible with their state of incorruption. It is, then, to show their incapacity for suffering that the Apostle says: 'It is sown in corruption, it shall rise in incorruption.' (I Corinthians 15:42)

Furthermore, the soul which is enjoying God will cleave to Him most perfectly, and will in its own fashion share in His goodness to the highest degree; and thus will the body be perfectly within the soul's dominion, and will share in what is the soul's very own characteristics so far as possible, in the perspicuity of sense knowledge, in the ordering of bodily appetite, and in the all-round perfection of nature; for a thing is the more perfect in nature, the more its matter is dominated by its form. And for this reason the Apostle says: 'It is sown a natural body, it shall rise a spiritual body.' (I Corinthians 15:44) The body of the risen will be spiritual, indeed, but not because it is a spirit – as some have badly understood the point – whether in the sense of a spiritual substance, or in the sense of air or wind; it will be spiritual because it will be entirely subject to the spirit.

Saint Thomas expressed a central Christian idea, long adhered to in Catholic dogma, when he said the risen body of the just 'will be spiritual, but not because it is a spirit – as some have badly understood the point.' No, it will truly be *body*. He passionately upheld the idea, in spite of its apparent absurdity, that our present body, the very one we have now, will be glorified if our works are good. It is not enough that the souls of the just will enjoy beatitude; their bodies must participate, too. Indeed, it is against the nature of the soul to exist without its physical counterpart, as he says in *Summa Contra Gentiles* 2.68, 83; 4.79. Soul separate from body is *imperfect*. The resurrection is natural in that it reunites the two, though its cause is supernatural (*Summa Contra Gentiles* 4.81). Saint Thomas and other Christian thinkers felt an intuitive rightness in this vision, even though it contradicted the obvious facts of bodily decay. That intuitive rightness weighed against conceptual difficulties such as these: If our bodies will be glorified centuries or millenia after their decomposition, from what material will they be reconstituted? Which stage of their development will become their form for eternity? Will people disfigured from birth be given body parts they did not possess on Earth? And what about innocent children who die? Will they be children in heaven?

In spite of conceptual difficulties and apparent absurdities such as these, many Christian theologians maintained their belief in glorified embodiment. Some of them were confirmed in this by reports of bodily radiance, levitation, stigmata, and other extraordinary physical phenomena associated with the early desert fathers and saints such as Francis of Assisi, Joseph of Cupertino, John of the Cross, and Teresa of Avila (see Part Two). Though the doctrine of resurrection is embedded in a pre-scientific worldview and is supported by plain superstition, it has persisted, we propose, because intelligent and sensitive thinkers have intuited the body's potential for transformation and have been supported in their view by the extraordinary powers of mystics and saints. Reframing Christian vision from the developmental perspective proposed in this book, doctrines of bodily glorification can be seen to symbolize a new evolutionary advance, and 'risen bodies of the just' might represent luminous embodiment.

Origen, the third-century theologian held by many to be the greatest Christian thinker of his day, wrote about the glorified body with daring and imagination. As a thought experiment, again, read the following passages while remembering the evidence for extraordinary human functioning we have described.

Our flesh indeed is considered by the uneducated and by unbelievers to perish so completely after death that nothing whatever of its substance is left. We, however, who believe in its resurrection, know that death only causes a change in it and that its substance certainly persists and is restored to life again at a definite time by the will of its Creator and once more undergoes a transformation.

Into this condition, therefore, we must suppose that the entire substance of this body of ours will develop at the time when all things are restored and become one and when 'God shall be all in all.' We must not think, however, that it will happen all of a sudden, but gradually and by degrees, during the lapse of infinite and immeasurable ages, seeing that the improvements and correction will be realized slowly and separately in each individual person.

For the faith of the Church does not accept the opinion derived from certain Greek philosophers, that besides this body which is composed of the four elements, there is a fifth body which is entirely other than and diverse from our present body; since we can neither produce from the holy scriptures the least suspicion of such an opinion, nor can its acceptance be allowed as a logical inference, particularly as the holy apostle clearly lays it down that no new bodies are to be given to those who rise from the dead, but that they are to receive the same ones which they possessed during life, only transformed from a worse to a better condition. For he says, 'It is sown a natural body; it will rise a spiritual body' and 'It is sown in corruption; it will rise in incorruption; it is sown in weakness; it will rise in power; it is sown in dishonour; it will rise in glory.'

The whole argument, then, comes to this, that God has created two universal natures, a visible, that is, a bodily one, and an invisible one, which is incorporeal. These two natures each undergo their own different changes. The invisible, which is also the rational nature, is changed through the action of the mind and will by reason of the fact that it has been endowed with freedom of choice; and as a result of this it is found existing sometimes in the good and sometimes in its opposite. The bodily nature, however, admits of a change in substance, so that God the Artificer of all things, in whatever work of design or construction or restoration he may wish to engage, has at hand the service of this material for all purposes, and can transform and transfer it into whatever forms and species he desires, as the merits of things demand. It is to this, clearly, that the prophet points when he says, 'God who makes and transforms all things.'

Origen anticipated proposals such as those in this book by his intuitive vision of our possibilities for extraordinary life; by his belief that material substance can undergo 'every kind of transformation'; by his insistence that the glorified body would arise, however mysteriously, from our present body, not a 'fifth body' such as that proposed by some Greek philosophers; and by his belief in a gradual development toward glorification during the 'lapse of infinite and immeasurable ages.' Though scholars still debate the sources of his thought, attributing them variously to Christian, Neoplatonist, and gnostic inspirations, we find a strong resonance in Origen with later Christian visions of the Glorified Body. Like Saint Paul before him and Saint Thomas Aquinas one thousand years later, he anticipated the idea that human nature, including both mind and flesh, can realize a beatific existence.

That the doctrine of the Glorified Body remains central to some Christian thinkers today is evident in the following passages from the twentieth-century Catholic writer Romano Guardini:

To be man is to be spirit expressed and made active through the body. To be man is to be a bodily organism, subject to the operation of a personal spirit that bestows on that organism a form and capacity which of itself it is powerless to attain to; to be man is to occupy a specific place in history, in which the spirit with its dignity and responsibility takes its stand. Resurrection therefore signifies that the spiritual soul, true to its nature again becomes the soul of a body-indeed that only now is it fully liberated and empowered to inform the body. Resurrection signifies that the matter from which the soul has departed becomes once more personalized, spiritualized corporeality, that is, human body, though no longer limited by time and space, but become, as Paul says, a spiritual, a 'pneumatic' body.

In all of these different kinds of existing things we find 'body' – in the crystal, the apple tree, the horse and birds, and in the man I am addressing. At each stage physical matter is put at the service of a new principle that gives it not only fresh qualities and capacities, but indeed at every stage a new character. Stage by stage it overcomes inertia, weight, bondage, muteness, and gains lightness, space, height, freedom; its sphere of operation broadens and the operations themselves increase in importance. Both the power to act and the scope for action are enlarged.

Does this line of development stop with man as we know him? Our intuitive feeling tells us it must proceed further. Humanity is not a blind alley. The possibilities of what we call body are inexhaustible. A clear and direct indication of what they are is furnished by the rising stages the body reaches in man himself.

For the human body is not a finished, arrested form; it is ever in process of becoming. That a healthy body kept in condition by care and exercise is more 'body' than a neglected one is self-evident. But does the body reach its greatest dignity and perfection in the face and carriage of a man who lives among noble objects and pursues a thinking life, or in the trained and healthy but anti-intellectual and superficial man? If the question surprises us, it is because we are in the habit of looking at the human body much as we look at the animal body, as nature merely. But the human body is definitely determined by spirit. The face of a man who is passionately searching for truth is not only more 'spiritual' than that of the man with a dulled mind, it is also more of a face, that is to say, it is more genuinely, more intensively 'body.' And there is not only more 'spirituality' in the bearing of a man with a free and generous heart than in that of a crude and selfish person, there is a more responsive body. With man begins a wholly new scale of development. The body as such becomes more animated, more vibrating, as it is more strongly informed by the life of the heart, mind and spirit . . .

What, then, will not be possible when eternity breaks into time and divine strength and holiness holds unrestricted sway, setting the spirit free in its absolute purity and power?

Saint Paul, Origen, Saint Thomas Aquinas, and Romano Guardini, each of them reflecting the same Christian view though they lived in different times and places, believed that the body as well as the soul can realize a state of beatitude. The soul, they believed, leads the body toward this end but cannot do so unless it opens to the Transcendent. As we have seen, in the ways of growth we have reviewed, the same principle holds. Our greater attributes, including the body's capacity for more luminous form, must be guided by our intention, imagination, and opening to guidance and energies from a power and intelligence beyond the ordinary self.

TAOIST DOCTRINES OF BODILY TRANSFORMATION

The scholar David T. Hansley in his book *Subtle Bodies* described ancient wisdom traditions that taught humans to become 'co-creators' of the universe. Such initiates can learn, for example, to control the natural energies of the body.

Taoist adepts taught that to become immortal man must learn to be one with the Primal Force. This force was described as Light, which if concentrated upon and circulated in a correct manner through the subtle anatomy, brought all the powers of the body and lower self before the throne of the Heavenly Heart in the forehead. This culminated in the prolongation of life and the creation of an immortal body.

In his *Taoism: The Road to Immortality*, John Blofeld, a student of Chinese esoteric practice, described the 'yogic alchemy' by which immortal bodies are created. By the sublimation of *ching* (semen or psychological essence), *chi* (breath or vital force), and *shen* (mind or spirit), the adept forms a 'spirit-child' or 'spirit-body,' the vehicle of ever-lasting life. Such teachings reflect the long-standing Taoist belief that humans can advance to higher forms of embodiment, in this flesh or a substance created within it. This belief is based on a lore of bodily transformation that came in part with Buddhism from India, in part from an earlier shamanism that existed in China and Siberia, and in part from the ongoing experience of Taoist mystics. Again, such doctrines combine intuitions of our greater capacities and manifestations of them in various saints and sages.

SHAMANIC TRANSFORMATIONS OF THE BODY

Shamans around the world, though their ethnic backgrounds have differed in many ways, have long shared a wide range of practices, among them rituals of symbolic dismemberment and resurrection that aim to renew both body and soul. Consider, for example, the following activities described by Mircea Eliade:

> The ecstatic experience of dismemberment of the body followed by a renewal of the organs is known to the Eskimo. They speak of an animal that wounds the candidate, tears him to pieces or devours him; then new flesh grows around his bones. [T]he majority of Eskimo shamans seek ecstatic initiation and in the course of it

undergo many ordeals, sometimes very close to the Siberian and Central Asian shaman's dismemberment. In these cases there is a mystical experience of death and resurrection induced by contemplating one's own skeleton.

Among the Warburton Range Aborigines (of West Australia) initiation takes place as follows. The aspirant enters a cave, and two totemic heroes (wildcat and emu) kill him, open his body, remove the organs, and replace them with magical substances. They also remove the shoulder bone and tibia, which they dry, and before putting them back, stuff them with the same substances. During this ordeal the aspirant is supervised by his initiatory master, who keeps fires lighted and observes his ecstatic experiences.

Imagined dismemberment such as this is practiced, too, in the Americas, Africa, and Indonesia, where according to Eliade, 'Dream sickness or initiation ceremony [has the same central element]: death and symbolic resurrection of the neophyte, involving cutting up of the body performed in various ways (dismemberment, gashing, opening the abdomen, etc.).' Eskimos of Siberia, Greenland, and Labrador also have practiced rituals of death and rebirth. The great arctic explorer Knud Rasmussen described interviews with shamans in his *Intellectual Culture of the Iqlulik Eskimos.* He wrote:

Though no shaman can explain to himself how and why, he can, by the power his brain derives from the supernatural, as it were by thought alone, divest his body of its flesh and blood, so that nothing remains but his bones. And he must then name all the parts of his body, mentioning every single bone by name; and in so doing, he must not use ordinary human speech, but only the special and sacred shaman's language which he has learned from his instructor. By thus seeing himself naked, altogether freed from the perishable and transient flesh and blood, he consecrates himself, in the sacred tongue of the shamans, to his great task, through that part of his body which will longest withstand the action of the sun, wind and weather, after he is dead.

These initiations enable the shaman through direct experience to realize the ego-transcendent identity and awareness we have described in this book, which outlasts all insults or threats to mind and body. Such practices enable the initiate, who has survived imagined dismemberment, to maintain high energy, focus, strength, and acuity through both spiritual and physical ordeals. Once initiated, the shaman can fully 'inhabit' his body in all circumstances imbued with supernatural power.

However, within these initiatory aims and results, which most students of shamanism recognize, there is, we propose, another less-acknowledged aspiration. Shamanic initiations, like the Roman Catholic Doctrine of Glorification and Taoist beliefs in psychophysical transmutation, express an intuition that the body can not only transcend the world's vicissitudes but grow into a more luminous entity that shares the soul's ecstasy and liberation. Humans, in short, have since the Stone Age sensed the body's capacity to live in ever-closer alignment with the Transcendent, thus acquiring new freedom from the elements, new capacities for earthly activities, and a joyous, life-giving radiance.

This intuition is congruent with the evolutionary vision proposed in this book. As we have seen, the various attributes of animal organisms have developed in concert since life appeared on Earth, and they have continued to do so among human beings. Mind and body have co-evolved since our primate ancestors began their advance to Homo sapiens and can, we believe, continue that advance toward forms of embodiment as luminous as the spirit we know in our highest moments. It is impossible to say how long it might take for such transformations to unfold, but the prospect of further advance they give us could inspire new creativity, determination, and excitement among those of us drawn to the evolutionary adventure.

Part Four

Practices
and Readings

16

TRANSFORMATIVE PRACTICE

Viewed in the light of our spiritual awakenings, evolution reveals its secret face. In our deepest moments we see that a higher Presence inhabits the universe, attracting and impelling it toward higher ends. And that Presence is calling us. It summons us because like the world at large each of us is matter and spirit at once, both the result and agent of evolution's advance. But evolution meanders as it progresses, and thus our future is not guaranteed. Both history and common sense tell us that our further advance depends on us.

This rule applies to the development of all of our capacities. The emergent attributes reviewed in this book will not flourish unless we cultivate them. They will not deliver their gifts unless we turn toward the greater life they reveal and nurture them through constant acknowledgment and intelligent, long-term practice. In this chapter, we will outline a program of such discipline that can be adapted to fit your interests, abilities, and circumstances, and that can be expanded in various ways. Follow your deepest leadings in this.

The program suggested here is meant only as a guide, for we believe that each attribute of our emergent nature carries within itself the elements of a transformative practice. Each time we experience moments of greater perception, communication, knowing, love, or identity, such as those we have discussed, the memory of them remains as a seed that can be cultivated. Intention, perseverance, and expectation of success are crucial factors in this. Without dedication and practice, our emergent capacities will not blossom.

BASIC PRINCIPLES OF TRANSFORMATIVE PRACTICE

Transformative practice involves inherited physical, biological, and social processes that all of us have cultivated to some extent in the course of everyday life. We can improve body awareness and control, for example, because we have been required to do so all our lives in learning how to walk, speak, and perform other necessary physical acts. We can improve our abilities to concentrate and relax because we have done so already, at least once in a while, at work or in leisure activities. Each of us can strengthen and refine our will, visualize desired capacities, deepen our self-reflection, detach ourselves from particular emotions and thoughts, and raise our center of consciousness through prayer because we have done these things to some degree, whether instinctively or through practice, since early childhood. The basic elements of transformative practice, in other words, are inherent to our developing nature as it has been formed by the evolution of life on this planet. Many spiritual teachers have emphasized this. The Indian philosopher Sir Aurobindo, for example, said that 'all life is yoga,' by which he meant that all of us, at every turn, can realize more of our latent divinity.

But the same processes that facilitate our growth can also retard it. Our powers of intention, for example, can be warped by destructive impulses, our imagination can be charged with negative thoughts, our self-reflection can be fragmented by useless distractions, and our prayers can be narrowly self-centered. Moreover, it is often hard for us to change because we are creatures of habit, which is the case in large part because we need stability in the midst of life's vicissitudes. Without homeostasis, our inherited capacity for self-regulation, our body's intricate systems could not maintain their balance as our physical environments and levels of exertion fluctuate. And without basic mental and emotional stability, we cannot function in the shifting circumstances of work and family life.

For these reasons, we are simultaneously empowered and held fast by the functioning of our mind and body, which through their long evolution are adapted to the complexities of life on Earth. This long-standing tension of our animal-human nature, its simultaneous resistance to life-threatening change and capacity for dynamic restructuring, must be wisely and skillfully negotiated during transformative practice. We must respect our basic tendencies as we begin to restructure them. Such restructuring takes time and is often difficult, but its rewards can be great.

Indeed, practice can become its own reward, a challenging but deeply satisfying activity. And more than that, it is often assisted by agencies that seem to come from beyond the ordinary self. These spontaneous empowerments – call them the graces of God, the workings of Buddha Mind, or the flow of the Tao – answer our calls for a greater life and confirm our aspirations for it.

We want to emphasize this. As both products and agents of the evolving universe and its guiding Presence, we must build on what our past has given us in the light of a higher leading. In this, the sacred traditions have much to teach us. The great Zen master Dogen famously said that Zen practice is more than a means to an end; it *is* enlightenment. In the Christian life of virtue and prayer, it is said that 'practice rewards nature, and is in turn rewarded by grace.' In Taoism, one 'guides the world where it most deeply wants to go.' Or as the celebrated Indian mystic Sri Ramakrishna put it, 'The winds of grace are always blowing, but we must raise our sails.' These various admonitions point to the same fundamental principles: first, that our present nature, if respected, will support our cultivation of its latent capacities; and second, that we are assisted in this by a higher presence or power.

And these two principles involve a third. To nurture all of our emergent attributes, we can turn to practices that produce many positive changes at once. Most of the exercises we suggest here are especially good for that. Meditation, for example, can simultaneously calm the mind, promote hormonal balance, sharpen thought, release the imagination, lift the emotions, help strengthen volition, and open ways to greater states of consciousness. With similar synergistic effect, fitness training can at the same time strengthen the heart, improve circulation, lower blood pressure, strengthen bone and skin, promote emotional stability, help clarify thought, and increase vitality. These and other practices do many good things for us, all at once. Like good business deals or scientific theories, they can yield great return on investment.

And furthermore, they can be joined with other exercise to yield even greater results. Numerous studies have shown, for example, that physical fitness enhances meditation and, conversely, that meditative techniques promote fitness. The research physician Herbert Benson has found that most people can, by repeating a word such as 'one' while exercising on a treadmill, automatically increase their muscular and cardiorespiratory capacity, and the sport psychologist Richard Suinn has demonstrated a similar effect by having subjects 'run relaxed.' This synergy of physical and mental training is appreciated now by meditation teachers and sportspeople around the world.

The same principle holds for other practices. Psychotherapy is recommended now by Roman Catholic, Jewish, and Buddhist teachers for certain monks and lay students because the self-awareness it can provide facilitates the mindfulness and self-liberation that contemplative prayer and meditation are meant to promote. Conversely, many psychotherapists now advise their clients to practice meditation so that they might acquire greater detachment from their emotions, impulses, and thoughts. Disciplines that stand the tests of time typically have this synergistic effect, producing several beneficial results at once, because all of our capacities are connected and therefore influenced for better or worse by significant changes in any part of our body or mind. *The efficiency of practice, in other words, arises from the underlying unity of human nature and its emergent attributes.* We have returned to this thesis again and again: In spite of human nature's shortcomings and perversities, which are vividly apparent to us all, its many attributes can and eventually must participate in our further development because that is their destiny, their most basic intent. Human nature, we believe, is meant for integral transformation. The winds of grace are blowing for all of our attributes, but we must raise a sail large enough to catch them. The program we outline here is based on this fundamental principle.

But a reminder before we begin: Because this is an integral practice with broadly encompassing aims, it must be approached as a long-term activity. It is a program for lifelong learning, and for that reason it works best when approached for its own sake as well as for its particular results. In his book *Mastery*, George Leonard has described ways in which human growth is cut short by a failure to persevere in self-discipline. There is an antidote to such failure, though, in the recognition that improvements usually come in spurts after long periods of little or no advance. By enjoying 'the long plateaus of the learning curve,' as Leonard puts it, and by embracing practice for its own sake, we are more likely to succeed in transformative practice than if we demand immediate results. To paraphrase Dogen, practice *is* transformation when undertaken in this spirit.

BASIC ELEMENTS OF TRANSFORMATIVE PRACTICE

In spite of differences that arise from their different origins and philosophies, transformative disciplines around the world share several basic elements. Contemplative prayer, for example, involves the same instinctive opening to the Transcendent in Hindu, Jewish, Christian, and Islamic cultures. Witness meditation, during which one observes thoughts, impulses, and emotions with liberating detachment, is practiced by Theravada Buddhists, Zen Buddhists, Indian yogis, Sufis, and contemporary psychologists. And though they are described in different ways and given different names, focused intention and affirmations are required in all such disciplines.

Because these fundamental activities, moves, or modalities of practice take different forms, they are best thought of as sets or families. Here we will emphasize five such 'practice-families' that, we believe, are especially important for the cultivation of our emergent attributes.

1. FOCUSED INTENTION, AFFIRMATIONS, AND VOWS

Without this family, or set, of activities, no transformative practice can succeed. Though our emergent attributes often appear spontaneously, they must be deliberately cultivated if we want them to last, and for this we need focused intention and a persistent will to actualize them.

To reinforce such intention and perseverance, every sacred tradition requires vows from its members to pursue virtue, goodness, enlightenment, or oneness with God. That is why Alcoholics Anonymous and the various 'twelve-step' programs of modern times require affirmations by their participants and why sports-people practice 'self-talk,' visualization, and concentration exercises to improve their fitness and performance. *The Life We Are Given* by George Leonard and Michael Murphy outlines an integral transformative practice similar to the kind we are proposing here; it describes the use of affirmations, which:

. . . are clear, straightforward statements of positive change in body, being, and performance. They represent a firm contact with ourself. They focus our best conscious efforts on transformation while seeking to enlist powers beyond our conscious understanding. They are written in the present tense to describe conditions as you intend them to be at some specified time in the future.

To take an example: Say you're a person who is often too busy or preoccupied to consider other people's feelings. You want to develop more empathy. Your affirmation could be, 'I enjoy a profound empathy for other people that sometimes appears to be telepathic.' Present tense. It would not be, 'I will develop my powers of empathy' or 'I intend to be a more empathic person' or 'To be more empathic.'

By employing the present tense, the affirmation, 'I enjoy a profound empathy for other people that sometimes appears to be telepathic' might seem to deny reality. Yes, right now, in the life you lead, you are by no means an empathic person. But your affirmation is not a denial of that reality. Rather, it is an instrument for creating a parallel, present-day reality in your consciousness, a precondition for the affirmation work we use in integral transformative practice.

This consciousness of yours is nothing you can touch or photograph or measure with any known instrument, but it is nonetheless real. It exists in the universe. It is organized. It produces results. Your job is to create the condition of being an empathic person in the realm of your consciousness. This may be accomplished through language (repeating the affirmation silently or aloud), imaging (creating a strong image of yourself as an empathic person), and emotion (feeling what another feels). In this example, some part of the change can be accomplished simply through practicing being empathic with loved ones, acquaintances, or strangers – even if that practice seems at first pro forma. It's also important to open yourself to the magic of grace, that mysterious, seemingly unearned mediation that often comes when least expected. But whether the mediation is practical and easily understandable or mysterious, the concentrated intentionality triggered by the affirmation process is central.

Such affirmations can be practiced through words, images, emotions, and deliberate acts. And they are real. If firmly held, they become more than 'figments of the imagination' as they exert real energies for change. Indeed, they can become *increasingly* real if reinforced through constant practice, and for that reason must be chosen with care. To paraphrase the ancient adage, be careful what you pray for because you may well get it. As you will see, the exercises described below involve constant intentions, which can be reinforced through images, language, and other means.

2. SELF-OBSERVATION, WITNESS MEDITATION, AND LIBERATING DETACHMENT

To develop our emergent attributes, we need to move toward the greater awareness revealed by disciplined self-observation and witness meditation. This awareness, which both transcends and embraces our psychological and bodily functioning, grows as we deliberately detach ourselves from all images, thoughts, impulses, feelings, and sensations. It comes into its own, so to speak, through non-interfering self-observation that relinquishes attachment to both inner and outer events. As it grows, this witnessing awareness provides new freedom from mental, emotional, and physical habits, as well as brief moments of joy and recognitions of a deeper freedom still. With long-term cultivation, it opens onto larger vistas and becomes a boundless subjectivity that realizes unity everywhere.

This fundamental awareness is its own reward and one of the supreme results of transformative practice, but it is also necessary for practical success in both the early and later stages of integral development. Its ever-renewing freedom cushions the shocks, readjustments, and restructurings required for high-level change. Its spaciousness, clarity, and constancy helps us sustain deep and lasting change. As it develops through meditation and ongoing self-observation, it blossoms into the transcendent knowing and identity discussed in this book, revealing our deepest being, in which we find the source of our synchronicities, emergent attributes, and premonitions of extraordinary life. This, of course, is the secret of the best modern therapy and the ancient practice of contemplative meditation. From the undivided, inclusive, ever-buoyant awareness we find in self-observing meditation, we can bring our various attributes into contact and eventual integration. Abiding in it, we discover new sources of creativity, spontaneous right action, and direct contact with our deepest source.

Such awareness can be cultivated in all circumstances, including transitions between different states of consciousness. The Indian philosopher Sri Aurobindo wrote:

> It is even possible to become wholly conscious in sleep from beginning to end or over large stretches of our dream-experience; then we are aware of ourselves passing from state after state of consciousness to a brief period of dreamless rest, which is the true restorer of the energies of the waking nature, and then returning by the same way to the waking consciousness.

We can also develop such awareness during transitions to states other than sleep. A few Indian yoga schools have even permitted the use of alcohol as part of their discipline, encouraging their followers to maintain self-awareness while intoxicated. Some Sufi groups emphasize self-observation during manual labor, intense exercise, and other conditions in which attention typically falters. And *The Tibetan Book of the Dead*, as well as other manuals for dying, give instructions for the maintenance of consciousness through stages of death. By extending unbroken awareness through all of our activities, such practices open connections between – and help integrate – our dissociated parts. They give us more command of habitual behaviors, promote access to our spiritual depths, and begin to reveal our deepest self within all mental and physical events.

3. CONTEMPLATIVE PRAYER

The fundamental awareness, or knowing, we have just described can be realized as well through the practice of spiritual devotion. Such devotion, called bhakti yoga by Hindus, is fundamental to Christian contemplative life, as well as to Jewish and Islamic mysticism. In her mystic text *The Seven Manners of Loving*, Beatrijs of Nazareth (ca. 1230–68) wrote:

> When love for God is awakened in the soul, it joyfully arises and stirs itself in the heart. The heart then is so tenderly touched in love, so powerfully assailed, so wholly encompassed and so lovingly embraced in love that the soul is altogether conquered by love. Then it feels a great closeness to God and a spiritual brightness and a wonderful richness and a noble freedom and a great compulsion of love, and an overflowing fullness of great delight. The soul feels that all its senses and its will have become love, that it has sunk so deeply and been engulfed so completely in love that it has itself entirely become love. Love's beauty has adorned the soul, love's power has consumed it, love's sweetness has submerged it, love's righteousness has engulfed it, love's excellence has embraced it, love's purity has enhanced it, love's exaltedness has drawn it up and enclosed it, so that the soul must be nothing else but love and do nothing else.

The great Sufi master Jalaluddin Rumi wrote: 'I, you, he, she, we – in the garden of mystic lovers, these are not true distinctions.' In the realization produced by spiritual devotion, everything begins to be seen as God's glory and goodness. Praising God in song and prayer, meditating on God's magnificence, and repeating

God's name, leads to a purification that can remove all barriers between lover and Beloved, and the two become One.

In this oneness, this joy, the great Indian mystic Sri Ramakrishna discovered the same essential identity, the same fundamental and eternal ground, that he had experienced through contemplative meditation. He was not alone in equating the two kinds of realization. According to spiritual adepts such as Rumi and the poet Kabir, the God we know through loving prayer is the same as the One we know through self-observation. 'For ages I knocked at God's door,' Rumi wrote. 'But when it opened at last, I saw I was knocking from inside.'

Frederic Myers, the pioneering psychical researcher, viewed prayer from the perspective of his research with paranormal phenomena and the subliminal mind. Prayer, he wrote, resembles deep hypnosis and other self-suggestive techniques in that it makes 'a draft upon the Unseen.' He wrote:

> I have urged that while our life is maintained by continual inflow from the World-soul, that inflow may vary in abundance or energy in correspondence with variations in the attitude of our own minds. [The] supplication of the Lourdes pilgrims, the adoring contemplation of the Christian Scientists, the inward concentration of the self-suggesters, the trustful anticipation of the hypnotized subject – all these are mere shades of the same mood of mind – of the mountain-moving faith which can in actual fact draw fresh life from the Infinite.

Like Myers, William James wrote about prayer in nonsectarian language. The further limits of human nature, he wrote:

Plunge into an altogether other dimension of existence from the sensible and merely 'understandable' world. Name it the mystical region, or the supernatural region, whichever you choose. So far as our ideal impulses originate in this region (and most of them do originate in it, for we find them possessing us in a way for which we cannot articulately account), we belong to it in a more intimate sense than that in which we belong to the visible world, for we belong in the most intimate sense wherever our ideals belong. Yet the unseen region in question is not merely ideal, for it produces effects in this world. When we commune with it, work is actually done upon our finite personality, for we are turned into new men, and consequences in the way of conduct follow in the natural world upon our regenerative change. But that which produces effects within another reality must be termed a reality itself, so I feel as if we had no philosophic excuse for calling the unseen or mystical world unreal. God is real since he produces real effects.

If asked just where the differences in fact which are due to God's existence come in, I should have to say that in general I have no hypothesis to offer beyond what the phenomenon of 'prayerful communion' . . . immediately suggests. The appearance is that in this phenomenon something ideal, which in one sense is part of ourselves and in another sense is not ourselves, actually exerts an influence, raises our centre of personal energy, and produces regenerative effects unattainable in other ways. If, then, there be a wider world of being than that of our everyday consciousness, if in it there be forces whose effects on us are intermittent, if one facilitating condition of the effects be the openness of the 'subliminal' door, we have the elements of a theory to which the phenomena of religious life lend plausibility. I am so impressed by the importance of these phenomena that I adopt the hypothesis which they so naturally suggest. At these places at least, I say, it would seem as though trans-mundane energies, God, if you will, produced immediate effects within the natural world to which the rest of our experience belongs.

We have noted many kinds of experience that suggest, as James put it, that something beyond the ordinary self 'actually exerts an influence, raises our centre of personal energy, and produces regenerative effects unattainable in other ways.' In our most inspired moments, we typically feel as if something greater – call it God, Buddha Mind, or the Tao – is moving through us, and we are naturally called to the 'prayerful communion' with it that James described. Such prayer is instinctive in us and can empower all transformative practice.

4. CATHARSIS

The word 'catharsis,' which comes into English and other modern languages from ancient Greek, means a purifi-cation or cleansing of the mind and emotions that relieves both psychic and physical tension. In the healing temples of ancient Greece, the cathartic power of drama was so esteemed that it was regularly prescribed as a cure for disease. Indeed, Aristotle saw catharsis as a central func-tion of drama, and his view has influenced many thinkers since.

In modern psychology, catharsis has been used since Freud's time to relieve emotional conflicts and gain access to unconscious contents of the mind. It is an active com-ponent of political rallies, sports events, movies, and humor, and it is a basic element of much transformative practice, including therapeutic dialogue, intense meditation and prayer, strenuous athletic training, and role-playing in various kinds of therapy. The recommended exercises that follow sometimes trigger catharses, whether mild or intense. If they are troubling or difficult to understand, we recommend that you discuss them with a therapist, spiritual counselor, or trusted friend. Be assured, however, that they are a common by-product of newly discovered capacities and spiritual growth.

5. MENTAL IMAGERY

As we are using the term here, 'mental imagery' refers to quasi-sensory experience that occurs in the absence of physical stimuli. On a cold winter night, for example, while imagining a summer day at a beach, you can view inward pictures of surf accompanied by sensations of warmth on your skin, the sounds of gently rolling waves, smells of the sea, and the taste of beer or lemonade. You can do this because mental imagery can produce effects that resemble those of ordinary vision, hearing, taste, smell, and touch. Many scientific studies have shown that all people have some capacity for it, to varying degrees, and that all of us have a night-and-day stream of it to which we may or may not attend. For better or worse, imagery inhabits our reveries, our dreams, and our deliberate thought. It has a constant influence on our body, emotions, intentions, and reason. 'As a man thinketh,' said Jesus, 'so is he.'

We constantly communicate with mental images, which is why we are sometimes advised to 'lighten up,' 'come down,' or 'see the light.' Recognition of imagery's power is embedded in our common language. Knowing this, shamans, yogis, Zen masters, Christian spiritual directors, counselors, coaches, and other teachers have long employed it in their disciplines. They have done so because, like other elements of practice that have stood the tests of time, it can alter many aspects of human nature at once. It can facilitate powers of will, enrich emotions, help improve sensori-motor skills, and promote access to greater states of mind through the enlistment of countless psychological and bodily processes all at once, even when most such processes operate outside of ordinary consciousness. Like the other basic elements of practice we have noted, it can be highly efficient, which is why athletes and actors employ it to enhance performance, why clients in therapy use it to picture desired behaviors, and why many contemplatives imagine the higher presence or power with which they want to unite.

TRANSFORMATIVE EXERCISES

The exercises described below correspond to the emergent attributes explored in Part Two, but we have not framed them in a tightly systematic way. Since we believe that each person's way of growth is unique, we do not advocate a step-by-step program here. Listen to friends who share your interest in such practices as well as to teachers you respect, but follow your own leadings, too. While persistence is necessary for success in any discipline, improvisation is important as well. Be creative. There are many ways to work with the suggestions we make in the pages that follow.

EXPANDING PERCEPTION

In Chapter Three, we described different kinds of expanded perception ranging from improvements of the five senses to increased body awareness to glimpses of extrasensory energies and entities. Within all such perceptions, however, there resides a fundamental awareness that can be amplified – or 'revealed' – by self-observing meditation. Because it is crucial to the emergence of our greater attributes, we will begin with the cultivation of this underlying awareness.

First, however, we must note that for some people this involves what seems to be a paradox. The awareness we are talking about is both immediately available – indeed, we cannot be conscious without it – and yet capable of what seem to be sudden flowerings. It is right here, right now, as a condition of reading this book, and yet it has endless depths that can be revealed through long-term practice. It is, as many teachers have said, 'closer than our own skin,' but at the same time 'larger than the world.' If such statements seem paradoxical or confusing, we suggest they might make better sense as you practice this kind of meditation.

Witness Meditation
In a quiet place where you will not be disturbed, sit on a cushion or chair and simply observe your feelings, impulses, sensations, and thoughts. You can either close your eyes for this or keep them focused, with a relaxed gaze, on a point in front of you. Readjust your posture if you are uncomfortable, but sit erect to prevent sleep or drowsiness. If you sit on a cushion, you should cross your legs as yogis or Buddhist monks do; but whether you sit on a cushion or chair, keep your spine straight. If you slump you are likely to lose concentration.

Don't be concerned if thoughts come and go. Your commitment is simply to watch them. If emotions rise, let them pass or fluctuate. They, too, move with the stream of your consciousness. If sounds intrude, regard them as birds in flight through the sky of your larger being. If a sensation bothers you, if a hand tickles or starts to itch, try letting the feeling pass. All day, after all, such feelings rise and pass away.

And if you suddenly see that you've been caught in

reverie or a chain of habitual thoughts, come back to your witnessing self. You can always do this, no matter how far your mind has wandered, no matter what inner storm has passed. You can always come home to this basic awareness.

Remember, you need not be a slave to your feelings or thoughts. They need not be your master. Simply observe them now and persevere. If a valuable image or insight comes, eventually let it go. If it has real value, it will return when this exercise is done. In time you might notice that you are relieved as an image or feeling passes, relieved to let go of a particular thought. There is a new kind of freedom here, an ever-renewable sense of release.

Keep this up for fifteen minutes. Eventually you can make it longer. If at first it is hard to start meditating, it might eventually be hard to *stop.* Meditation itself, as the Zen master Dogen said, is its own reward. It is a first form of enlightenment. It reveals a self-existent delight.

But the exercise isn't finished yet.

When your meditation is done, you can remain self-observant. The freedom you have glimpsed, this relief from unnecessary feelings and thoughts, can pervade your everyday life. It can bring spaciousness to your relationships and new pleasure to leisure and work. And it can bring you back, again and again, to the deeper wells of your being. In Taoism and Zen it is said that 'meditation in action is a hundred, no a thousand, no a million, times greater than meditation in repose.' It is greater because the joy, the power, and the knowing it reveals should not be limited to the few hours or minutes we practice it.

Sensing

In a quiet place outside – in a garden, park, field, or woods – sit or stand for a moment in meditation, observing your thoughts and emotions as we've suggested, until you feel a growing balance and clarity. Then turn your attention to the things around you and the quality of your perception. Become aware of the colors and forms you see, the sounds and smells, and the sensations in your body. Observe how you sense the temperature and feel the breeze. Now ask for help in prayer as you actively intend to perceive with more depth and clarity. How much beauty begins to blossom? Can you see more than you did before?

Now open to deeper, more vibrant color. Pay attention to the uniqueness of forms. See how each tree's spray of limbs, each flower, each blade of grass forms a distinctive pattern. Notice shadows on the rocks, the light they radiate, and the enchantment that pervades the location. Use your powers of intention to move beyond ordinary hearing toward sounds you hadn't heard before. Do the same with smells and skin sensations. Discover some you hadn't noticed.

Now look for fleeting luminosities. Can you see auras or tiny points of light? Hold onto these sensations for as long as you stay, remaining in the witness position. Then carry this sense of expanded perception as you move to another location.

Remote Viewing
Ask a friend to visit a location unknown to you at a time you both agree upon and act as a target for this experiment with clairvoyance, or 'remote viewing.' They should remain there for ten or fifteen minutes, closely observing prominent characteristics of the place and writing them down for future reference. While your friend is doing this, go to a quiet and secluded place, close your eyes, relax, and begin to meditate. Assume the witness position and be ready to observe any forthcoming

experience. As your mind quiets and comes into clearer focus, extend your perception toward your friend with a focused intention to see where he is and what he is perceiving. Stay in the witness position as you notice the perceptions that come spontaneously to mind. Let your impressions form as they will without interfering with them, unless they are obstructed by habitual trains of imagery or thought. Let what you begin to see come more clearly into view without assuming too quickly what it is. Renew your intention to find your friend, and let your emerging impressions continue to rise until they seem to form a pattern. But again, don't force a pattern on them. Even if you don't see a particular place, you might be sensing some of its features. Do this for fifteen minutes or more, making notes about the things you perceive and your spontaneous associations to them. Then compare your perceptions with the list of the location's features and other observations about the experiment provided by your friend.

MOVEMENT

Moving from Center

Many martial arts and forms of dance cultivate movement from one's center, a point several inches below the navel. This practice promotes grace, coordination, and balance in part because it keeps our focus on the whole of our bodies rather than on individual muscles or moves. Begin this practice by choosing a dance step, sports maneuver, or other familiar movement. Concentrate your attention on a point below your navel and visualize the initiation of all movements from this location. Now try the movement itself, keeping your focus on your center as you move. Use your powers of intention to help your body move more freely and in perfect coordination from this center. As you practice this technique, check whether you are experiencing a new lightness and freedom from effort. When you are finished, vow to carry this technique into all your movements.

Moving with a Mantra

Repeating a word or sound in cadence, too, can promote new freedom of bodily movement while you are exercising. Any sound or word can be used for this as long as it facilitates calm, good rhythm, and focus, but you might try something suggestive such as 'one,' 'flow,' or 'smooth.' This is like chanting a spiritual phrase in that it centers you in a deeper, more energizing place.

As you move while repeating your mantra, see if your consciousness assumes a new poise, or station, beyond your ordinary points of physical reference. This might happen gradually or too subtly to notice at first. But wait to see if it will happen. In Taoism it is said that surrender to the Tao gives rise to a 'spirit-child,' which is made of spirit-matter. Conceivably, the new center you find while moving with a rhythmically repeated word gives hints of such a birth.

Visualization of Movement

Choose a familiar but difficult movement from sports, dance, or another activity you would like to improve. After quieting your mind, visualize it in great detail, seeing it first in your mind's eye, then sensing it throughout your body. Now attempt to accomplish the movement exactly as you saw and felt it. Repeat the procedure several times, noticing whether your actual movement conforms to your image of it. As you continue, add color and precision to your visualization. Make it more vivid and more immediate. Then observe what effect it has on the maneuver you are trying to master.

The development of communication skills requires that we grow in empathy, self-awareness, and freedom from defensiveness, competitiveness, passive-aggressive behaviors, and other destructive attributes. Many of us find help in this from personal counseling or therapy that explores unexamined tendencies that keep us from realizing more creative contact with others.

Observing Reciprocal Interaction in a Group
Before you engage in your next group interaction, whether it be a family reunion, work meeting, or informal gathering, practice using your powers of intention to view the coming interactions from your witness (observer) position. Remember that in healthy group interaction the discussion will move freely from one individual to another without anyone monopolizing the conversation because of a hidden agenda. During the meeting, observe yourself and each group member in this way, remembering to watch and listen from a detached point of view, without judgment or condemnation. This kind of observation can help sensitize us to the many psychological problems that come up between people, as well as alert us to unnoticed patterns that impede our relations with others.

Telepathic Sensitivity
Communication sometimes seems to involve telepathy. To develop such sensitivity, you might practice guessing who is calling when the telephone rings. At the first ring, take a few seconds to adopt the witness position, focusing on the person who calls. What impressions come? Can you guess who it is? Do this for an entire day and track how often you are right. Intend that your accuracy will

improve, then compare the first day's attempts with those made on days that follow.

OPENING TO HIGHER ENERGY

Visualizing Energy
After choosing a serene outdoor setting, sit down, close your eyes, and relax your mind and body. Now open your eyes and look at your surroundings. Intend to see more beauty and luminosity in the forms around you. Then close your eyes again and intend to see everything in its quantum reality, as dancing patterns of energy, each emanating from the same energetic source. Affirm that you are intimately connected with this energy, as though all the universe is part of you looking through your eyes. Breathe this higher source into your own body and mind.

Now stand up from your center, attempting to feel this constant, ever-renewing power. See yourself filled with it and floating up. Move as though rising from your center, affirming that you have an unlimited source of energy emanating from the core of your being. Carry this feeling with you for the rest of your day.

Uplifting the Energy of Others
In a group setting, attempt the following exercise, which demonstrates and builds on the higher connection that exists between us all. As each person speaks, visualize a stream of energy flowing from the Transcendent through you to the one who speaks, raising them into greater alignment with their own higher potential and source. Notice any difference in what is said or in their general demeanor.

This practice can also be attempted when all group members are committed to performing this technique. While one person talks about an issue that is important to them, the others visualize him or her being filled with energy and lifted into their greater wisdom and knowing. After each person has taken a turn, discuss the experience.

Silent Intervention
It is also possible to help strangers or passing acquaintances through telepathic outreach. One can do this in a restaurant or store, for example, when someone sitting or standing nearby, or someone serving you, seems depressed or upset. As in the exercise described above, lift the person in your imagination, bringing power from a higher source through you to them. See if their mood or attitude changes. Note how they react to those around them. You might be surprised at the results.

PLEASURE, JOY, AND ECSTASY

Noticing Subtle Pleasures
Pick an unhurried moment and intend to notice the subtler pleasures of life. Begin by slowing your breath and feeling the pleasure that the burst of oxygen gives you. Stand on your toes and reach high with both arms. Hold the position for a long moment. Then sit, focusing on the pleasure relaxation brings. Feel this pleasure through your body. Savor it deeply. Think of other small pleasures and intend to savor them as you do now.

Pleasures of Completion
Choose a moment when you are nearing completion of a job. It can be a creative work by which you are inspired or something more ordinary, such as cleaning the kitchen. When you've finished, take a moment to consider what you've accomplished. Explore the feelings you have about it, intending to notice the pleasure its completion brings. Make a conscious decision to be aware of such

pleasure with every task you complete for the rest of the day, however small it might be. When the day is done, make a vow to make such awareness a constant part of your experience.

Conscious Smiling and Laughter

Sometime when your energy is low, move to a place where you cannot be heard or seen. Then force a smile, imagining that your mood is more upbeat. Laugh out loud for a several seconds, remembering how it feels to be fully amused. Now laugh in a more animated way a minute or more. Embrace and integrate this new mood of intentional happiness. Hold on to it for the rest of the day.

LOVE

Remembering Love

Go to a quiet place, close your eyes, and relax. Repeat a favorite phrase, lyric, verse, or scripture to open yourself to higher intuitions and memories. Then remember a feeling of love you had at some time in your earlier life, perhaps love for a parent when you were a child, or for a favorite pet, or for a friend or spouse. Once the feeling of love is recalled, bring it into the current moment without connecting it to any person or cause. Simply bring yourself to love as a primary state. Then vow to keep it for the rest of the day.

Returning to Love

Pick a time when you are emotionally upset, whether with anger, frustration, disappointment, or general irritation. Then sit down and remember a special time when you experienced love. Visualize what you felt then in the current moment, intending to feel it deeply. Embrace the feeling as if it were closer to your true self than the emotion that disturbs you. Then release the negative feelings from your body as if they were dissolving in your love. Hold this state throughout the day.

TRANSCENDENT KNOWING

Clarifying Intuitions

After practicing meditation as we suggested in the first exercise, observe everything that occurs with detachment. As you go through your day, continue to observe your feelings and thoughts. Observe what might be called analytical thoughts, those you consciously direct to analyze a particular problem. But at the same time pay attention to those that seem to come as if from nowhere - a sudden thought of a friend or work associate, an idea to buy an item you've wanted, or a reverie about something strange. Ask yourself why the thought came now. What does it connect to? Does it carry seeds of an intuition related to the problem you are trying to solve? Possibly it is there to guide you toward the solution you've been looking for.

TRANSCENDENT IDENTITY

Discovering Mission

Begin by closing your eyes, relaxing, and reviewing your life. Start at the beginning, with your family, and play your life forward in your mind as if watching a movie. Note the events that come to memory, but stay detached. Look for connections among them, and higher meanings they suggest. What did you learn from your early family experience that bears upon your deepest aims? What interpersonal styles and problems did you see? How did you react?

Now move forward and look at your educational years. What teachers did you like or dislike? And why? Why did you make the close friends you had? What were you learning about? Look at the key synchronistic events of those years and the experiences they led to. What early jobs did you seek? How did you get them?

Look at your career and romantic choices up to the present moment. What have you learned? What have you missed? What has the theme of your movie been? Ask yourself what, from all the experiences you've just recalled, you would tell others if you were advising them how to live more fully?

And last, compare this assessment with your deepest and most heartfelt dream of what you want to accomplish in life. Relate it to the central thing you want to do, the largest gift you want to give the world at large. How do your life circumstances relate to this general sense of mission? Do they help or hinder you? What comes to mind that you should do next?

WILL BEYOND EGO

Recalling Zone Moments
Review the times in your life in which key actions seemed to come spontaneously, as if from a deeper place – during a sports activity perhaps, or while giving a speech, or performing in some other way. Remember how your actions and words suddenly came to you, as if from a larger self, a greater being and capability. Now go on with your life, intending to move closer to this level of functioning.

THE EXPERIENCE OF INTEGRATION AND SYNCHRONISTIC FLOW

Synthesizing Identity, Energy, and Knowing
Sit down in a favorite place and relax, assuming the witness position. Visualize the universe as flowing from

one divine source, making up your larger body, and looking through your eyes out on itself. Feel that source as an energy that wells up within you, overflowing into everything you see. At the same time let this source flowing through you reveal your essential identity and how you can best enrich the world. After this visualization, watch your thoughts carefully for guidance from your deepest self and pointers to immediate actions that serve your essential mission.

Integral Flow
In quiet meditation, simply watch time pass, observing your life from a perspective above your sensations, feelings, and thoughts. Now go on with your life, go to work, out to dinner, or whatever you would ordinarily do, but continue to observe events closely, including your feelings and thoughts. Distinguish habitual thoughts from those that seem to come from a deeper, more inspired place, and if they prompt you to a spontaneous and potentially creative act, follow them in the spirit of exploration. If, for example, your thought is to go somewhere unexpected and to do so is not especially difficult, follow your intuitive prompting. Does something magical happen? When you've done this, pay careful attention to what happens next. Are the events that follow in any way meaningful or synchronistic? Ask yourself why these events might be happening now. Do they have anything to do with larger goals in your life? But take care not to jump to easy conclusions and keep a balance between openness and healthy caution. Experience teaches us that often we must wait for the true meaning of events to become clear. Always find a positive, 'silver lining' in whatever occurs. See if what you have just done stimulates another spontaneous intuition. Keep the flow going as long as you can.

*　　*　　*

REMEMBER, these exercises can be adapted to your interests and circumstances in many ways. Evolution has brought each of us to the brink of transformation. At no other time has there been such wide acknowledgment of our greater potentials, such abundance of resources for vision and practice, or such openness toward the spiritual mysteries of existence. Through balanced and dedicated practice, all of us can more fully participate in – and contribute to – the world's evolutionary adventure.

A door has been opened for us. It is our destiny to walk through it.

17

A GUIDE TO THE LITERATURE OF TRANSFORMATION

New understandings of our greater nature have appeared in various cultures since the beginning of human history. Though many of these have been lost for long periods of time, they are being recovered by students of ancient texts, historians, and religious scholars so that they are now available in unprecedented abundance. And in modern times, as we have seen, many of them have been supplemented, expanded, and refined by discoveries in the physical, biological, and human sciences. Today we possess the greatest literature of human transformation that has ever existed on Earth.

In the pages that follow, we present a sample of this burgeoning literature that includes many of its enduring classics. Our attempt here is not to be exhaustive but to reflect the richness and power of our extraordinary heritage. Whereas several of the titles we include have a wide readership, others do not, and some are out of print. Nevertheless, we feel it is important to list hard-to-find books if they are central to the advance of self-knowledge. It is likewise important that they not be lost as spiritual resources, either for us or for future generations.

We have divided these works according to the chapters for which they have special importance. A few are cited in more than one chapter and appear more than once.

A commitment to practice is best sustained when we stand on firm intellectual ground, supported by humankind's great scientists, philosophers, saints, and sages. These books can help create that foundation.

CHAPTER ONE: THE MYSTERY OF OUR BEING

Alexander, Samuel. *Space, Time, and Deity*. Volumes I & II. Peter Smith, 1979. In this, his major work, Alexander described his philosophic approach, called 'empirical metaphysics,' by which he meant a broad-ranging philosophy dealing with spiritual issues that was based upon verifiable data. For Alexander, our developing world has five basic levels: space-time, matter, life, mind, and deity, each emergent from the others.

Bergson, Henri. *Creative Evolution*. Translated by A. Mitchell. Henry Holt, 1913. The French philosopher wrote in a fluent, nontechnical style that won him a wide readership as well as the Nobel Prize for literature. In this, his best-known book, he proposed that the *elan vital*, or 'vital impetus,' which can be viewed as a 'supra-consciousness or God,' drives the evolution of animals, plants, and human beings. In later works such as *The Two Sources of Morality and Religion*, Bergson proposed that mystics participate more fully than others in God's love for humankind, and for that reason form the vanguard of evolution. However, their spirits must become universal to ensure our further development, and to that end societies must be 'open,' not authoritarian, and tolerant of radical spiritual ideas.

Berry, Thomas and Brian Swimme. *The Universe Story*. HarperSanFrancisco, 1992. Berry is a cultural historian and Roman Catholic priest, Swimme a philosopher and mathematical cosmologist. This book is their deeply felt meditation on the evolving universe and its spiritual dimensions. For Berry, such reflections constitute a kind of 'epic literature.'

Bohm, David. *Wholeness and the Implicate Order.* Routledge, 1973. David Bohm, a leading figure in quantum theory, develops a view of physics that treats the totality of existence, including matter and consciousness, as an unbroken whole. Bohm proposes that every independent element in our universe contains within it the sum of all elements, i.e the sum of all existence itself.

Broad, C. D. *The Mind and Its Place in Nature.* Routledge and Kegan Paul, 1925. In this book, Broad, an eminent British philosopher, related evolutionary emergence to matter, mind, and evidence that consciousness survives bodily death.

Chaisson, Eric. *Cosmic Dawn.* Little, Brown, 1981. A history of evolution from the birth of the universe to life on earth.

Darwin, Charles. *The Correspondence of Charles Darwin.* Volumes I-III. Cambridge University Press, 1985.

—— *The Descent of Man and Selection in Relation to Sex.* Random House, 1871. Here Darwin extended his proposals regarding evolution and natural selection to the development of humans from our primate ancestors.

—— *The Expression of the Emotions in Man and Animals.* The University of Chicago Press, 1872, 1965. An historic and still-revealing study of emotional expressiveness in humans and animals based on Darwin's comparative study of infants (including his own), painting, sculpture, animals, and people in different cultures.

—— *The Origin of Species By Means of Natural Selection or the Preservation of Favored Races in the Struggle for Life.* Random House, 1859. This landmark book, one of the greatest in the history of science, prompted the acceptance by scientists around the world of evolution as a fact and natural selection as one of its chief mechanisms. When it was published, it electrified both the scientific world and the general public in Europe and America.

—— *The Voyage of the Beagle.* Viking, 1989. This is the journal Darwin kept on his famous voyage to South America and the Galapagos Islands in the 1830s. It records many observations that would lead to his theories of evolution.

Davies, Paul. *The Cosmic Blueprint: New Discoveries in Nature's Creative Ability to Order the Universe.* Simon & Schuster, 1988. Davies, a mathematician and physicist, presents his ideas about the self-organization through which both inorganic and living systems evolve into more elaborate forms, and shows how these ideas can be applied to the universe as a whole.

—— *The Mind of God: The Scientific Basis for a Rational World.* New York: Simon & Schuster, 1992. An exploration of purpose and order in the evolving universe. Davies provides evidence that there is some sort of telos in evolution, a fundamental tendency of the universe to move toward higher levels of complexity.

Eldridge, Niles. *Reinventing Darwin: The Great Debate at the High Table.* John Wiley, 1995. An illuminating discussion of evolutionary theory and how it has been argued in the scientific community. Eldridge is the evolutionary theorist who, with Stephen Jay Gould, developed the model of *punctuated equilibria.*

Elgin, Duane. *Awakening Earth.* William Morrow, 1993. A visionary exploration of the evolution of human culture and consciousness from the ancient past to the distant future.

Ferris, Timothy. *The Whole Shebang: A State-of-the-Universe(s) Report.* Simon & Schuster, 1998. Ferris is a prize-winning science writer. This is his authoritative, clearly written account of cosmic evolution, including its beginning in the Big Bang, the development of galaxies, stars, planets, and the Earth.

Gebser, Jean. *The Ever Present Origin. Part One: Foundations of the Aperspectival World. A Contribution to the History of The Awakening of Consciousness. Part Two: Manifestations of the Aperspectival World. An Attempt at the Concretion of the Spiritual.* Ohio University Press, 1986. Second Edition. A sweeping overview of both individual and collective human development from Stone-Age times to the present, joining the perspectives of aesthetics, sociology, anthropology, psychology, religious studies, and other fields. Gebser sees humanity giving rise to a new 'aperspectival' or 'integral' consciousness that goes beyond the collective consciousness of ancient times and the ego-bound individuality of post-Renaissance modernity. This emergent consciousness embraces the world in a more inclusive and integral way than the mentalities that preceded it, experiencing spiritual realities with greater intensity while apprehending both time and eternity. We are, wrote Gebser, 'shaped and determined not only by today and yesterday, but by tomorrow as well.'

Glass, Bentley, et al., ed. *Forerunners of Darwin 1745–1859.* Johns Hopkins Press, 1959. An overview of eighteenth-century notions about evolution that preceded and set the stage for Darwin's discoveries.

Goudge, T. A. *Emergent Evolution* in *The Encyclopedia of Philosophy.* Volume Two. Macmillan, 1967. The article summarizes the chief ideas about evolutionary emergence as developed by various philosophers, including Alexander, Morgan, and Polanyi.

Gould, Stephen Jay, ed. *The Book of Life.* Revised edition. Norton, 2000. A richly illustrated collection of essays by eminent scientists about the history of life on Earth from its origins to *Homo sapiens.* This book is both authoritative and easy to understand, with drawings, photographs, and diagrams that dramatize the immense panorama of life on Earth.

—— *Hen's Teeth and Horse's Toes.* Norton, 1983. This book includes an essay, 'Evolution as fact and theory,' which is cited in Chapter One.

—— *Ontogeny and Phylogeny.* Harvard University Press, 1977. This book, which can be found in many libraries, provides an authoritative 190-page history of ideas about evolution from the ancient Greeks to modern times. Gould shows that for more than two thousand years certain philosophers and naturalists glimpsed the fact of evolution as well as certain aspects of current evolutionary theory. Reading his account, you will see that humankind's discovery of evolution has been marked by inspired intuitions and that it has taken some fascinating twists and turns.

Graham, Peter W., ed. *The Portable Darwin.* Penguin, 1993. A useful introduction to Charles Darwin's most important writings, with clear and accessible summaries of his thought and historical importance.

Hegel, G. W. F. *The Phenomenology of Mind.* Translated by J. B. Baillie. Harper Torchbook, 1967. *Phenomenology of Spirit.* Translated by A. V. Miller with an analysis of the text and foreword by J. N. Findlay. Oxford University Press, 1977. In this immensely influential book, Hegel proposes that the world is a dialectical unfoldment of *Geist* (mind or spirit) from unreflective nature to human selfconsciousness, an evolution by which *Geist* comes to know itself. In Hegel's view, each new stage of development subsumes *(aufheben)* the stages that preceded it, both annihilating and fulfilling them.

Kauffman, Stuart. *At Home in the Universe.* Oxford University Press, 1995. Kauffman is a pioneer in complexity theory, the science of large, complex systems. In this book, he presents a compelling case that self-organization is a robust natural feature of the inorganic, biological, and human domains. Spontaneous order, he argues, arises in nearly every complex system, from snowflakes to bacteria to humans to business corporations.

Lamb, Simon, and David Sington. *Earth Story.* Princeton University Press, 1998. An illustrated, clearly written history of the Earth's geological evolution and its relation to the development of plant and animal species.

Lovejoy, Arthur O. *The Great Chain of Being: A Study of the History of an Idea.* Harvard University Press, 1974. The American philosopher-historian Arthur Lovejoy was the chief promoter in the United States of 'the history of ideas' as a field of inquiry. In this, his most famous and influential book, he explores the idea of the Great Chain of Being (the hierarchy of inanimate, animal, human, and super-human forms) from Plato and Aristotle into the nineteenth century, tracing its influences in ancient, medieval, and modern times.

Mayr, Ernst. *The Growth of Biological Thought, Diversity, Evolution, and Inheritance.* Harvard University Press, 1985. A comprehensive history of biological thought by one of the world's most eminent authorities on the development of evolutionary theory.

Morgan, C. Lloyd. *Emergent Evolution*. Henry Holt and Company, 1923. Morgan pioneered the idea of evolutionary emergence, and proposed that our world has four successive levels: psychophysical events, life, mind, and spirit or God. Each 'emergent' level of the world: 1) arises from and supervenes upon what already exists; 2) is genuinely new in the universe; 3) occurs in ways that could not be predicted from the laws and conditions that preceded it; and 4) cannot be explained naturalistically but must be accepted with 'natural piety.'

Murphy, Michael. *The Future of the Body: Explorations into the Further Reaches of Human Nature*. Tarcher/Putnam, 1992. This book, which grew out of the Esalen Institute archives on extraordinary human functioning (now housed at Stanford University's School of Medicine), describes a wide range of human attributes and their supernormal expressions in an evolutionary context.

Polanyi, Michael. *Personal Knowledge*. Harper & Row, 1958. This is one of the twentieth century's greatest books on the philosophy of science. Polanyi, who was an eminent scientist as well as a philosopher, demonstrates the crucial role of subjectivity in human knowledge. He also produces powerful arguments for the emergent nature of evolutionary progress.

Satprem. *Sri Aurobindo or The Adventure of Consciousness*. Auromere, 1996. A spirited biography of Aurobindo, with colorful descriptions of the great philosopher's mystical realizations, philosophical vision, and Integral Yoga.

Schelling, Friedrich. *System of Transcendental Idealism*. University Press of Virginia, 1964. Schelling, a German philosopher, was among the first to 'temporalize' the Great Chain of Being (to use the phrase of Arthur Lovejoy), conceiving nature to be the progressive manifestation of God. For Schelling the world was a 'slumbering spirit,' or *Deus Implicitus*, by stages returning to its divine source, *Deus Explicitus*. Schelling, who published this work in 1801, strongly influenced his friend Hegel.

Sheldrake, Rupert. *A New Science of Life*. Tarcher/Putnam,1981. Sheldrake does not see the universe operating like a machine; instead, he sees it as much like a living organism.

He asks: What is the nature of life, and how are the shapes and instincts of living organisms determined? Sheldrake's hypothesis, 'Formative Causation,' proposes that form and function of all living things are passed to succeeding generations by 'morphogenetic fields' that extend through space and time.

Simpson, George Gaylord. *The Meaning of Evolution: A Study of the History of Life and of Its Significance for Man.* Yale University Press, 1961. A classic account of evolutionary theory and what it suggests about humankind's possibilities for further progress.

Stebbins, G. L. *The Basis of Progressive Evolution.* University of North Carolina Press, 1969. Here Stebbins outlines his estimates of evolutionary 'graduations' (advances in grade) by which living creatures have advanced from single-celled organisms to humankind.

Swimme, Brian. *The Universe is a Green Dragon.* Bear & Company, 1985. A fictional dialogue between a young person and an older storyteller about the mysteries, beauty, and promise of the evolving universe. This is a book for readers young and old.

—— *The Hidden Heart of the Cosmos.* Orbis, 1996. A lyrical, often passionate series of reflections on the unfolding cosmos and its spiritual depths.

Thompson, D'arcy Wentworth. *On Growth and Form.* Abridged Edition. Cambridge University Press, 1961. A beautifully written account of biological processes that can be read as a companion to Stuart Kauffman's *At Home in the Universe.* In the words of one commentator, it lovingly describes 'the shape of horns, teeth, and tusks, jumping fleas and slipper limpets, buds and seeds, bees' cells and drops of rain, a film of soap and bubble of oil, and the splash of a pebble in a pond.' Thompson was a great man of science, and was also a gifted poet.

Teilhard De Chardin, Pierre. *The Phenomenon of Man.* With an introduction by Julian Huxley. Harper & Row, 1959. A Jesuit paleontologist, Chardin joined scientific expertise and spiritual intuition in a vision of the world's evolution through the 'lithosphere,' or inorganic world, the 'biosphere' of living things, and the 'noosphere,' or world of mind, toward the 'Omega Point,' in which the world would be joined more closely with God. Like Hegel, Schelling, and Aurobindo, he conceived the world to be a progressive manifestation of its implicit divinity.

Wallace, Alfred Russel. *My Life; A Record of Events and Opinions. Volumes I-II.* Dodd, Mead and Company, 1905. Wallace discovered natural selection at approximately the same time Darwin did, but believed that spiritual as well as material influences were involved in human evolution. In these volumes he describes, among other things, his thinking about human development in relation to higher powers.

Weiner, Jonathan. *The Beak of the Finch.* Vintage, 1994. The story of two scientists who, in studying the finches that Darwin described on the Galapagos Islands, concluded that evolution can happen much faster than Darwin believed. The book describes interesting changes in biological method and theory since Darwin's day.

Whitehead, Alfred North. *Process and Reality: An Essay in Cosmology.* Edited by David Ray Griffin and Donald W. Sherburne. The Free Press, 1978. Whitehead, a world-famous mathematician as well as a speculative philosopher, took creativity to be the primary feature of the universe, and proposed that all entities, whether inanimate, animal, or human, 'prehend' (remain in contact with) one another. Even inanimate things, he argued, have some degree of subjectivity and freedom through which they can move toward closer alignment with the divine attraction. As living things evolve to higher complexity, their subjectivity and freedom, grow, which enables them to come closer, if they choose, to God's life and purposes. This is Whitehead's major philosophical work.

Wilber, Ken. *A Brief History of Everything.* Shambhala, 1996. Wilber, one of the world's leading systematic philosophers today, relates evolution to God and higher human possibilities. This book, which is written in a playful dialogue format, provides a way into all of his work.

—— *No Boundary.* Shambhala, 1981. Human development is here viewed by one of the world's leading philosophers.

—— *Sex, Ecology, Spirituality. The Spirit of Evolution.* Shambhala,

1995. Wilber's most comprehensive book. It brings the discoveries of the physical, biological, and human sciences, as well as comparative religious studies, the arts, and other fields, into a comprehensive view of our evolving universe in relation to spirit. Wilber can be seen to participate in the lineage of 'evolutionary panentheism' (the doctrine that the divine both transcends and inhabits the evolving universe) that began with Hegel and Schelling and includes Bergson, Gebser, Teilhard, and Sri Aurobindo. You can read it selectively, choosing sections that attract your interest.

CHAPTER TWO: A HISTORY OF HUMAN AWAKENING

Adler, Mortimer. *Aristotle for Everybody: Difficult Thought Made Easy*. Bantam, 1978. This little volume, by one of the twentieth century's most honored educators, makes the great Greek philosopher's work more accessible.

Aquinas, Saint Thomas. *Basic Writings of St. Thomas Aquinas*. Edited by A. C. Pegis. 2 vols. Random House, 1947–48. A superb collection of the writings of the great Christian theologian of the late Middle Ages, illustrating his grand synthesis of theology and philosophy.

—— *Summa Theologica*. Translated by the English Dominican Fathers. 3 vols. Benziger, 1947–48. One of the most influential works in Christian theology, Aquinas's magnum opus reveals his quest to summarize all that can be known about God using the powers of both faith and reason.

Arberry, A. J., trans. *The Koran Interpreted*. 2 vols. George Allen & Unwin, 1955. Some believe that Arberry has succeeded better than anyone in bringing the richness, beauty, and poetic power of the Arabic original into English. Arberry also provides a fascinating preface on the history and difficulties of translating the Koran, with an interpretation informed by modern critical scholarship.

Aristotle. *The Complete Works of Aristotle: The Revised Oxford Translation*. Edited by J. Barnes. 2 vols. Princeton University Press, 1984. An authoritative collection of writings by the Greek philosopher, who was a student of Plato and mentor to Alexander the Great. Described by Dante as 'the master of those who know,' the range of Aristotle's intellect still astonishes. It embraced natural philosophy, metaphysics, art, drama, ethics, rhetoric, and politics.

Armstrong, Karen. *Buddha*. HarperSanFrancisco, 2001. A highly accessible and poetic evocation of Buddha's life and teaching.

—— *Muhammed: A Biography of the Prophet*. HarperSanFrancisco, 1992. A fresh look at Muhammed from a prolific contemporary religious scholar and writer.

Arnold, Edwin. *The Light of Asia*. Altemus, 1879. A poetic rendering of the life of the Buddha by a Victorian Englishman. This book enjoyed tremendous popularity in the late nineteenth and early twentieth centuries and deservedly so. It captures something precious in this ancient story and delivers it with great power and feeling.

—— *The Song Celestial*. David McKay Company, 1934. Some think this to be the poetic translation that comes closest to conveying the feeling of the original Sanskrit of the Bhagavad Gita.

Assagioli, Robert. *Psychosynthesis*. Penguin, 1965. Assagioli was the founder of psychosynthesis, which joins modern psychology and dynamic psychiatry with both Eastern and Western spiritual practices. In this, his main book, he presents a comprehensive guide to the principles and techniques of psychosynthesis.

Augustine, St. *Confessions*. Catholic University Press, 1953. The great scholar of mysticism, Evelyn Underhill, once wrote of this book, '. . . no one can read the *Confessions* without being struck by the intensity and actuality of his spiritual experience, and the characteristically mystical formulae under which he apprehended Reality . . . No mere literary genius could have produced the wonderful chapters in the seventh and eighth books, or the innumerable detached passages in which his passion for the Absolute breaks out. Later mystics, recognizing this fact, constantly appeal to his authority, and his influence ranks next to that of the Bible in the formation of the medieval school.'

Aurelius, Marcus. *Meditations.* Penguin Classics, 1964. The great Roman Emperor (121–180 C.E.) was also a Stoic philosopher. His philosophy, which joins social, political, and spiritual wisdom, resonates with the vision of integral transformation we present in this book.

Aurobindo, Sri. *The Collected Works of Sri Aurobindo.* Sri Aurobindo Ashram, 1972. These include all of Aurobindo's poetry, and his many books, articles, and letters about philosophy, psychology, political events, literary criticism, and the varieties of transformative practice. These collected works include an immense lore about the evolution of human nature, including the body.

—— *The Essential Aurobindo.* McDermott, Robert, ed. Lindisfarne Press, 1987. An updated collection of Aurobindo's works with a spirited and lucid afterword by the editor, which clarifies the relevance of Aurobindo's work for people in the West.

—— *A Greater Psychology: An Introduction to the Psychological Thought of Sri Aurobindo.* Dalal, A. S., ed. Tarcher/Putnam, 2001. In his foreword to this masterly anthology, Ken Wilber writes, 'When it comes to a "greater psychology" – one that includes body, mind, soul, and spirit – Aurobindo has much to teach us . . . This book is surely the finest overview of Aurobindo's psychological thought.'

—— *The Life Divine.* India Library Society, 1965. This is the most comprehensive statement of Aurobindo's philosophy and perhaps the world's greatest exposition of 'evolutionary pantheism.'

Bacon, Francis. *Advancement of Learning: Novum Organum; The New Atlantis.* In Great Books of the Western World. Vol. 30. Encyclopaedia Britannica, 1952. In this massively ambitious work, Bacon outlined his means of inductive thinking, which became essential to the scientific method as it developed during the Renaissance and European Enlightenment.

Bamford, Christopher, ed. *Homage to Pythagoras: Rediscovering Sacred Science.* Lindisfarne Press, 1994. A collection of nine essays that reexamines Pythagoras as the 'presiding genius of our culture' and a symbol of the reconciliation of scientific and religious sensibilities.

Barnstone, Willis. *The Poetics of Ecstasy: Varieties of Ekstasis from Sappho to Borges.* Holmes & Meier, 1983. A rhapsodic form of literary analysis proposing that ecstasy has been a vital essence in the work of major authors since ancient times.

Barnstone, Willis, trans. *The Poems of St. John of the Cross.* New Directions, 1972. One of the most fiery translations we have of the great ecstatic saint.

Basham, A. L. *The Wonder That Was India.* Grove Press, 1959. Widely acclaimed as the finest introduction to the development of Indian culture from its Indus Valley origins to about 1000 C.E.

Bateson, Gregory. *Mind and Nature.* Dutton, 1979. This is an outstanding introduction to Gregory Bateson, the pioneering anthropologist and social theorist. In this book, Bateson explores the mind-body relationship, artificial intelligence, evolutionary biology, epistemology, philosophy, logic, and cognitive science.

Becker, Ernest. *The Denial of Death.* The Free Press, 1973. A Pulitzer Prize-winning exploration of the psychological grip of death in our lives, and its role in stimulating art, creativity, and heroism.

Bible, authorized King James Version. In many editions. This version of the Bible is one of the greatest translations ever written, in any culture, at any time, of any scripture.

Black Elk. *Black Elk Speaks.* As told to John Neihardt. Washington Square Press, 1959. Originally published in the early 1930s, this is generally regarded as one of best books about American Indian spirituality.

Blake, William. *The Poetry and Prose of William Blake.* Edited by D. V Erdman. Commentary by Harold Bloom. Doubleday, 1970. Blake is one of the world's great visionary artist-poets. His vision resonates today for those of us seeking to transcend what he called 'Newton's sleep,' a life of strict materialism, habitual perception, and mechanistic thought.

Buber, Martin. *I and Thou.* Charles Scribner's Sons, 1958. Written by the best-known teacher of Hasidism in the twentieth century, Buber here explores the nature of 'I-Thou' relationships, in which people meet one another at a level beyond ordinary needs, desires, and mechanical responses, regarding one another for their unique and inimitable nature and for their intrinsic and eternal worth.

—— *The Way of Man*. Citadel Press, 1966. By the eminent author of *I and Thou*, this book explores the nature and purpose of life and our relationship with God, and incorporates the teachings of many Jewish spiritual masters.

Burckhardt, Jacob. *The Civilization of the Renaissance in Italy*. Translated by Torchbook, 1958. For decades this has been considered a definitive work on the Renaissance. The Swiss historian Burckhardt's essential idea was that the city-states of Italy had transcended the former feudal conditions of Europe and created the unique atmosphere in which individualism and the Renaissance flourished.

Burckhardt, Titus. *Alchemy*. Translated by William Stoddart. Fons Vitae, 1997 (revised edition). An artful and deeply learned summary of the symbolism and major strands of Western esoteric thought that fall under the name 'alchemy.' The teachings of alchemy, as brilliantly illustrated in Burckhardt's classic, were a kind of code in which much of the West's transformative thought was preserved.

Burr, A. H. *The World's Rim: Great Mysteries of the North American Indians*. University of Nebraska Press, 1953. A highly regarded introduction to the spiritual sensibilities of Native-American peoples.

Butler's Lives of the Saints. Complete Edition (in four volumes), edited, revised, and supplemented by Herbert Thurston, S. J. and Donald Attwater. Christian Classics, 1956. This monumental work was originally assembled and published in several volumes between 1756 and 1759. Thurston, who edited this updated version of the work, was a Jesuit scholar and the leading Roman Catholic authority of the twentieth century on the paranormal phenomena of Christian sanctity.

Cahill, Thomas. *How the Irish Saved Civilization*. Doubleday, 1996. An innovative look at early European history, showing how Irish monks painstakingly copied classical Roman and Greek texts, then carried them to monasteries on the continent, thereby keeping the knowledge intact until the scholars of Renaissance Italy rediscovered them.

Campbell, Joseph. *The Hero with a Thousand Faces.* 2nd ed. Princeton University Press, 1968. This is one of mythologist Joseph Campbell's best-known books and has influenced filmmakers, artists, sculptors, dancers, poets, and general readers alike. In it, Campbell proposes that there exists a 'monomyth,' literally 'one story,' at the heart of the worldwide quest for self-knowledge.

—— *The Masks of God, Volume I: Primitive Mythology.* Viking, 1959. An exploration of myths from our prehistoric past and the mental environments of our earliest hunting and planting ancestors.

—— ed. *The Mysteries: Papers from the Eranos Yearbooks.* Bollingen Series. Princeton University Press, 1955. A collection of essays by leading historians of religion and mythology surveying the mystery cults of ancient India, Greece, Iran, and the Middle East.

Campbell, Joseph and Bill Moyers. *The Power of Myth.* Anchor, 1988. With wit and wisdom, this extraordinary conversation explores how myths help us understand ourselves and our world through stories ranging from 'modern marriage to virgin births, from Jesus to John Lennon.'

Capra, Fritjof. *The Tao of Physics: An Exploration of the Parallels Between Modern Physics and Eastern Mysticism.* Shambhala, 2000. This essay examines the meeting of East and West, the parallels between modern physics and Eastern philosophy, and the insights that emerge from this meeting.

Cassian, John. *Dialogues.* In *Cassian: Library of Nicene and Post-Nicene Fathers.* Cassian's record of conversations during his seven-year pilgrimage among Christian monks in the Egyptian desert. This work influenced St. Benedict (d. 47), whose Rule influences monastic constitutions to this day, and St. Gregory the Great (540–604), whose writings were an important influence on later Christian contemplatives.

Cellini, Benvenuto. *The Autobiography of Benvenuto Cellini.* Translated by J. A. Symonds. Modern Library, 1985. This work is to autobiography what Montaigne's *Essays* are to the essay form: the revelation of a recognizable personality that could be walking our streets today. It is a defining work of the Italian Renaissance. In his bold affirmation of self, Cellini, a famous artisan, reflects the liberating and sometimes amoral spirit of the Renaissance in its turn away from the pieties of medieval Europe.

Cicero, Marcus Tullius. *The Basic Works of Cicero*. Edited by M. Hadas. Modern Library, 1951; and *De Republica (On the Commonwealth)*. Translated by George H. Sabine and Stanley B. Smith. Macmillan, 1976. Given credit for transforming Latin from a utilitarian language into a rhetorical one fit for statesmen, Cicero was one of the most convincing orators in history and these works help show why.

Cleary, Thomas. *Awakening to the Tao*. Shambhala, 1990. An erudite but accessible introduction to the genius of the Taoist traditions by a an excellent translator of Eastern spiritual texts.

Cleary, Thomas, trans. *The Essential Confucius*. HarperCollins, 1992. This introduction to the core teachings of the great Chinese sage, philosopher, educator, and social critic provides solid philosophical and historical background as well as aphorisms and commentaries by Confucius on a wide variety of subjects.

—— *The Essential Koran*. HarperCollins, 1993. This is an accessible, annotated translation of the Koran's spiritual wisdom. Designed for non-Muslim Westerners, Cleary's selections and translation reveal the central ideas, beauty, and power of Islamic spirituality.

Coleridge, Samuel Taylor. *The Complete Poems*. Penguin Classics, 1997. Coleridge joined a soaring metaphysical imagination and mystical insight in much of his literary work. This is a complete edition of his often magnificent poetry.

Conze, Edward. *Buddhism: Its Essence and Development*. Philosophical Library, 1951. A solid introduction to Buddhist thought and practice by a great Western scholar of Buddhism.

Copernicus, Nicolaus. *On the Revolutions of the Heavenly Spheres*. Translated by C. G. Wallis. In Great Books of the Western World, Vol. 16. Encyclopaedia Britannica, 1952. In this, one of humankind's most revolutionary books, the Polish astronomer overwhelmed the thousand-year-old Ptolemaic view of the Earth-centered universe. With the proposals he advanced here that the Earth revolved around the sun, Copernicus helped set the stage for modern science by challenging ancient astronomers and theologians alike.

Corbin, Henri. *Creative Imagination in the Sufism of Ibn Arabi.* Translated by Ralph Manheim. Bollingen Series 41. Princeton University Press, 1969. Ibn Arabi, the great Islamic mystic-metaphysician, joined direct spiritual experience with a luminous and imaginative metaphysics. In this book, Henri Corbin, one of the leading religious scholars of the twentieth century, helps the reader understand Ibn Arabi's vision by comparing Islamic mysticism to other forms of Western spiritual experience with scholarly rigor and authentic spiritual insight.

—— *The Man of Light in Iranian Sufism.* Shambhala, 1978. Here Corbin describes the 'polishing' of perceptual ability by which a Sufi adept can see auras and other spiritual energies. In the texts Corbin cites, it is clear that such ability has been acknowledged in the Sufi tradition for many centuries.

Cousineau, Phil, edited with an introduction. *Soul: An Archaeology: Readings from Socrates to Ray Charles.* HarperSanFrancisco, 1995. A sweeping view of the concept and imagery of soul from Egyptian gnosticism and classical Greek philosophers to artists such as Wassily Kandinsky and musicians such as Ray Charles.

Crossan, John Dominic. *The Historical Jesus: The Life of a Mediterranean Jewish Peasant.* HarperSanFrancisco, 1992; and *Jesus: A Revolutionary Biography.* HarperSanFrancisco, 1994. Crossan is a man of great learning and wit. These contemporary scholarly studies of Jesus are provocative, controversial, and engrossing. The first book is lengthy; the second is a shorter and more popular version of it.

Dante. *The Divine Comedy.* Translated by C. S. Singleton. 3 vols. Princeton University Press, 1973–75. One of the greatest works of genius in all the world's literature as well as one of humankind's most sweeping and trenchant pictures of the transcendent realms.

Descartes, Rene. *The Philosophical Works of Descartes.* Translated by E. S. Haldane and G. R. T. Ross. 2 vols. Dover, 1955.

Required reading for those who are interested in exploring the basis for modern rationalism in the work of the great French philosopher.

Deussen, Paul. *The Philosophy of the Upanishads*. T. and T. Clark, 1906; and Dover, 1966. A classic written at the turn of the century and in some respects never bettered. This is a comprehensive, well-documented, and highly engaging study that brings alive the thought-world of the Upanishads.

Dickinson, Emily. *The Complete Poems of Emily Dickinson*. Edited by Thomas H. Johnson. Little, Brown, 1967. Dickinson's vision and verse are in the tradition of American Transcendentalists from Jonathan Edwards to Ralph Waldo Emerson. Her poems radiate the presence of genius, soul, and spirit.

Dodds, E. R. *The Ancient Concept of Progress*. Clarendon Press, 1973. A discussion of ideas about progress in Greek and Roman times by a great British classicist.

Doyle, Brendan, ed. *Meditations with Julian of Norwich*. Bear & Company, 1983. A moving translation of the celebrated fourteenth-century English mystic.

Durkheim, Emile. *Elementary Forms of the Religious Life*. University of Chicago Press, 1947. This is a classic work by one of the founders of the sociology of religion. In it, Durkheim gives a theoretical account of totemism among Australian aboriginal peoples as a basis for his major thesis that religion is an outgrowth of the human need for social order and cohesion.

Eckhart, Meister. *The Essential Sermons, Commentaries, Treatises, and Defense*. Translated with an introduction by E. Colledge and B. McGinn. Paulist Press, 1981. Widely considered to be one of Christianity's greatest mystics, Eckhart deeply influenced philosophers such as Hegel, Fichte, and Heidegger. In Eckhart's mystical experience and metaphysics (which celebrates the essential unity of the soul with God), we find strong correspondences with Eastern philosophy and spiritual practice.

Edgerton, Franklin, trans. *Bhagavad-Gita*. Harper Torchbook, 1964. Unsurpassed if one is looking for literal translation with syllable by syllable accuracy, this translation of

India's great scripture is accompanied by a ninety-page contextual and interpretive essay of great authority, clarity, and power. The Bhagavad Gita is one of humankind's supreme works of spiritual insight.

Einstein, Albert. *The World as I See It.* Translated by Alan Harris. The Wisdom Library, 1979. A series of sometimes surprising reflections on spiritual matters – and life in general – by the great scientist.

Eliade, Mircea. *Shamanism, Archaic Techniques of Ecstasy.* Translated by Willard R. Trask. Bollingen Series 76. Princeton University Press, 1964. A landmark study of shamanism among Stone-Age cultures around the world. Eliade, who defines the shaman as a 'specialist in techniques of ecstasy,' provides a thorough, though unannotated, bibliography.

Eliot, T. S. *Complete Poems and Plays.* Harcourt, Brace & World, 1971. The American-born Eliot captured like few others the spiritual hollowness and purposelessness of modern life. Yet this caustic vision is balanced by one of the great spiritual poems of the twentieth century, *Four Quartets.*

Emerson, Ralph Waldo. *The Best of Ralph Waldo Emerson.* Walter J. Black, Inc., 1969. Variously called the 'Hindu-Yankee' and 'a Plotinus Montaigne,' Emerson was deeply influenced by Schelling's Idealism and India's great scripture the Bhagavad Gita. With Henry David Thoreau, he is America's most famous Transcendentalist philosopher, known worldwide for this belief in self-reliance and the 'oversoul.'

Epictetus. *The Art of Living: The Classic Manual on Virtue, Happiness, and Effectiveness.* A New Interpretation by Sharon Lebell. HarperSanFrancisco, 1998. This unpretentious yet timeless book by the great Stoic philosopher (who was also a slave for many years) has recently been given a graceful new life by editor Sharon Lebell, who celebrates virtue, inner freedom, and practical wisdom at once.

Evans-Wentz, W. Y. *Tibet's Great Yogi Milarepa.* Oxford University Press, 1928, 1969. Milarepa is revered by Tibetans as one of their greatest mystic-poets and spiritual adepts. This biography translated from the Tibetan was edited and annotated by the American religious scholar Evans-Wentz.

Fadiman, James and Robert Frager, eds. *Essential Sufism.* HarperCollins, 1997. This readable introduction to Islamic mysticism contains more than three hundred fables, poems, and prayers from Sufi prophets, poets, teachers, and sages both ancient and modern.

Ficino, Marsilio. *Letters.* 3 vols. Shepheard-Walwyn, 1975. The great Platonist philosopher, mentor, and translator of Renaissance Florence was also a marvelous letter writer. This collection reveals his mystical insight, soaring imagination, creative metaphysics, and great capacity for friendship. Like Plotinus, Ibn-Arabi, and other realized mystics who were also gifted thinkers, Ficino points the way toward a revelatory metaphysics for our time.

—— *The Book of Life.* Translated by Charles Boer. Spring Publications, 1980. This was one of the most important and secretly influential books of the Italian Renaissance, offering soul-centered advice on food, depression, astrology, health, and longevity.

Frazer, Sir James. *The Golden Bough: A Study in Comparative Religion.* 12 vols. Macmillan, 1911–15. An enormously influential work on 'primitive' religion and magic written at the turn of the century. It is also available in an abridged version edited by Theodore Gaster.

French, R. M., trans. *The Way of a Pilgrim.* HarperSanFrancisco, 1991. Thought to be the record of the inner life of a simple nineteenth-century Russian layman who takes up the practice of the Prayer of the Heart, this is a moving and beautiful glimpse into the depth of one Christian life.

Freud, Sigmund. *The Standard Complete Works of Sigmund Freud.* Edited by J. Strachey. 21 vols. Hogarth, 1955–61. Freud is one of the great revolutionaries of modern life. Nearly every field of knowledge has come under his influence, from psychology and anthropology to art, religion, education, history, and biography. Though his overemphasis on the importance of childhood trauma and sexuality is widely acknowledged, his discoveries about the human unconscious, psychological defense mechanisms, and the healing possibilities of psychotherapy and self-inquiry are now essential – and indispensable – for knowledge regarding the human potential.

Galilei, Galileo. *Dialogue Concerning the Two Chief World Systems Ptolemaic and Copernican.* Translated by S. Drake. University of California Press, 1989. The great Italian astronomer and physicist went far beyond publishing his discovery of Jupiter's moons, sun spots, and newly visible stars. In a bold but dangerous defense of Copernicus, he published the infamous *Dialogue* and paid for its publication by being sentenced by the Inquistion to house arrest during the last years of his life. Galileo, as much as anyone else, was a principal founder of modern science.

Gibbon, Edward. *The Decline and Fall of the Roman Empire.* 3 vols. Modern Library, 1977. In this, one of humankind's great works of history, British historian Edward Gibbon traced the Roman empire's glories and decline from its earliest days into the Middle Ages.

Ginzberg, L. *Legends of the Bible.* Jewish Publication Society of America, 1956. This is a brilliant one-volume abridged version of the author's monumental seven-volume study of what Jewish imagination has done with its biblical heritage.

Goethe, Johann Wolfgang von. *Faust.* Translated by Alice Raphael. The Heritage Press, 1930. One of the world's greatest and most influential literary works, *Faust* has entered the modern imagination as an allegorical tale about the selling of one's soul to the devil for the gift of knowledge.

Govinda, Lama. *The Way of the White Clouds: A Buddhist Pilgrim in Tibet.* Shambhala, 1970. Written by a famous convert to Buddhism, this account of spiritually adventurous travels in Tibet and India is by turns wondrous, strange, and informative. Govinda, born German, first took his Buddhist robes in the Southern (Theraveda) school but later found his home in the Tibetan tradition.

Green, Elmer and Alyce Green. *Beyond Biofeedback.* Knoll Publishing, 1977. In this pioneering investigation of biofeedback, the Greens present their own research and its broader implications, examining self-regulation in creativity, meditation, healing, and the powers of psychics, healers, and mystics.

Griffiths, Bede. *Universal Wisdom: A Journey Through the Sacred Wisdom of the World.* HarperSanFrancisco, 1994. A superb large anthology of sacred scriptures, with a thirty-page general introduction and shorter section introductions, by a Catholic monk who spent much of his life in India and was deeply influenced by its spiritual traditions.

Gurdjieff, G. I. *Meetings with Remarkable Men.* Penguin Arkana, 1999. A picaresque glimpse of the mystic Gurdjieff's life and teachers. Gurdjieff's 'fourth way,' or path to enlightenment in everyday life, has attracted more and more followers in recent decades in Europe and the Americas.

—— *All and Everything: Beelzebub's Tales to His Grandson.* Penguin Arkana, 1999. Gurdjieff's magnum opus contains a wealth of esoteric knowledge, a rascal's humor, great compassion for our human condition, and descriptions of an extraordinary path toward spiritual awakening.

Guthrie, W. K. C. *The Greek Philosophers: From Thales to Aristotle.* Harper Torchbook, 1960. Guthrie was a great and prolific English scholar of Greek philosophy. For those interested in the roots of the thinking that led to the Athenian explosion of Socrates, Plato, Aristotle, the Stoics, and Epicureans, this is a good place to start.

Hafiz. *The Gift.* Translations by Daniel Ladinsky. Penguin Arkana, 1999. A celebratory work that brims with the Sufi mystic-poet's exuberance and joy.

Hanh, Thich Nhat. *The Heart of the Buddha's Teaching: Transforming Suffering into Peace, Joy & Liberation.* Broadway, 1999. A simple, poetic introduction to the core teachings of Buddhism, including the Four Noble Truths, the Noble Eightfold Path, and various sutras. The famous Buddhist monk assembles stories from classic Buddhist literature and contemporary anecdotes, offering commentaries on their essential meaning.

Harner, Michael. *The Way of the Shaman.* HarperCollins, 1990. Anthropologist Michael Harrier, who studied under South-American sorcerers, is both a scholar and practitioner-advocate of shamanism. This is an excellent short introduction to the guiding ideas and practices of shamanism by a man who has embraced it as a living tradition.

Harvey, Andrew, ed. *The Essential Mystics: The Soul's journey into Truth.* HarperSanFrancisco, 1996. This collection includes testimonies to the mystic's relationship with the divine from all major world traditions. Included are teachings from Native-American, Australian, and African visionaries as well as from Taoist, Buddhist, Jewish, Christian, Hindu, Islamic, and ancient Greek sources. All of these echo the same longing of the soul to merge with the divine – and a simultaneous need to be fully engaged in the world to effect such union. This book is an easy read and offers practical insights to numerous mystical traditions.

Heinberg, Richard. *Memories and Visions of Paradise: Exploring the Universal Myth of a Lost Golden Age.* Quest, 1995. In this overview of humankind's legends and dreams of a lost Golden Age, the author distinguishes simple nostalgia for an imagined past from the enduring human urge to find or create a better way of life.

Heschel, Abraham. *God in Search of Man.* Jewish Publication Society, 1956. Jacob Neusner, a twentieth-century giant of Jewish scholarship, has said that this book is 'an account of classical Judaic theology written with love and immense learning, the single best introduction to the intellectual heritage of Judaism.'

Hick, John. *An Interpretation of Religion.* Yale University Press, 1989. The author is one of the greatest contemporary philosophers of religion. A Christian, he studied the world's other religious traditions with both sympathy and erudition. This book is his magnum opus, a brilliant exposition of his belief that religion is a culturally varied respond to an actual, many-named Transcendent reality.

—— *Death and Eternal Life.* Harper & Row, 1976. Nowhere do religions seem more in conflict than in their doctrines of postmortem survival. Hick enters this morass and with consummate scholarship produces a new theory of humankind's afterlife destiny. Whether or not you agree with Hick's ultimate conclusion, this book overflows with insight and imaginative speculation.

Hildegard of Bingen. *Hildegard of Bingen: Mystical Writings.* Edited and translated by F. Bowie and O. Davies. Crossroad, 1992. This twelfth-century Benedictine abbess, musical composer, poet, painter, theologian, healer, biographer, playwright, and mystic is increasingly influential among religious seekers today.

Hillman, James. *Re-visioning Psychology.* Harper & Row, 1975. By 're-visioning psychology,' psychologist James Hillman means rediscovering the soul and bringing it back to its primary place in life, as well as turning from a focus in psychotherapy on pathology to an emphasis on creativity and imagination.

Hixon, Lex. *Coming Home: The Experience of Enlightenment in Sacred Traditions.* Anchor, 1978. In this beautifully written book, religious scholar Les Hixon explores the enlightenment experiences of central figures in Tantric Hinduism, Zen, Christianity, Judaism, Sufism, and Taoism.

—— *Great Swan: Meetings with Ramakrishna.* Shambhala, 1992. This beautiful introduction to the luminous mind and spirit of the great Bengali mystic Sri Ramakrishna (1836–86) offers practical instruction, spiritual inspiration, and a vivid picture of Ramakrishna's ecstasies and magnetic presence.

Homer. *The Iliad.* Translated by Robert Fitzgerald. Doubleday, 1974; and *The Odyssey.* Translated by Robert Fitzgerald. Doubleday, 1961. These two epic poems are permanent parts of the Western world's cultural foundation. They are inexhaustible sources of history, psychology, and art, reminding every generation of great literature's timeless beauty and power.

Huddleston, Roger, ed. *Little Flowers of St. Francis.* Templegate, 1988. A collection of legendary accounts of St. Francis. An uplifting glimpse at possibly the most universally loved of Christian saints, including the fables, legends, and folk tales that gathered around Francis like birds on his shoulders.

Hume, R. E., trans. *The Thirteen Principal Upanishads.* Oxford University Press, rev. ed., 1931. One of the most comprehensive, scholarly, and useful Upanishad translations into

English, with an excellent introductory essay and explanatory notes.

Huxley, Aldous. *The Doors of Perception.* Harper & Row, 1970. Inspired by William Blake's famous epigram, 'When the doors of perception are cleansed, every thing would appear to man as it is, infinite,' Huxley's essay explores the spiritual dimensions of both normal and supernormal perception.

—— *The Perennial Philosophy.* Harper & Row, 1944. An essay on the spiritual unity within the deep structure of all religions. It contains a thematic compilation of quotations from various traditions with Huxley's superb commentaries.

Isherwood, Christopher. *Ramakrishna and His Disciples.* Simon & Schuster, 1959. An excellent introduction to the life and work of one of the world's greatest mystics by an eminent essayist and novelist.

James, William. *The Varieties of Religious Experience.* Penguin Classics, 1982. A much-quoted and influential classic in the psychology of religion by the eloquent philosopher and father of American psychology, with essays on mysticism, conversion experience, and pathologies of the religious life.

Jung, C. G. *Memories, Dreams, Reflections.* Translated by Richard and Clara Winston. Random House, 1961. This colorful and memorable autobiography, told to Aniela Jaffé, is remarkable for its disclosures of Jung's inner world, including a tantalizing collection of dreams, premonitions, synchronicities, alchemical investigations, and strange details of his midlife soul crisis.

—— *Synchronicity: An Acausal Connecting Principle.* Translated by Series 8. Princeton University Press, 1973. The first and still definitive book on what Jung described as 'meaningful coincidences.' Often difficult reading because originally intended for the scientific community, it is balanced by a series of fascinating examples of precognition, clairvoyance, and telepathy that Jung believed were only understandable through the notion of synchronicity.

Khan, Inayat and H. J. Witteveen, ed. *The Heart of Sufism: Essential Writings of Hazrat Inayat Khan.* Shambhala, 1999.

Hazrat Inayat Khan brought Sufism to the West and founded a Sufi Order in 1910. Witteveen, executive supervisor of the International Sufi Movement, distills the core of Khan's spirituality from the Sufi master's sixteen-volume collected works. Included in this collection are Khan's teachings on the great Sufi poet, Rumi. Khan writes: 'It is not by self-realization that man realizes God; it is by God-realization that man realizes self.'

Kahn, Pir Vilayat. *Awakening: A Sufi Initiation*. Tarcher/Putnam, 1999. Sufi master Pir Vilayat Khan, the son of Hazrat Inayat Khan, guides the reader beyond the self through meditative practices, visualization, whirling, and *dhikr*, the traditional Sufi ritual for inviting the Divine Presence into the heart. *Awakening* is Pir Vilayat's most accessible work on the principals of Sufism and self-transformation.

Kandinsky, Wassily. *Concerning the Spiritual in Art*. Dover, 1977. The great painter Kandinsky describes the artist's role as one in which he or she divines the inner life of all things. In language reminiscent of Eastern yogic descriptions of the kundalini, Kandinsky claims that the function of art is to 'raise the spiritual triangle.'

Kant, Immanuel. *Critique of Pure Reason*. Translated by N. K. Smith. Macmillan, 1968. One of the milestone books of Western philosophy, in which the great German philosopher argued that we cannot directly know *the ding an sich*, the 'thing in itself,' because our knowledge is shaped by intrinsic mental categories through which we apprehend the world at large.

Kapleau, Philip. *The Three Pillars of Zen*. Boston: Beacon Press, 1967. A lively description of how Zen is practiced in modern Japan, with lectures by Zen masters, interviews with Zen students, letters, and testimonials.

Kavanaugh and O. Rodriquez. *The Collected Works of St. John of the Cross*. ICS Publications, 1973. St. John of Cross, with St. Teresa of Avila, helped reform the Carmelite order in Spain and is generally considered to be one of Christianity's greatest mystics. His collected works comprise one of humankind's greatest accounts of the contemplative life.

Kempis, Thomas. *The Imitation of Christ*. Translated by C. F. Atkinson. Thomas Nelson and Sons, 1988. A classic

271

spiritual guide and source of inspiration for over five centuries to Christians and non-Christians alike.

Kerenyi, Carl. *Eleusis: Archetypal Image of Mother and Daughter.* Translated by Ralph Manheim. Bollingen Series 55. Princeton University Press, 1967. A study of the ancient mystery cult and its implications for modern psychology.

Knitter, Paul. *No Other Name? A Critical Survey of Christian Attitudes Toward World Religions.* Orbis, 1985. For the Christian who wishes to learn about theories of religious unity and the history of Christian attitudes toward other religions, there is no better book than this. Its author, a Christian, argues the need for a new global theology in which Christianity cannot claim a privileged position.

Kripal, Jeffrey. *Kali's Child: The Mystical and the Erotic in the Life and Teachings of Sri Ramakrishna.* Second edition. University of Chicago Press, 1998. A groundbreaking study of Sri Ramakrishna in which Professor of Religion Jeffrey Kripal explores the homoerotic dimensions of the great Indian mystic's life and works.

Kuhn, Thomas S. *The Structure of the Scientific Revolution.* Second edition. University of Chicago Press, 1970. A classic critique of scientific method and its practice, pedagogy, and established customs, in which Kuhn introduced the term 'paradigm shift' to describe watershed transitions in scientific theory.

Lao-Tzu. *Tao To Ching: A New English Version.* Translated by Stephen Mitchell. HarperCollins, 1992. A beautiful translation by author and poet Mitchell of Lao Tzu's classic manual on the art of living.

—— *Tao Te Ching: The Definitive Edition.* Translated by Jonathan Star. Tarcher/ Putnam, 2001. Star's edition provides the first comprehensive verbatim translation of each character in the *Tao Te Ching,* giving Western readers a unique tool to plumb the text for its deepest meanings.

Le Mee, Jean, trans. *Hymns of the Rig Veda.* Knopf, 1975. Thoughtfully selected and well translated, this survey presents portions of the Rig Veda in a visually aesthetic format. Beautiful photographs on every page add to the richness of the book.

Leonardo da Vinci. *Leonardo da Vinci.* Edited by G. Nicodemi et al. Reynal. William Morrow, 1956. No investigation of the Renaissance is complete without at least a glance at the collected writings, art, and scientific sketches of da Vinci. Leonardo, as much as anyone, defined the 'renaissance man.' He was a painter, sculptor, architect, engineer, scientist, poet, musician, inventor, and experimenter without peer.

Lin Yutang. *The Wisdom of Confucius.* Modern Library, 1938. An engaging introduction to the great sage with commentaries by a famous expositor of Chinese philosophy. The book includes representative portions from most of the key Confucian texts.

Luther, Martin. *Basic Theological Writings.* Edited by T. F. Lull. Fortress Press, 1989. Luther's 'protesting' of abuses by the Church during the sixteenth century was a central cause of the Protestant reformation. This collection provides an overview of Luther's faith and belief.

Mann, W. Edward, and Edward Hoffman. *Wilhelm Reich: The Man Who Dreamed of Tomorrow.* Tarcher/Putnam, 1980. A biography of the pioneering Austrian psychoanalyst who described the role of 'body armor' (largely unconscious muscular tension) in human personality, the destructive effects of authoritarian social and political regimes, and the release of vital energies through psychotherapy, self-inquiry, and somatic disciplines.

Mascaró, Juan, trans. *The Bhagavad Gita.* Penguin Classics, 1965. A rendition of the classic treatise on the numinous dialogue between Krishna and Arjuna on the nature of good and evil, love and war, Atman and Brahman.

—— *The Dhammapada: The Path of Perfection.* Penguin Classics, 1974. A memorable version of the classic Buddhist wisdom book.

—— *Upanishads.* Penguin Classics, 1965. Less exacting and authoritative than Hume's translation, but in its own special way an effective rendering of seven Upanishads and parts of five others. The introductory essay relates upanishadic thought to other mystical literature.

Maslow, Abraham. *Toward a Psychology of Being.* D. Van Nostrand Company, 1968. This is one of humanistic and transpersonal psychology's foundational texts.

273

—— *The Farther Reaches of Human Nature.* Viking, 1971. A seminal work exploring our highest potentials by one of the founders of humanistic and transpersonal psychology.

Merton, Thomas. *Contemplative Prayer.* Image, 1971. This little gem of a book, newly issued with a foreword from the Vietnamese Zen teacher Thich Nhat Hanh (who knew Merton in the 1960s) distills Merton's own reading and long experience with contemplative prayer. The book draws on St. John of the Cross, Eastern desert monasticism, and other great exemplars of Christian mysticism.

.—— *The Seven Story Mountain.* Harvest Books, 1999. Thomas Merton's first book describes his early doubts, his conversion to a Catholic faith of extreme certainty, and his decision to take life vows as a Trappist. It has been one of the most influential works of twentieth century Christian contemplative life.

Meyer, Marvin W., ed. *The Ancient Mysteries: A Sourcebook of Sacred Texts of the Mystery Religions of the Ancient Mediterranean World.* HarperSanFrancisco, 1987. A collection of sacred texts that dramatizes the power of ritual, ceremony, and holy space to trigger transformational experience.

Milton, John. *Paradise Lost.* Penguin Classics, 2000. In this epic poem, perhaps the greatest in the English language, Milton describes Man's creation, fall, and redemption. Read in the light of spiritual awakenings such as those described in this book, it reveals layer after layer of new meaning and beauty.

Mitchell, Stephen. *The Gospel According to Jesus: A New Translation and Guide to His Essential Teachings for Believers and Unbelievers.* HarperCollins, 1991. Mitchell presents the life and teachings of Jesus in a new translation of what might be called the Essential Gospel. Eliminating passages added by the early church, Mitchell has drawn from Matthew, Mark, Luke, and John with his own discerning and insightful commentary.

Montaigne, Michel de. *The Selected Essays of Montaigne.* Edited and with an introduction by Lester G. Crocker. Pocket Library, 1959. Montaigne is generally credited with the invention of the essay form as we know it today, and his essays have been constantly in print since they were first published in 1580. Significantly, Montaigne chose the word *essais*, which in French means trials, attempts, or probings, in reference to his basic purpose, which was to know himself and the world with greater clarity and depth.

Needleman, Jacob. *The Heart of Philosophy: An Introduction to Philosophy with the Magic Left In.* HarperSanFrancisco, 1982. With genuine warmth and a scholar's depth, Needleman explores the most vital and relevant teachings of the world's great philosophers, showing us that philosophy is an invaluable tool for modern personal transformation.

Newton, Sir Isaac. *Principia Mathematica.* One of the most influential books in history, in which the great physicist presents his historic discoveries about gravity and the laws of motion.

Nicholson, R. *Studies in Islamic Mysticism.* Cambridge University Press, 1967 reprint of 1921 edition; *The Idea of Personality in Sufism.* Cambridge University of Press, 1923; and *The Mystics of Islam.* G. Bell & Sons, 1914. Nicholson's celebrated erudition and the literary quality of his scholarship still make these important and helpful works. Some students of Islam feel that the latter work in combination with Arberry's *Sufism* comprise the best introduction to the field.

Novak, Philip. *The World's Wisdom.* HarperSanFrancisco, 1994. A clearly written and elegantly selected anthology of passages from the sacred scriptures.

Otto, Rudolf. *The Idea of the Holy.* Translated by John W. Harvey. Oxford University Press, 1923. An influential study of the numinous dimensions of religious experience by the eminent German religious scholar.

Ouspensky, P. D. *In Search of the Miraculous.* Harcourt, Brace, Jovanovitch, 1949, 1977. Ouspensky begins the book with an account of his first meeting with Gurdjieff in a Moscow lecture hall in 1915 and from there proceeds to a colorful account of what he learned from Gurdjieff over the next eight years. Ouspensky's orderly mind, philosophical acumen, and profound sense of spiritual adventure make this a good book with which to begin an investigation of Gurdjieff's teachings.

—— *The Fourth Way*. Vintage, 1957, 1971. A collection of verbatim extracts from Ouspensky's talks, with his answers to students' questions, between 1921 and 1946.

—— *The Psychology of Man's Possible Evolution*. Vintage, 1950. This serves as an introduction to the teaching of the great master G. I. Gurdjieff and is a primer to Gurdjieff's psychological ideas on consciousness and spiritual development.

Ovid. *Metamorphosis*. Edited by E. J. Kenney. Oxford University Press, 1986. This poem has been honored for centuries as a foremost source of information about Greek antiquity, as well as for its psychological insight into the constant 'metamorphoses' of human nature.

Pagels, Elaine. *The Gnostic Gospels*. Vintage, 1981. Emerging from the discovery in 1945 of Gnostic Christian texts at Nag Hammadi in Egypt, this accessible book on gnosticism presents self-knowledge as the route to union with God and shows that Christianity might have developed differently if gnostic texts had become part of the Christian canon.

Pannikar, Raimundo. *The Vedic Experience: Mantramanjari*. University of California Press, 1977. A rich introduction to Vedic thought, superbly selected, translated, introduced, and analyzed, that gives the reader a vivid sense of the Vedic mind.

Paracelsus. *Paracelsus: Essential Readings*. Translated by Nicholas Goodrick-Clarke. Crucible, 1990. Paracelsus, a celebrated physician who was steeped in the astrology, mysticism, and occultism of the Renaissance, reflected the cultural transition in Europe from the age of faith to the Enlightenment.

Patanjali. *Yoga Sutras*. Translated by I. K. Taimni as *The Science of Yoga*. Theosophical Publishing House, 1967. One of the finest translations of India's foremost yoga text, with an accessible and useful commentary. There is perhaps no better way into Patanjali's sutras for English readers than through this book.

Plato. *The Collected Dialogues of Plato.* Edited by E. Hamilton and H. Cairns. Bollingen Series 71. Princeton University Press, 1963. All Plato's Dialogues and letters, expertly translated, in a single volume.

—— *The Phaedo: The Trial and Death of Socrates.* Translated by Benjamin Jowett. Oxford University Press, 1963. Plato's account of Socrates's last hours, with an inspiring dialogue between the philosopher and his friends on the immortality of the soul.

—— *Symposium.* Translated by A. Nehamas and P. Woodruff. Hackett Publishing, 1989; translated by Benjamin Jowett. Oxford University Press, 1928. One of the most beloved of Plato's dialogues, the *Symposium* is an exploration of the nature of love that climaxes in two speeches: one by Socrates, who describes the transformative journey of love as an ascent to Beauty, and one by Alcibiades, in praise of Socrates into which Plato pours his profound love for the man.

Plotinus. *The Enneads.* Translated by Stephen Mackenna. Larson Publications, 1992. Variously described as a 'bible of beauty' and the most precious book in the Western spiritual canon, this is, in Huston Smith's words, an 'exalting' translation of the third-century Greek philosopher's writings. Plotinus, one of the world's greatest mystic-metaphysicians, was the founder of Neoplatonism, which profoundly influenced subsequent pagan, Christian, Jewish, and Islamic mysticism.

Progoff, Ira, trans. *The Cloud of Unknowing.* Dell, 1957. Progoff's splendid introduction readies the reader for a glimpse into the mind of the anonymous spiritual classic, which espoused a condition of complete openness and 'unknowing' to find the living presence of God.

Radhakrishnan, S. *The Principle Upanishads.* Harper & Brothers, 1953. One of the twentieth century's best-known Indian philosophers here provides the complete Sanskrit texts of eighteen Upanishads, with excellent translations into English, an erudite historical and philosophical introduction, and explanatory notes.

Ramakrishna, Sri. *The Gospel of Sri Ramakrishna.* Translated by Swami Nikhilananda. Ramarishna-Vivekananda Center,

1977. A stunning record of conversations between Ramakrishna and his disciples and visitors between the years 1882 and 1886, recorded by his disciple 'M.'

Rousseau, Jean-Jacques. *Confessions.* Translated by J. M. Cohen. Penguin Classics, 1953. A historically central work by a father of the Enlightenment and French Romanticism.

Rumi, Jelaluddin. *The Essential Rumi.* Translations by Coleman Barks, with John Moyne. HarperSanFrancisco, 1995. These popular translations and renditions have helped make Rumi one of the most popular poets in the world today, seven centuries after his death.

Satprem. *Sri Aurobindo or the Adventure of Consciousness.* Harper & Row, 1968. A lively introduction to the extraordinary life, work, and philosophy of the great Indian mystic and philosopher Sri Aurobindo.

Schelling, Friedrich. *System of Transcendental Idealism.* University of Virginia Press, 1978. This is the book in which the great German philosopher introduced his 'evolutionary pantheism,' the doctrine that our evolving universe is an unfolding of 'slumbering spirit,' a passage from *dens implicitus*, the 'implicit divine,' to *dens explicitus*, God made fully manifest.

Schimmel, Anne-Marie. *Mystical Dimensions of Islam.* University of North Carolina Press, 1975. An extensive and authoritative historical survey of Islamic mysticism by a major contemporary scholar with a superb bibliography.

Scholem, Gershom. *Jewish Gnosticism, Merkabah Mysticism, and Talmudic Tradition.* Jewish Theological Seminary of America, 1965; and *Major Trends of Jewish Mysticism.* Schocken Books, 1961. Two classic overviews of Jewish mysticism by one of the field's greatest scholars.

Schuon, Frithjof. *Spiritual Perspectives and Human Facts.* Faber and Faber, 1954; *Light on Ancient Worlds.* Perennial Books, 1975; *Logic and Transcendence.* Harper & Row, 1975; and *Gnosis: Divine Wisdom.* Murray, 1961. The Swiss-born Sufi teacher and brilliant student of the world's mystical traditions does not so much argue or persuade as he asserts and proclaims. This style does not endear him to all readers, but few can deny that, for those readers convinced of a spiritual unity from which all religions emanate, Schuon's books are singularly powerful, beautiful, and compelling.

Shah, Idries. *The Tales of the Dervishes: Teaching – Stories of the Sufi Masters over the Past Thousand Years.* Dutton, 1970. Richly layered with multiple meanings and essential truths at their core, these exquisite and entertaining dervish tales should not be dismissed as mere fables, legends, or items of folklore. They are genuine teaching stories, presented in this book in ways that challenge common assumptions about everyday life and spiritual practice.

—— *The Sufis.* Anchor, 1971. First published in 1964, this book explores the spiritual and psychological tradition of Sufism. Shah traces its impact on the development of Western civilization from the seventh century and shows that many of the greatest traditions, ideas, and discoveries of the West can be traced to the teachings of Sufi masters working centuries ago. More than an historical account, this is a teaching book in the tradition of the great Sufi classics.

Shakespeare, William. *The Complete Works of Shakespeare.* The Cambridge Edition Text, edited by W. A. Wright. Doubleday, 1936. Acclaimed by literary critic Harold Bloom as the 'inventor of the human,' Shakespeare remains the greatest playwright who has written in English and one humankind's greatest psychologists.

Smith, Huston. *The World's Religions.* HarperSanFrancisco, 1991. In print for more than forty years, this book has introduced countless people to the major religions. Smith doesn't try to tell us everything about each religion, but he has a great gift for getting eloquently to the heart of each tradition. In the slim volume, *Forgotten Truth* (Harper and Row, 1976), Smith eloquently presents his understanding of the common deep structure of traditional religious worldviews, and offers a critique of both the power and the limitations of modern science as a mode of understanding the world.

—— *Why Religion Matters: The Fate of the Human Spirit in an Age of Disbelief.* HarperSanFrancisco, 2001. A passionate exploration of the need for spiritual life in what the author regards as a suffocating, spiritually illiterate, materialistic postmodern world increasingly narrowed by scientism.

Smith, Wilfred Cantwell. *The Meaning and End of Religion.* Fortress Press, 1991; *Faith and Belief.* Princeton University Press, 1979; and *Towards a World Theology.* Westminster Press, 1981. Great erudition and profound sympathy pervade every page of these reflections on the spiritual unity of humankind by one of the twentieth century's greatest scholars of comparative religion.

Sogyal Rinpoche. *The Tibetan Book of Living and Dying.* HarperSanFrancisco, 1992. Bringing ancient teachings to modern minds, Tibetan teacher Sogyal Rinpoche presents anecdotes and stories from religious traditions East and West. He introduces the reader to the fundamentals of Tibetan Buddhism, and then progresses to the subject of death and its power to touch the heart and awaken consciousness.

Suzuki, Daisetz. *Essays in Zen Buddhism.* Rider, 1949, 1950. A treasury of information and insights by the Japanese scholar who made Zen an English word.

Suzuki, Shunryu. *Zen Mind, Beginner's Mind.* Weatherhill, 1970. Luminous and practical Soto Zen sermons by the Zen master who founded the San Francisco Zen Center. This book is an excellent introduction to Zen Buddhist practice.

Tarnas, Richard. *The Passion of the Western Mind: Understanding the Ideas That Have Shaped Our World View.* Harmony, 1991. A grand survey of the history of Western thought in one volume incorporating a transpersonal point of view.

Teresa of Avila, Saint. Translated and edited by E. Allison Peers. *The Interior Castle.* Image, 1961. According to Harvard theologian Harvey Cox, '[This is] a capstone spiritual classic of Western Christianity by a woman who combined energetic activity in the world with profound inwardness. Unmatched for its subtle insights into the labyrinth of the soul.'

Thibaut, George, trans. *The Vedanta Sutras of Badarayana with the commentary by Shankara.* Dover, 1962.2 vols. Reprint of Sacred Books of the East, v. XXXIV and XXXVIII. *The Vedanta Sutras (a.k.a. Brahma Sutras)* are a compendium of terse aphorisms summarizing the teaching of the

Upanishads. The great Indian philosopher Shankara's commentary on them is the major work in which he develops his *advaita* (nondualist) position.

Tillich, Paul. *The Courage to Be.* Yale University Press, 1952. In this influential book, one of the world's most eminent theologians describes the dilemma of modern man and points a way to the conquest of the problem of anxiety. Working with metaphors of Christian faith, he argues that being, above all else, requires courage . . . the courage to resist the lure of appearance and open to the mystery, power, and fundamental enchantment of being.

Torrance, Robert M. *The Spiritual Quest: Transcendence in Myth, Religion and Science.* University of California Press, 1994. The author suggests that the spiritual quests in Stone-Age and developed traditions are different in nuance but not in essence, and that the spiritual quest itself has deep roots in human biology, psychology, and language. Fascinating, highly informed, thorough, and readable, with a comprehensive bibliography.

Underhill, Evelyn. *Mysticism: A Study in the Nature and Development of Man's Spiritual Consciousness.* Oneworld, 1993. Published nearly a century ago, this is among the most celebrated books on Christian mysticism and, according to many scholars and commentators, an original contribution to the world's spiritual literature.

Waley, Arthur. *The Analects of Confucius.* Macmillan, 1938. Now some sixty years old, this translation remains the favorite of many. Waley also provides an excellent introduction to Confucian practice and thought.

—— *The Way and Its Power.* George Allen and Unwin, 1934. An excellent introduction to philosophical Taoism.

Walsh, Roger. *The Spirit of Shamanism.* Tarcher/Putnam,1990. Shamanic practices are explored in light of their relevance to growth and healing and as tools for working with the world's ecological crises.

—— *Essential Spirituality: Seven Practices Common to the Great World's Religions.* Tarcher/Putnam, 1999. In simple language and with frequent anecdotes, this psychiatrist, philosopher, and student of the world's religions not only describes the seven practical aims he finds common to the world's wisdom traditions but also provides the reader with specific exercises for moving toward them. This is a self-help book with unusual depth.

Watts, Alan. *The Supreme Identity: An Essay on Oriental Metaphysic and the Christian Religion.* Vintage, 1972; and *Behold the Spirit: A Study in the Necessity of Mystical Religion.* Vintage, 1947, 1971. Watts was chiefly known as an interpreter of Zen Buddhism and Taoism to the West, but he was also a profoundly articulate expositor of Christian mysticism and the universal themes it shared with other traditions. These are two of the best of his many books.

—— *Tao: The Watercourse Way.* Pantheon, 1975. This is Watts's last book, a beautiful work of scholarship and art. Watts draws on ancient and modern sources to interpret the Chinese philosophy of Tao for the West.

—— *The Way of Zen.* Vintage, 1954. With great clarity, insight, richness, and depth, Watts takes the reader through the history and background of Zen to its unique expression in Japanese art and life.

Whitman, Walt. *Leaves of Grass.* Signet, 2000. *Leaves of Grass* was first published in 1855 with only twelve poems. Over the long expanse of Whitman's life, the book reappeared in many versions, becoming richer and more far-reaching in parallel with Whitman's growing experience. Ralph Waldo Emerson proclaimed it to be '. . . the most extraordinary piece of wit and wisdom that America has yet contributed.'

Wiesel, Elie. *Souls on Fire: Portraits and Legends of Hasidic Masters.* Translated by Marion Wiesel. Summit, 1972. The brilliant post-Auschwitz Jewish writer retells stories and legends of the Hasidic masters.

Wordsworth, William. *Selected Poetry of William Wordsworth.* Modern Library, 2001. The great British poet wrote some of the greatest mystical poetry in the English language. This single-volume edition of his work was edited by literary critic and Pulitzer Prize-winning poet Mark Van Doren.

Yampolsky, Philip. *Zen Master Hakuin: Selected Writings.* Columbia University Press, 1971. A study in English of

Hakuin, the great Zen master, by a highly respected translator and interpreter of Zen.

Yeats, W. B. *The Poems of W B. Yeats*. Macmillan, 1961. Yeats was one of the twentieth century's greatest poets as well as one of the masterminds behind the Celtic Revival in Ireland, which brought together spiritual, literary, linguisitic, mythological, and political concerns.

Yogananda, Paramahansa. *Autobiography of a Yogi*. Self Realization Fellowship, 1979. Yoganada's life story has influenced millions of readers and is considered to be a modern religious and spiritual classic.

Zimmer, Heinrich. *Philosophies of India*. Bollingen Foundation and Princeton University Press, 1974. A highly learned yet rollicking survey of Indian philosophical thought, written colorfully and energetically.

Zweig, Connie, and Jeremiah Abrams. *Meeting the Shadow: The Hidden Power of the Dark Side of Human Nature*. Tarcher/Putnam, 1991. Spiritual teachers, psychologists, and social commentators explore the power and hidden potentials of human nature's dark side.

CHAPTER THREE: OUR EXPANDING PERCEPTION

Ackerman, Diane. *A Natural History of the Senses*. Random House, 1990. A celebration of the human senses that is both poetic and scientifically well-informed, with descriptions of intense, liberating, deeply pleasurable sensory experience. Ackerman divides such experience into six classes, involving smell, touch, taste, hearing, vision, and synesthesia (crossing of the senses, as when one hears a flower blossoming).

—— *The Taste of Vanilla*. Random House, 1992. Here Ackerman focuses on the sense of taste, with many vivid reports about deeply sensuous moments that show we can cultivate an extraordinary richness of sensory experience.

Campbell, Don. *The Mozart Effect: Tapping the Power of Music to Heal the Body, Strengthen the Mind, and Unlock the Creative Spirit*. Avon, 1997. A lyrical study of classical music's healing effects on our physical, emotional, and spiritual well-being, whether in classrooms, maternity wards, or mental health clinics.

Castenada, Carlos. *The Teachings of Don Juan.* Washington Square Press, 1974. The original story of Castaneda's experiences with the Yaqui Indian sorceror Don Juan Matus retains its power and originality. Don Juan's teaching offers a new perception of reality and opens doors to realms beyond our everyday life.

Dossey, Larry. *Recovering the Soul: A Scientific and Spiritual Search.* Bantam, 1989. Dossey proposes that our minds are 'non-local,' which means that they are connected to a universal consciousness unconfined to our bodies. As a physician and leading reformer of medicine, he presents compelling medical, scientific, and spiritual evidence for the concept of 'one mind' and the extraordinary implications this has for us personally and for humanity as a whole.

Droscher, V *The Magic of the Senses.* Dutton, 1969. A well-informed review of exceptional sensory experiences, with both firsthand accounts and summaries of scientific studies.

Gurney, Edmund, Frederic Myers, and Frank Podmore: 1886, 1970. *Phantasms of the Living.* Scholars' 2 vols. Facsimiles & Reprints. A landmark collection of case studies involving apparitions of the living and the dead, with accounts of other paranormal phenomena.

Huxley, Aldous. *The Art of Seeing.* Creative Arts, 1982. First published in 1942, this is an account in Huxley's wonderfully lucid prose of his own recovery from a bout of near-blindness, with an exploration of ways in which memory, imagination, fear, anxiety, and preconceptions affect human visual capacity.

LaBerge, Stephen. *Lucid Dreaming.* Bantam, 1985. Written by a leading sleep researcher who more than anyone else has established research on lucid dreaming (dreaming with awareness that you are dreaming), this work provides an overview of his research as well as practices for opening to the vast realm of dreams.

Lindbergh, Charles. *The Spirit of St. Louis.* Scribners, 1953. In this classic account of his history-making solo flight across the Atlantic, Lindbergh describes his vivid experience of heightened perception.

Milne, L., and M. Milne. *The Senses of Animals and Men.* Atheneum, 1972. A wide ranging, well-informed review of anecdotal and scientific accounts of both animal and human sensory capacities.

Murphy, Michael, and Steven Donovan. *The Physical and Psychological Effects of Meditation.* Institute of Noetic Sciences, 1997. A review of nearly two thousand scientific meditation studies, some of which show that meditation can improve vision, hearing, and other senses.

Murphy, Michael, and Rhea White. *In the Zone: Transcendent Experience in Sports.* Penguin Arkana, 1995. A survey of extraordinary feats, perceptions, and altered states of consciousness in athletic activity, with an examination of sport as a transformative practice.

Oh, Sadharu, and David Falkner. *Sadharu Oh: A Zen Way of Baseball.* New York: Vintage, 1985. This is not only a fine sports biography, but a landmark account of extraordinary functioning and heightened perception in sport. Oh, Japan's greatest baseball player for many years, studied aikido and other transformative practices in his quest for athletic greatness.

O'Neil, Eugene. *Long Day's Journey into Night.* Yale University Press, 1955. One of the greatest psychological portraits of the loneliness that plagues urban life in the twentieth century.

Reda, Jacques. *The Ruins of Paris.* Translated by Mark Treharne. Reaktion Books, 1996. A series of short essays and prose poems about the effects of the author's practice of seeing his hometown streets in a new way every Sunday afternoon.

Rogo, D. Scott. *NAD; A Study of Some Unusual 'Other-World' Experiences.* Vol. I. University Books, 1970; and *NAD; A Psychic Study of the 'Music of the Spheres.' Vol. 11.* University Books, 1972. Two collections of firsthand accounts of supernormal hearing. These include stories of music, voices, and other sounds for which there was no apparent physical source.

Targ, Russell, and Keith Harry. *The Mind Race: Understanding and Using Psychic Abilities.* Villard, 1984; and Targ, Russell, and Harold Puthoff. *Mind-Reach: Scientists Look at Psychic Ability.* Delta, 1977; and Targ, Russell, Charles Tart, and Harold Puthoff. *Mind at Large.* Praeger,1979. These three books describe the studies of clairvoyance, or 'remote viewing,' conducted at SRI International with support from the United States Department of Defense. Drawing on their research, the authors describe ways in which remote viewing can be cultivated.

Tart, Charles. *States of Consciousness.* Psychological Processes, 1983. A systematic exploration of how and why altered states and heightened perceptions can come about and their place in our evolving nature. This remains a classic study of human consciousness and its further reaches.

van der Post, Laurens. *The Lost World of the Kalahari.* Harcourt Brace & Company, 1986. A rare glimpse into living Paleolithic culture, by one of the great voices of conscience in the twentieth century.

Walsh, Michael, ed. *Butler's Lives of the Saints.* Concise Edition Revised & Updated. HarperSanFrancisco,1991. One of the classics of world spiritual literature. (See the annotation in Chapter 2.)

CHAPTER FOUR:
THE MYSTERY OF MOVEMENT

David-Neel, Alexandra. *Magic and Mystery in Tibet.* Penguin, 1971. A first-hand account of David-Neel's adventurous travels in Tibet during the early twentieth century with descriptions of supernormal capacities she witnessed among Tibetan mystics.

Feurerstein, Georg. *The Yoga Tradition: Its History, Literature, Philosophy and Practice.* Foreword by Ken Wilber. Hohm Press. 1998. A comprehensive illustrated overview of the Yoga tradition, with its history from ancient shamanism to its modern expression in Hinduism and Buddhism. The book contains both theoretical commentary and practical guidance in yoga.

Govinda, Lama. *The Way of the White Clouds.* Hutchinson, Second Edition, 1968. A firsthand account by the German religious scholar of his adventures and spiritual experiences in Tibet and India.

Ming-Dao, Deng. *Scholar Warrior: An Introduction to the Tao in Everyday Life.* HarperSanFrancisco, 1990. An introduction to a Taoist spiritual path, including lore about supernormal movement abilities, that blends physical, mental, and spiritual exercises.

Myers, Frederic. *Human Personality and Its Survival of Bodily Death.* 2 vols. Longmans, Green and Co, 1903, 1954. One of the world's greatest works on extraordinary human capacities, by the man who helped found modern psychical research and invented the word 'telepathy.' Out-of-body excursions, which Myers describes in considerable detail, comprise one type of supernormal movement as we have defined the phenomenon in this book.

CHAPTER FIVE:
ENHANCING COMMUNICATION

Dossey, Larry. *Healing Word: The Power of Prayer and the Practice of Medicine.* HarperSanFrancisco, 1993. In this groundbreaking book, physician Larry Dossey shares the latest evidence connecting prayer, healing, and medicine. Using real-life examples and personal anecdotes, Dossey offers proof that prayer can contribute to health and healing.

—— *Prayer is Good Medicine: How to Reap the Healing Benefits of Prayer.* HarperSanFrancisco, 1996. Dossey, a pioneering physician, describes both clinical and experimental studies of prayer's healing power and provides practical advice about it.

Ehrenwald, Jan. *Telepathy and Medical Psychology.* Norton, 1948. Ehrenwald, a psychiatrist, builds on Freud's proposal that telepathy is screened from awareness by the same defense mechanisms involved in the processing of sensory information. In this book, he describes how telepathy and our defenses against it operate in psychotherapy and every-day life.

Grof Stanislav and Christina Grof, eds. *Spiritual Emergency: When Personal Transformation Becomes a Crisis.* Tarcher/Putnam, 1989. A collection of essays by the Grofs and other well-known psychologists and spiritual teachers exploring the dynamics of the transformational crisis called 'spiritual emergency.'

Keating, Thomas. *Intimacy with God.* Crossroad, 1994. This beautiful, profound, and practical book is filled with insight and wisdom, showing us how centering prayer can deepen our intimacy with God and lead us to the life-transforming power of love in relationship with the Divine.

Ullman, Montague, Stanley Krippner, and Alan Vaughn, eds. *Dream Telepathy: Experiments in Nocturnal ESP.* McFarland & Co. Inc, 1989. A description of landmark studies by Ullman and Krippner, which strongly suggest that tele-pathic communication occurs between people in dreams.

CHAPTER SIX:
OPENING TO A GREATER ENERGY

Benson, H. *Beyond the Relaxation Response.* Times Books, 1984. This book describes research by a Harvard University team with Tibetan lamas who exhibited marked control of their bodily temperatures.

Brunton, Paul. *A Search in Secret India.* Samuel Weiser, 1970. A fascinating travel account of both inner and outer journeys of discovery, including Brunton's encounter with the great Indian sage Ramana Maharshi.

Eliade, Mircea. *Shamanism.* Bollingen Series. Princeton University Press, 1964. A celebrated study of shamanism and its implications for modern psychology by the renowned professor of religious history. Eliade describes 'magical heat' and other kundalini-like phenomena that are prevalent among shamans in many parts of the world.

Gendlin, Eugene. *Focusing.* Bantam, 1981. Focusing is a tech-nique that shows you how to listen to your body (or rather, body/mind) as your best teacher on all matters of the heart and soul. It teaches you how to get in touch with your body/mind – the part of you that feels and knows without using logic, morality, guilt, or blame.

Katz, Richard. *Boiling Energy: Community Healing Among the Kalahari Kung.* Harvard University Press, 1982. An account by anthropologist Richard Katz of healing and initiatory practices among the Kung people of the Kalahari desert in southern Africa. Many such practices involve 'boiling n/um,' an extraordinary energy that resembles the 'magical heat' described in Eliade's *Shamanism* (see above) and the kundalini experiences of Hindu-Buddhist yoga.

Sanella, Lee. *The Kundalini Experience: Psychosis or Transcendence?* Integral Publishing, 1987. Psychiatrist Lee Sanella describes experiences among contemporary Americans that strongly resemble traditional accounts of the kundalini experiences produced by Hindu-Buddhist yoga.

Thurston, Herbert. *The Physical Phenomena of Mysticism.* Burns Oates, 1952. A celebrated overview of physical phenomena such as 'the fire of love' and stigmata, which are by-products of mystical experience. The author was a leading Catholic authority on the supernormal powers produced by the contemplative life. See especially Chapter VIII, 'Incendium Amoris.'

CHAPTER SEVEN: ECSTASY

Abram, David. *The Spell of the Sensuous: Perception and Language in a More-Than-Human World.* Vintage, 1996. The author, a philosopher and practiced magician, joins shamanism, myth, storytelling, environmental consciousness, and poetry in calling for human beings to return to their natural place in the world.

Ackerman, Diane. *A Natural History of the Senses.* Random House, 1988. A celebration of sensory pleasure and the sensuous evolution of the human body.

Aurobindo, Sri. *The Collected Works of Sri Aurobindo.* Sri

Auribindo Birth Centenary Library. Volumes I-XXX. Sri Auribindo Ashram, 1972. Sri Aurobindo, India's greatest philosopher of the twentieth century as well as a deeply realized mystic, writes with eloquence and great detail about the immense variety of ecstasies produced by transformative practice.

Barnstone, Willis. *The Poetics of Ecstasy: Varieties of Ekstasis from Sappho to Borges*. Holmes & Meier, 1983. A compelling analysis of ecstasy's role in the poetic act and creative activity in general. The book includes essays on Sappho, Dickinson, Cavafy, St. John of the Cross, and Borges.

Baker-roshi, Richard. *Original Mind: Zen Practice in the West*. Riverhead, 2002. A landmark work of Buddhist insight and practice by the Western world's most creative living Buddhist teacher.

Campbell, Joseph, with Bill Moyers. *The Power of Myth*. Edited by Betty Sue Flowers. Doubleday, 1988. One of the most influential popular books on Campbell, featuring the great scholar of mythology in dialogue with the famed PBS documentary filmmaker. Their conversation soars between the soul's high adventures in mythology, art, and literature and the ongoing conflict between science and spirituality. In these conversations, Campbell elaborates his famous admonition to 'follow one's bliss.'

Johnson, Robert A. Ecstasy: *Understanding the Psychology of Joy*. Harper & Row, 1987. A highly readable, yet eminently wise book by the Jungian psychologist on the nature and virtue of ecstasy and the tragic consequences of its long repression in Western society.

Kabir. *The Kabir Book: Forty-Four of the Ecstatic Poems of Kabir*. Translated by Robert Bly. Beacon Press, 1977. The ecstatic Islamic poet is translated here in beautiful and accessible language by the poet Robert Bly.

Murphy, Michael. *The Future of the Body: Explorations into the Further Evolution of Human Nature*. Tarcher/Putnam, 1992. An examination of supernormal human attributes and their relation to evolution, with an analysis of transformative practices that promote them.

CHAPTER EIGHT: LOVE

Fromm, Eric. *The Art of Loving: An Enquiry into the Nature of Love.* Harper & Row, 1956. The author writes sensibly, poetically, and convincingly about different forms of love as well as the tragic consequences that come from the alienation that marks modern life.

Gilbert, Jack. *The Great Fires: Poems 1982–1992.* Knopf, 1992. An incendiary book of poems rooted in the agony and the ecstasy of love.

May, Rollo. *Love and Will.* Norton, 1969. The author, a celebrated humanistic and existentialist psychologist, makes a strong argument that dehumanization involves a failure to grasp the transformative powers of love.

Needleman, Jacob. *A Little Book on Love.* Delta, 1996. A practical, wise, and luminous essay on love, using the prisms of myth, philosophy, poetry, theology, and everyday life. Needleman, a philosopher, concludes that we are unknown to ourselves unless we learn to love.

Plato. *Symposium.* Translated by Benjamin Jowett. Oxford University Press, 1963. This classic dialogue explores love from different points of view: mythically through Phaedrus, sophistically through Pausanias, poetically through Agathon, comically through Aristophanes, and with historic philosophic eloquence by Plato's great teacher Socrates.

Rilke, Rainer Maria. *Letters to a Young Poet.* Translated by Stephen Mitchell. Random House, 1984. Written by the great European poet, these exquisite letters illuminate the vocation of writing, the nature of poetry, and ways in which we are called to more love and life.

Steindl-Rant, David. *Gratefulness: The Heart of Prayer.* Paulist Press, 1984. A member of the Calmaldolese order of monks, Steindl-Rant explores the relationship between prayer and the gratefulness that comes with love, which is at the very center of what it means to be human. 'To bless whatever there is, and for no other reason but simply because it is, that is what we are made for as human beings,' he writes. Connecting contemplation and action, he affirms that contemplation may best be realized by 'acting in love.'

Welwood, John. *Journey of the Heart: The Path of Conscious Love.* HarperCollins, 1990. An exploration of intimate relationship as an unfolding process of spiritual discovery, the challenges of which awaken our deepest strengths and resources.

Wiesel, Elie. *Souls on Fire: Portraits and Legends of Hasidic Masters.* Translated by Marion Wiesel. Summit, 1972. A collection of loving tales about masters of Jewish mysticism, including the Baal Shem Tov, the Maggid of Mezeritch, and Israel of Rizhin.

CHAPTER NINE: TRANSCENDENT IDENTITY

Almaas, A. H. *Essence: The Diamond Approach to Inner Realization.* Samuel Weiser, 1986. Almaas's work involves a synthesis of Western and Eastern approaches to psychological and spiritual development, drawing from ancient and modern spiritual traditions and current psychological theory. *Essence* explores essential reality as the truth of who we are when we move beyond ego.

Emerson, Ralph Waldo. *The Essays of Ralph Waldo Emerson.* The Heritage Club, 1959. Essays by the great American transcendentalist philosopher, ranging in their subject matter from history to love, friendship, poetry, and politics. See especially 'The Oversoul' for an account of transcendent identity.

Hesse, Herman. *Siddhartha.* Translated by Hilda Rosner. New Directions, 1951. A classic retelling of the life of the Buddha through the eyes of a troubled young Indian youth attempting to work out his own destiny.

Huxley, Aldous. *The Perennial Philosophy.* Harper & Row, 1988. A survey of mysticism East and West that explores the unitive knowledge of God, self-knowledge, spiritual liberation, transcendent identity, prayer, and contemplative meditation.

Mitchell, Stephen, trans. *Bhagavad Gita: A New Translation.* Harmony, 2000. In this great spiritual fable, the god

Krishna can be seen as the protagonist of Arjuna's transcendent identity or self.

Nikhilandananda, Swami. Translated and with an Introduction. *The Gospel of Sri Ramakrishna.* Ramakrishna-Vivekanananda Center, 1942, 1977. A famous firsthand account of the great Indian mystic by his disciple 'M.,' with an excellent sketch of his life by Swami Nikhilananda. See especially Nikhilananda's account of Ramakrishna's initiation of his famous disciple Narendra (later Swami Vivekananda), which involves Narendra's shattering experience of transcendent identity.

Peace Pilgrim. *Peace Pilgrim: Her Life and Work in Her Own Words.* Ocean Tree, 1994. The testament of a woman who had a midlife epiphany to make continual pilgrimages across America until there was peace in the world. In this epiphany and her subsequent life, she became her 'true self' or 'transcendent identity.'

Plotinus. *The Enneads.* Translated by Stephen Mackenna. Larson Publications, 1992. Plotinus claimed that each of us has an eternal identity that is rooted in *Nous,* the divine world of forms. His descriptions of that identity resonate deeply with those moments we instinctively call recognitions of our 'true self' or 'real L'

Rumi. *The Essential Rumi.* Translations by Coleman Barks with John Moyne. HarperCollins, 1995. One of the world's greatest literary and philosophical figures, Rumi is today one of the world's most popular poets. That Rumi recognized transcendent identity is evident in the lines 'For years I knocked at God's door/ and when it opened at last/ I saw I was knocking from the inside.'

CHAPTER TEN: TRANSCENDENT KNOWING

Bateson, Gregory, and Mary Catherine Bateson. *Angels Fear: Towards an Epistemology of the Sacred.* Bantam, 1988. Gregory Bateson and his daughter Mary Catherine Bateson explore religious insight and the aesthetic sensibility with the proposition that these ways of knowing are as valid as those of science and logic.

Bucke, Richard. *Cosmic Consciousness*. Dutton, 1969. This still-popular 1901 classic studies the evolution of the human mind and its journey to 'cosmic consciousness.' Bucke bases his views on several famous spiritual awakenings, including those of Plotinus, Jesus, the Buddha, Emerson, and Walt Whitman.

Frankl, Viktor. *Man's Search for Meaning*. Translated by Ilse Lasch. Beacon Press, 1992. Frankl's autobiographical story of his years at Auschwitz is a landmark in spiritual litera-ture. In it, he describes moments of spiritual insight that confirm one's religious faith and commitment to life, even in the most difficult circumstances.

James, William. *The Varieties of Religious Experience*. New York: Mentor Books, 1958. A famous and highly influential study of mysticism, religious conversion, pathologies of the spiritual life, and the relations between belief and tran-scendent knowing.

Koestler, Arthur. *The Act of Creation*. Macmillan, 1964. An ex-ploration of discovery in art, humor, and science, which, Koestler shows, often involves insights that seem to come from beyond the ordinary self.

Mandela, Nelson. *Long Walk to Freedom*. Abacus Books and Little, Brown, and Company, 1994. A monumental work of conscience, love, and courage. Mandela's own words testify to the political will that can be summoned by a life grounded in philosophical vision and transcendent knowing.

Nasr, Seyyed Hossein. *Knowledge and the Sacred*. State University of New York, 1989. This brilliant work by an eminent religious scholar explores the sacred quality of knowledge and the relations between spiritual realization and essential intelligence.

Vaughan, Frances. *Awakening Intuition*. Doubleday, 1979. This excellent study of intuition examines both its personal and transpersonal aspects and offers commentary and prac-tical guidance for its development.

Yates, Francis A. *The Art of Memory*. University of Chicago Press, 1966. A treatise on the ancient Greek and Roman system of 'artificial memory,' which was used by orators, artists, playwrights, actors, and scientific philosophers.

CHAPTER ELEVEN: A WILL BEYOND EGO

Chuang-Tzu. *The Way of Chuang-Tzu*. Translated and edited by Thomas Merton. New Directions, 1965. A book of writings by the humorous Chinese sage, edited by the American contemplative Thomas Merton, that brims with wit, intuition, and spiritual insight. Chuang-Tzu describes ways in which we can find the Tao in everyday life and go with it toward goodness, harmony, and joy.

Csikszentmihalyi, Mihaly. *Optimal Experience*. Cambridge University Press, 1988; *Flow: The Psychology of Optimal Experience*. Harper & Row, 1990; and *Creativity: Flow and the Psychology of Discovery and Invention*. HarperCollins, 1996. A vital trio of books that explore 'optimal experience' and 'flow,' the state of creative consciousness that the author and his colleagues have studied in cultures around the world. As Cskszentmihalyi defines it, 'flow' involves what we have termed 'will beyond ego.'

Dass, Ram. *Be Here Now*. Lama Foundation, 1979. Heartfelt guidance for a spiritual life is presented in this classic story of a Western psychologist's encounter with Eastern mysticism.

Daumal, René. *Mount Analogue*. Pantheon, 1960. This adventure novel is an extraordinary account of the search for the meaning of life. An exquisite tale steeped in beauty, poetry, and truth.

Dossey, Larry. *Healing Words: The Power of Prayer and the Practice of Medicine*. HarperSanFrancisco, 1993. A book that links spiritual power with medical science in the interest of providing empirical evidence for the role of prayer and belief in the healing arts.

Dostoyevsky, Fyodor. *The Brothers Karamazov*. Translated by C. Garnett. Modern Library, 1933. The story of Fyodor Karamazov and his sons, this final novel and masterpiece by Dostoyevsky explores the psychological and spiritual implications of the search for God and the nature of faith played out on the battlefield of love and hate.

Heraclitus. *Fragments: The Collected Wisdom of Heraclius*. Translated by Brooks Haxton with a Foreword by James Hillman. Pengiun, 2001. A long-needed modern version of the only remaining fragments of wisdom from one of the great philosophical treatises of Greek antiquity, *On Nature*. Heraclitus has influenced thinkers from Socrates to Heidegger, and his essential message – all things change, all things flow – anticipates modern philosophy and physics.

Hillman, James. *The Soul's Code*. Warner, 1997. In this work Hillman encourages us to 'grow down' into the earth, as an acorn does when it becomes an oak tree. He argues that character and calling are the result of 'the particularity you feel to be you,' the 'acorn' of our essential nature. In this, we are guided by a caretaker soul, or *daimon*, which leads us by fits and starts, but nonetheless inexorably, toward the realization of our particular calling.

Murphy, Michael, and George Leonard. *The Life We Are Given*. Tarcher/Putnam, 1995. A description of Integral Transformative Practice (ITP), an educational program to promote the balanced development of mind, body, heart, and soul. ITP involves the cultivation of will through affirmations and a 'focused surrender' to energies and transformative influences from beyond the ordinary self.

Redfield, James. *The Secret of Shambhala*. Warner, 1999. A fictional account of the experience of the power of prayer and intention, related to cultural transformation.

CHAPTER TWELVE:
THE EXPERIENCE OF INTEGRATION AND SYNCHRONISTIC FLOW

Bolen, Jean. *The Tao of Psychology: Synchronicity and the Self*. Harper & Row, 1979. A highly readable book that connects synchronicity with self-development, paranormal powers, and personal integration.

Goleman, Daniel. *Emotional Intelligence*. Bantam, 1995. This well-researched work draws on the latest findings in psychology and neuroscience to show how our emotional and rational faculties work together to influence our character and destiny. Goleman shows how to develop emotional intelligence in ways that can improve every area of our lives.

Jung, Carl. *Synchronicity: An Acausal Connecting Principle.* Translation by Series. Princeton University Press, 1960. In this essay, Jung introduced his notion of the 'meaningful coincidence,' which he believed held a key to an individual's destiny.

Progoff, Ira. *Jung, Synchronicity and Human Destiny.* Dell, 1973. This book illuminates Jung's often difficult ideas about synchronicity, placing the phenomenon in a context of personal growth and integration.

Redfield, James. *The Celestine Prophecy.* Warner, 1994. A fictional illustration of cultural and personal insights and their relationship to human purpose.

Tart, Charles. *Waking Up: Overcoming the Obstacles to Human Potential.* Shambhala, 1986. A charming introduction to Gurdjieff's work, with useful chapters on self-observation and self-remembering.

Weber, Renée. *Dialogues with Scientists and Sages: The Search for Unity.* Routledge & Kegan Paul, 1986. In this incisive discussion of the often difficult relations between science and spirituality, religious scholar Renee Weber interviews David Bohm, Rupert Sheldrake, the Dalai Lama, Bede Griffiths, Krishnamurti, and others in a search for common ground between different faiths and ways of acquiring knowledge.

CHAPTER THIRTEEN: TRANSFORMING CULTURE

Aristide, Jean-Bertrand. *Eyes of the Heart: Seeking A Path for the Poor in the Age of Globalization.* Common Courage Press, 2000. An anthology of short essays and stories by Haiti's first democratically elected president that combine passion and practicality in the search for an end to world hunger and poverty.

Bennis, Warren and Patricia Ward Biederman. *Organizing Genius: The Secrets of Creative Collaboration.* Perseus, 1998. Warren Bennis has written about leadership in works such as *Learning to Lead*, *Beyond Leadership*, and *On Becoming a Leader*. His aim in these books was to catalog the traits and styles of leadership that help individuals excel in their work. Here, Bennis discusses 'collaborative advantage' and the assembling of powerful teams. Drawing from six case studies that include Xerox's PARC labs, the 1992 Clinton campaign, and Disney animation studios, Bennis and co-author Patricia Ward Biederman distill the characteristics of successful collaboration, showing how talent can be pooled and managed for greater results than any individual is capable of producing.

Berry, Thomas. *The Dream of the Earth*. Sierra Club Books, 1998. A visionary celebration of the Earth that claims we have reached a defining moment of history that calls for a re-enchantment of nature and reverence for evolution as our new sacred story.

Collopy, Michael, and Jason Gardner, eds. *Architects of Peace: Visions of Hope in Words and Images*. Photography by Michael Collopy. Foreword by Walter Cronkite. New World Library, 2001. A striking collection of photographs and reflections of social activists and visionary political leaders, including Nelson Mandela, Cesar Chavez, Maya Lin, Mikhail Gorbachev, and Dr. Helen Caldicott.

Dass, Ram, and Paul Gorman. *How Can I Help?* Knopf, 1985. With moving accounts of suffering and goodness, this is an inspiring guide to compassionate action in everyday life.

Elgin, Duane. *Voluntary Simplicity*. Second edition. Quill/Morrow, 1993. This is an excellent book about a life of balance and voluntary simplicity that advocates the joining of ecological awareness and personal growth to better our lives and the planet at once.

Hanh, Thich Nhat. *Being Peace*. Parallax Press, 1987. This work presents spiritual practice as a form of social activism and a means of healing for oneself and the world.

Hawken, Paul. *The Ecology of Commerce: A Declaration of Sustainability*. HarperBusiness, 1993. A pioneering book that joins the hard realities of business with responsible innovation to promote ecological sustainability.

Keen, Sam. *Hymns to an Unknown God: Awakening the Spirit in Everyday Life*. Bantam, 1994. Keen invites us to explore new organizing myths for our time, new rituals to imbue our lives with meaning, and new ways to transform the ordinary into the sacred. He addresses our current crisis of meaning and provides a blueprint for bringing spirituality into everyday life.

Leonard, George. *Education and Ecstasy*. Delacorte, 1968. In this book Leonard proposes that to learn and keep learning from birth to death is the ultimate human destiny, and that learning, at its most effective, is a joyful activity. The book includes a spirited description of a highly interactive computerized learning environment designed to teach the basics to young children.

Muir, John. *The Wilderness World* of *John Muir*. Edited by Edwin Way Teale. Houghton Mifflin, 1954. The evocative power of Muir's writing is evident in this collection of his essays, which range in their focus from Yosemite to Alaska. With Thoreau, Muir is the spiritual father of America's environmental movement.

Orwell, George. *1984*. Signet, 1990; and Huxley, Aldous. *Brave New World*. HarperPerennial, 1998. Two satirical novels that attack the notion of utopia and progress. Their titles have entered the language as synonyms for the dangers of totalitarianism and soulless scientific and social advances.

Redfield, James. *The Celestine Vision*. Warner, 1998. A simple statement of various cultural and personal insights relating to human spiritual awakening.

Rozak, Theodore. *The Voice of the Earth: An Exploration of Ecopsychology*. Touchstone, 1992. An exploration of the connection between man's inner being and the outer world. Rozak examines topics such as the Anthropic Principle, the Gaia Hypothesis, mysticism, religion, and ecology, arguing that care of the soul and care for nature are essentially inseparable.

Senge, Peter. *The Fifth Discipline: The Art and Practice of the Learning Organization*. Doubleday, 1990. Using ideas that originate in many fields, including organizational development and contemplative practice, Senge explains why the learning organization matters, provides a summary of his management principles, offers some basic tools for practicing it, and shows what it's like to operate under this system. Senge was founder of the Center for Organizational Learning at MIT's Sloan School of Management.

CHAPTER FOURTEEN:
THE AFTERLIFE AND ANGELIC REALMS

Becker, Ernest. *The Denial of Death.* Free Press, 1973. Becker's central thesis is that our greatest problems as human beings begin by denying death and the terror of our mortality. He calls upon us to open to the transcendent as the only path that will liberate us.

Evans-Wentz, W. Y. *The Tibetan Book of the Dead.* Oxford University Press, 1960. Evans-Wentz's introduction and footnotes add clarity and depth to this ancient Tibetan manual to guide the soul at death through the *bardos,* or 'middle worlds,' between this life and ultimate liberation.

Godwin, Malcolm. *Angels: An Endangered Species.* Simon & Schuster, 1990. An examination of winged 'messengers' from the other world, from mythology and literature to religion and pop culture.

Grof, Stanislav, and Christina Grof. *Beyond Death: The Gates of Consciousness.* Thames and Hudson, 1980. An illustrated, poetically written survey of concepts regarding the moment of death and the afterlife in cultures throughout history. The Grofs suggest parallels between traditional accounts of postmortem existence, contemporary near-death episodes, and death-and-rebirth experiences of psychiatric patients.

Hastings, Arthur. *With the Tongues of Men and Angels: A Study of Channeling.* Henry Holt and Company, 1991. This thoughtful and discerning book examines the contributions of mediumship and other forms of channeling to the great spiritual traditions and explores its expression in modern times.

Head, Joseph, and S. L. Cranston. Reincarnation: *An East–West Anthology.* The Theosophical Publishing House, 1961. A collection of quotations, reflections, and speculations on the topic of reincarnation and life after death. More than four thousand world figures are cited, including Plotinus, Thoreau, Emerson, Frost, Lindbergh, and Walt Whitman.

Kübler-Ross, Elisabeth. *On Death and Dying.* Collier, 1970. It is here that Dr. Kübler-Ross first introduced the idea that there are five stages in our typical dealing with death: denial and isolation, anger, bargaining, depression, and acceptance. Through stories and interviews she explores how imminent death affects the patient, the professionals who serve the patient, and the patient's family.

Leeming, David Adams. *Flights: Readings in Magic, Mysticism, Fantasy and Myth.* Harcourt Brace Jovanovich, 1974. A brilliant gathering of material from literature, poetry, anthropology, and myth that reveals the enduring human fascination with what the author calls 'beyond the material.' The book includes essays on shamanism by John G. Neihardt and Black Elk; 'flights of shamanic poetry' from Coleridge, Yeats, Frost, Merton, and Walt Whitman; Jung's visionary encounters; accounts of the Salem Witch trials; tales of visionary experience in the Old Testament; Grimm's fairy tales; and fantasy stories from Poe, Vonnegut, and Fitzgerald.

Levine, Stephen. *Who Dies? An Investigation of Conscious Living and Conscious Dying.* Doubleday,1982. With wisdom and compassion, Levine shows us how to open to the enormity of living with death while engaging life as the perfect preparation for whatever may come next. He explores the sources of joy and suffering, with acceptance and responsibility as the key to both. He illustrates his points with stirring personal stories and keys to living a life of mindfulness and loving-kindness.

—— *Healing into Life and Death.* Doubleday, 1987. The healing power of merciful awareness is explored in this compassionate and beautiful work. Levine offers meditations and exercises for working with grief and pain.

Lindbergh, Charles. *The Spirit of St. Louis.* Scribners, 1953. In this classic account of his historymaking solo flight across the Atlantic, Lindbergh described his vivid experience of disembodied presences and heightened perception.

Meltzer, David, ed. *Death: An Anthology of Ancient Texts, Songs, Prayers, and Stories.* A wide-ranging study of ideas, rituals, ceremonies, and sacred texts that reveal the evolution of the idea of death and the afterlife. The 192 selections range from Neanderthal burial practices to Irish wakes, epic deaths in literature, dirges and laments, and charms and amulets.

Millasz, Gitta. *Talking With Angels.* Continuum Publishing Company, 1998. This extraordinary work is Gitta Mallasz's faithful recording of messages from voices describing themselves as angels who spoke to four spiritual seekers and friends each Friday for seventeen months during the unfolding horror of Nazi-occupied Hungary. Mallasz always rejected any notion of 'authorship' for this book, saying, 'I am merely the "scribe" of the angels.' The angels' message of personal responsibility is as meaningful and as urgent today as it was for its initial recipients half a century ago.

Mitchell, Stephen, trans. *The Book of Job.* HarperCollins,1992. A fresh version of the classic story of the 'voice from the whirlwind' and the angelic debate about the origins and meaning of suffering in the world.

Monroe, Robert. *Journeys Out of the Body.* Doubleday, 1971. Drawing on his own experience, Monroe explores out-of-body experiences and ways to induce them.

—— *Far Journeys.* Main Street Books, 1987. The sequel to Monroe's *Journeys Out Of the Body* reflects a decade of further research into realms beyond the known dimensions of physical reality. The author provides accounts of his own journeys beyond ordinary time and space, offers techniques to induce out of body experience, and provides a map for further exploration.

Moody, Raymond. *Life After Life: The Investigation of a Phenomenon – Survival of Bodily Death.* Mockingbird Books, 1975. Dr. Moody presents his pioneering study of more than one hundred people who experienced clinical death and were revived. Their testimonies have striking similarities and are overwhelmingly positive. These moving and inspiring accounts give us a glimpse of the 'other side' and descriptions of the unconditional love and peace that awaits us.

Myers, Frederick. *Human Personality and Its Survival After Death.* 2 vols. Longmans, Green and Co., 1903, 1954. A monumental study of human phenomena such as apparitions, telepathy, genius, and inspiration that bear upon the questions of postmortem existence and human personality's possibilities for survival of bodily death.

Osis, Karlis, and Erlander Haraldson. *At the Hour of Death.* Hastings House, 1986. A landmark study of visions, ecstasies, and apparitions at the time of death.

Poortman, J. J. *Vehicles of Consciousness: The Concept of Hylic Pluralism.* The Theosophical Publishing Company, 1978. The greatest survey, in any language, of doctrines of the spirit-body from ancient to modern times. Poortman, a Dutch philosopher, reviews the lore of extraphysical life in Stone-Age cultures; in ancient Egypt, India, Greece, Rome, and Persia; and in modern Europe, Asia, and the Americas.

Ring, Kenneth. *Life at Death: A Scientific Investigation of the Near-Death Experience.* Quill. 1982. Ring brings the rigors of science to this two-year study that includes interviews with more than one hundred survivors of near or clinical death.

Rinpoche, Guru, according to Karma Lingpa. *The Tibetan Book of the Dead: The Great Liberation Through Hearing in the Bardo.* Translation with commentary by Francesca Fremantle and Chogyam Trungpa. Shambhala, 1975. An ancient Tibetan manual for dying, which provides instruction to those attending the dying person for the soul's guidance in the realms beyond death.

Rogo, D. Scott. *NAD; A Study of Some Unusual 'Other-World' Experiences.* Vol. I. University Books, 1970; and Rogo, D. Scott. *NAD; A Psychic Study of the 'Music of the Spheres.'* Vol. II. University Books, 1972. Two colorful collections of firsthand accounts that involve supernormal hearing and apparent encounters with extraphysical realms.

Slocum, Joshua. *Sailing Around the World.* Dover, 1956. Slocum's robust firsthand account of his historymaking solo voyage around the world. In it he describes his encounter with a 'phantom sailor' who claimed to have helped him sail through a potentially disastrous storm. Such apparitions have long been reported by sailors, mountain climbers, and other adventurers.

Stevenson, Dr. Ian. *Reincarnation and Biology.* 2 vols. Praeger, 1997. A report of Stevenson's monumental research on memories 'of the reincarnation type,' which are typically reported by children, and his discoveries regarding lives that correspond to them. In this two-volume collection of case studies, he describes birthmarks and deformities that appear to correspond with events his subjects claim to remember, as for example when someone born with a missing finger 'remembers' losing one in a former life.

Tansley, David V. *Subtle Body: Essence and Shadow.* Thames & Hudson, 1977. A beautifully illustrated and densely written exploration of the elusive realms of the subtle energies and forms.

Thompson, Keith. *Angels and Aliens.* Addison-Wesley, 1991. The best interpretation of the so-called 'UFO experience,' which comes in many varieties. Thompson argues that many such experiences might be genuine encounters with extraphysical realms that are interpreted by their subjects as meetings with extraterrestrial beings.

Tyrell, G. N. M. *Apparitions.* Gerald Duckworth & Co., 1943. A classic study of apparitions, including an examination of their variety, consistencies across cultures, apparent causes, and effects on those who perceive them.

Williamson, C. J. 'The Everest Message.' The Journal of the Society for Psychical Research (Sept.), 48: 318–20. A description of the psychic events surrounding the 1975 British climb of Mount Everest.

CHAPTER FIFTEEN:
LUMINOUS EMBODIMENT

Blofeld, John. *Taoism: The Road to Immortality.* Random House, 2000. A survey of Taoist beliefs about bodily transformation and practices to achieve it.

Dodd, C. H. *The Meaning of Paul for Today.* Fontana Books, 1958.

A search for the living philosophy of Saint Paul and his significance for the modern world.

Fox, Matthew. *Sheer Joy: Conversations with Thomas Aquinas on Creation Spirituality.* Foreword by Rupert Sheldrake. Afterword by Bede Griffiths. HarperSanFrancisco, 1992. An innovative reevaluation of the work of one of the towering geniuses of medieval Europe, written in dialogue form and exploring ways in which to re-sacralize modern life.

Grosso, Michael. *Frontiers of the Soul: Exploring Psychic Evolution.* Quest, 1992. A wide-ranging exploration of paranormal phenomena, including intimations of bodily resurrection.

Guardrini, Romano. *The Lost Things.* Burns & Oates, 1954. Guardini, the twentieth-century Roman Catholic theologian, interpreted the Catholic dogma of glorification to suggest that it points to the further coevolution of body and soul toward their eventual divinization.

Tansley, David. V *Subtle Body: Essence and Shadow.* Thames & Hudson, 1984. A richly illustrated and evocatively written study of the ancient belief that the body is a reflection of the subtle anatomy. The author proposes that a deep experiential knowledge of the Self is needed for human beings to become cocreators in the universe with the Divine.

Walsh, Roger. *The Spirit of Shamanism.* Tarcher/Putnam,1990. Shamanic practices are explored in light of their relevance to growth and healing and as tools for working with the world's ecological crises.

CHAPTER SIXTEEN: PRACTICES

Almaas, A. H. *Diamond Heart Book One: Elements of the Real in Man.* The Diamond Heart Series, No 1. Diamond Books, 1987. This is the first in the four-book Diamond Heart series taken from seminars by A. H. Almaas. Through stages of increasing depth, Almaas leads the reader through a uniquely detailed and beautifully logical path to enlightenment.

Brussat, Frederic, and Mary Ann Brussat. *Spiritual Rx:*

Prescriptions for Living a Meaningful Life. Hyperion, 2000. A guide to spiritual practice, organized in alphabetical order, from Attention, Beauty, and Being Present to Transformation, Unity, Vision, Wonder, and Zeal. The book offers daily cues, reminders, vows, and blessings to the basic elements of practice, as well as suggestions for accessing videos, books, prayers, art, journal exercises, and mantras.

Cameron, Julia. *The Artist's Way: A Spiritual Path to Higher Creativity.* Tarcher/Putnam, 1992. A twelve-week program designed to access our natural creativity. It is filled with encouragement and daily reminders that joy should be at the heart of all practice.

Cleary, Thomas, trans. *Unlocking the Zen Koan.* North Atlantic Books, 1993. Cleary offers clever translations and analyses of ancient Chinese koans, but goes further by providing the reader with a five-step process to help unlock their mysteries. The practice can help readers delve deeper into any challenging reading.

Csikszentmihalyi, Mihaly. *Finding Flow: The Psychology of Engagement with Everyday Life.* Basic Books, 1997. The author supplements his earlier psychological studies of 'flow' by providing a number of insights about transformative practice and personal growth. These include changing the patterns of our everyday lives by controlling attention and finding the sacred aspect of our time.

DeRopp, Robert. *The Master Game.* Delacorte, 1968. DeRopp offers a roadmap for human awakening with revealing, often humorous insights into the human potential. This quirky, acerbic but thoughtful and well-written book, now hard to find, opens with a frank assessment of the possibilities that exist in all of life's 'games,' from the money game to the power game to the sex-pleasure game to the drug-high game, as a prelude to understanding the particular power, beauty, and danger of the 'highest' game, the master game of spiritual self-transformation.

Goldstein, Joseph. *The Experience of Insight: A Simple and Direct Guide to Buddhist Meditation.* Shambhala,1987. With practical guidelines for living, this book provides instruction for the practice of Buddhist insight *(vipassana)* meditation.

Goldstein, Joseph, and Jack Kornfield. *Seeking the Heart of Wisdom: The Path of Insight Meditation.* Shambhala,1987. A guide to insight meditation with specific exercises and discussions of them.

Johnson, Robert A. *Inner Work: Using Dreams & Active Imagination for Personal Growth.* Harper & Row, 1986. The Jungian psychologist suggests a four-step approach to accessing Active Imagination, including journaling, dreamwork, and ritual, in order to integrate our conscious and unconscious selves.

Kabat-Zinn, Jon. *Full Catatastrpohe-Living: Using the Wisdom of Your Body and Mind to Face Stress, Pain and Illness.* Delacorte, 1990. Drawn from vast experience, this is a practical and caring guide to mindfulness, meditation, and healing. The founder of the Stress Reduction Program at the University of Massachusetts Medical Center explains how to use mindfulness – moment-to-moment awareness – to work with any illness as well as the everyday frustrations of life.

—— *Wherever You Go, There You Are: Mindfulness Meditation in Everyday Life.* Hyperion, 1994. A poetic and heartfelt guide to the cultivation of attentiveness, mindfulness, and soulfulness in our daily lives.

Keen, Sam, and Anne Valley-Fox. *Your Mythic Journey: Finding Meaning in Your Life Through Writing and Storytelling.* Tarcher/Putnam, 1989. A collection of exercises for individuals and groups that facilitate the discovery and telling of stories about one's central course in life. The authors make the valuable distinction between traditional myths, which are often restrictive, and creative myths that allow people to reinvent their lives and grow beyond their circumstances.

Kornfield, Jack. *A Path with Heart: A Guide Through the Perils and Promises of Spiritual Life.* Bantam, 1993. Drawn from twenty-five years of practicing and teaching the path of awakening with heart, this is a warmly personal and practical guide to finding peace and truth in our daily lives. Written in a tone that embodies compassion and loving kindness, this book enlivens spiritual practice with teaching stories and down-to-earth explanations drawn personal experience.

Leonard, George. *Mastery*. Dutton, 1991. Leonard explores long-term practice (from aikido to gardening) as the royal road to growth and transformation. This is a wise and incisive book destined be a classic of transformative discipline.

Metzner, Ralph. *The Unfolding Self: Varieties of Transformative Experience*. Origin Press, 1998. A meditation on the central transformative paths that have existed in many cultures, each of which is organized around one or another of twelve widely used metaphors such as 'awakening from the dream,' 'freedom from captivity,' 'lifting the veil of illusion,' and 'moving from darkness to light.'

Murphy, Michael, and George Leonard. *The Life We Are Given*. Tarcher/Putnam, 1994. This book describes a program of integral transformative practice (ITP) to cultivate emergent attributes of body, mind, heart, and soul, which the authors conducted in 1992 and 1993. The book is now used by ITP groups around the world as well as by researchers at Stanford University who are studying the efficacy of long-term programs for personal growth.

Peck, M. Scott. *The Road Less Traveled*. Simon & Schuster, 1978. Peck integrates modern psychiatry and psychology with traditional Christian values of discipline and responsibility in an approach to personal growth and fulfillment.

Trungpa, Chogyam. *Cutting Through Spiritual Materialism*. Shambhala, 1973. Trungpa examines the self-deceptions, distortions, and sidetracks that imperil the spiritual journey as well as the awareness and fearlessness required for the true path. Spiritual practice is not about getting anywhere or achieving anything. It is, finally, its own reward.

—— *Shambhala: The Sacred Path of the Warrior*. Shambhala, 1988. This modern exploration of the path of the warrior explores ancient Tibetan practices that lead, through meditative awareness, to balance, compassion, bravery, and vulnerability in everyday life.

Uhlein, Gabriele. *Meditations with Hildegard of Bingen*. Foreword by Thomas Berry. Bear and Company, 1982. This modern translation of the medieval German mystic into English is also a wonderful book of 'centering' exercises or meditations based on her poetry.

Underhill, Evelyn. *Practical Mysticism*. Dover, 2000. The author condenses the insights of her classic work *Mysticism* into this book of essays on meditation and contemplation, which to her are the keys to the mystical life. For Underhill, diligent self-discipline gathers the forces of the soul and offers a 'loving gaze' to the presence of God in all creation.

Vaughan, Frances. *The Inward Arc: Healing and Wholeness in Psychotherapy and Spirituality*. New Science Library, 1985. A practical and comprehensive guide for the spiritual path, this study of transpersonal psychology presents numerous exercises for personal growth.

When author and therapist James Redfield self-published *The Celestine Prophecy* in 1993, a groundswell of enthusiasm from readers and booksellers made it one of the bestselling spiritual novels of all time. *The Celestine Prophecy* has spent more than three years on the *New York Times* bestseller list and two years as the bestselling American book in the world. In 1996 it was joined by *The Tenth Insight*, which also became an instant bestseller. Redfield's other *New York Times* bestsellers include *The Celestine Vision* and *The Secret of Shambala*. He lives in Florida and Arizona.

Michael Murphy began his quest into the nature of human potential in the early 1950s while a psychology major at Stanford University. In 1961 he co-founded what would become the leading growth centre in the world, the Esalen Institute, in Big Sur, California. In 1980 he helped to create the Esalen Institute's Soviet-American Exchange programme which promoted and foreshadowed greater communication between Soviet and American writers, social activists and political leaders; and hosted Boris Yeltsin during his first visit to the United States. Murphy is the author of such books as *Golf in the Kingdom*, *The Future of the Body* and *The Life We Are Given* (with George Leonard). He lives in Sausalito, California.

Sylvia Timbers has been involved in consciousness studies and training for over twenty-five years, developing multi-media projects and practices focused on psychological and spiritual development. She has worked as a counsellor to the terminally ill and is currently writing and co-producing a feature-length documentary about Tibet.

INDEX

314

315

317

A LIST OF OTHER JAMES REDFIELD TITLES AVAILABLE FROM BANTAM BOOKS

THE PRICES SHOWN BELOW WERE CORRECT AT THE TIME OF GOING TO PRESS. HOWEVER TRANSWORLD PUBLISHERS RESERVE THE RIGHT TO SHOW NEW RETAIL PRICES ON COVERS WHICH MAY DIFFER FROM THOSE PREVIOUSLY ADVERTISED IN THE TEXT OR ELSEWHERE.

40902 6	THE CELESTINE PROPHECY	£7.99
50370 7	THE CELESTINE PROPHECY: AN EXPERIENTIAL GUIDE *with Carol Adrienne*	£7.99
50551 3	THE CELESTINE PROPHECY: A POCKET GUIDE TO THE NINE INSIGHTS	£5.99
50418 5	THE TENTH INSIGHT	£7.99
50555 6	THE TENTH INSIGHT: AN EXPERIENTIAL GUIDE *with Carol Adrienne*	£7.99
50635 8	THE TENTH INSIGHT: A POCKET GUIDE	£4.99
50637 4	THE CELESTINE VISION	£7.99
50638 2	THE SECRET OF SHAMBHALA	£7.99
14343 X	THE CELESTINE PROPHECY (audio)	£9.99

Transworld titles are available by post from:

Bookpost, PO Box 29, Douglas, Isle of Man, IM99 1BQ

Credit cards accepted. Please telephone 01624 836000
fax 01624 837033, Internet http://www.bookpost.co.uk
or e-mail: bookshop@enterprise.net for details

Free postage and packing in the UK. Overseas customers: allow £1 per book (paperbacks) and £3 per book (hardbacks).